Language Learning, Gender and Desire

CRITICAL LANGUAGE AND LITERACY STUDIES
Series Editors: Professor Alastair Pennycook, *University of Technology, Sydney, Australia*; Professor Brian Morgan, *Glendon College/York University, Toronto, Canada*; Professor Ryuko Kubota, *University of British Columbia, Vancouver, Canada*

Critical Language and Literacy Studies is an international series that encourages monographs directly addressing issues of power (its flows, inequities, distributions, trajectories) in a variety of language- and literacy-related realms. The aim with this series is twofold: (1) to cultivate scholarship that openly engages with social, political and historical dimensions in language and literacy studies, and (2) to widen disciplinary horizons by encouraging new work on topics that have received little focus (see below for partial list of subject areas) and that use innovative theoretical frameworks.

Full details of all the books in this series and of all our other publications can be found on http://www.multilingual-matters.com, or by writing to Multilingual Matters, St Nicholas House, 31–34 High Street, Bristol BS1 2AW, UK.

Other books in the series
Collaborative Research in Multilingual Classrooms
Corey Denos, Kelleen Toohey, Kathy Neilson and Bonnie Waterstone
English as a Local Language: Post-colonial Identities and Multilingual Practices
Christina Higgins
The Idea of English in Japan: Ideology and the Evolution of a Global Language
Philip Seargeant
Gendered Identities and Immigrant Language Learning
Julia Menard-Warwick
China and English: Globalisation and the Dilemmas of Identity
Joseph Lo Bianco, Jane Orton and Gao Yihong (eds)
Language and HIV/AIDS
Christina Higgins and Bonny Norton (eds)
Hybrid Identities and Adolescent Girls: Being 'Half' in Japan
Laurel D. Kamada
Decolonizing Literacy: Mexican Lives in the Era of Global Capitalism
Gregorio Hernandez-Zamora
Contending with Globalization in World Englishes
Mukul Saxena and Tope Omoniyi (eds)
ELT, Gender and International Development: Myths of Progress in a Neocolonial World
Roslyn Appleby
Examining Education, Media, and Dialogue under Occupation: The Case of Palestine and Israel
Ilham Nasser, Lawrence N. Berlin and Shelley Wong (eds)
The Struggle for Legitimacy: Indigenized Englishes in Settler Schools
Andrea Sterzuk
Style, Identity and Literacy: English in Singapore
Christopher Stroud and Lionel Wee
Language and Mobility: Unexpected Places
Alastair Pennycook
Talk, Text and Technology: Literacy and Social Practice in a Remote Indigenous Community
Inge Kral

Language Learning, Gender and Desire

Japanese Women on the Move

Kimie Takahashi

MULTILINGUAL MATTERS
Bristol • Buffalo • Toronto

お父さんへ

Library of Congress Cataloging in Publication Data
Takahashi, Kimie.
Language Learning, Gender and Desire: Japanese Women on the Move/ Kimie Takahashi.
Critical Language and Literacy studies: 16
Includes bibliographical references and index.
1. English language—Social aspects—Japan. 2. Women—Japan—Identity.
3. Women—Japan—Language. 4. English language—Study and teaching—Japan.
5. Women—Japan—Social conditions—21st century. 6. Second language acquisition. I. Title.
P115.5.J3T35 2012
306.44082'0952–dc23 2012036457

British Library Cataloguing in Publication Data
A catalogue entry for this book is available from the British Library.

ISBN-13: 978-1-84769-854-4 (hbk)
ISBN-13: 978-1-84769-853-7 (pbk)

Multilingual Matters
UK: St Nicholas House, 31–34 High Street, Bristol BS1 2AW, UK.
USA: UTP, 2250 Military Road, Tonawanda, NY 14150, USA.
Canada: UTP, 5201 Dufferin Street, North York, Ontario M3H 5T8, Canada.

Copyright © 2013 Kimie Takahashi.

All rights reserved. No part of this work may be reproduced in any form or by any means without permission in writing from the publisher.

The policy of Multilingual Matters/Channel View Publications is to use papers that are natural, renewable and recyclable products, made from wood grown in sustainable forests. In the manufacturing process of our books, and to further support our policy, preference is given to printers that have FSC and PEFC Chain of Custody certification. The FSC and/or PEFC logos will appear on those books where full certification has been granted to the printer concerned.

Typeset by Techset Composition Ltd., Salisbury, UK.

Contents

Acknowledgements		vii
Transcription Conventions		ix
Series Editors' Preface		xi

1	Introduction	1
	1.1 'No Gossip, Please. I'm a Researcher!'	1
	1.2 'I Need a Man!'	2
	1.3 Identity, Desire and Power	4
	1.4 English Language Education and *Ryugaku*	9
	1.5 An Ethnographic Affair in Sydney	11
	1.6 Japanese Women on the Move	15
	1.7 Summary	19

2	Language Desire	20
	2.1 Introduction	20
	2.2 Media Discourses of Language Desire	20
	2.3 Dreaming of Tom Cruise and Brad Pitt	36
	2.4 Summary	40

3	*Ryugaku*	43
	3.1 Introduction	43
	3.2 English *Ryugaku* in the Media	43
	3.3 Australia as a Destination	46
	3.4 Summary	61

4	Desired Interlocutors	63
	4.1 Introduction	63
	4.2 Desires, Images and Realities	63
	4.3 Western Men = ELL Success	67
	4.4 Desirability of Interlocutors	72
	4.5 Summary	88

5 Agency   90
   5.1 Introduction   90
   5.2 Home as an ELL Opportunity   91
   5.3 Work as an ELL Opportunity   98
   5.4 The Choice to Work in the L2 Context   105
   5.5 Summary   108

6 Going Home   111
   6.1 Introduction   111
   6.2 Hybridity and the 'Cultural Supermarket'   112
   6.3 Media Images of Japanese Women Returning from *Ryugaku*   114
   6.4 Ambivalence   116
   6.5 Hybridity and Global Mobility   121
   6.6 Hybridity and Intercultural Relationships   130
   6.7 Summary   137

7 Conclusion   138
   7.1 Introduction   138
   7.2 Japanese Women on the Move Revisited   138
   7.3 Language Desire Revisited   143
   7.4 Implications   153

   Appendix: Description of Secondary Participants   164
   References   169
   Index   178

Acknowledgements

I conducted the doctoral research that forms the basis of this book in the Faculty of Education and Social Work at the University of Sydney. I began turning my thesis into *Language Learning, Gender and Desire* while I worked as a post-doctoral research fellow in the Department of Linguistics at Macquarie University, and finally completed the book shortly after I joined the Graduate School of English at Assumption University of Thailand in 2012. The research literally would not have happened if it were not for Gerard Sullivan who introduced me to the fascinating world of ethnography in the first place. Since I embarked on the project, I have been fortunate to have many colleagues who have encouraged me throughout the process; special thanks are due to Emily Farrell and Mike Dowman, and also to Adam Jaworski, Alexandre Duchêne, Angel Lin, Brian King, Deborah Cameron, Diane Hawley Nagatomo, Dominique Estival, Don Kulick, Donna Butorac, Emi Otsuji, Haruo Orito, Huamei Han, Jackie Chang, Jenny Zhang Zie, Lachlan Jackson, Masaki Oda, Muhammad Ali Khan, Samantha Pickering, Sarah Bedford, Sheila Pham, Shih-Wei Cheng, Vahid Parvaresh, Vera Williams Tetteh, Yukinori Watanabe, Yumiko Ohara and many others. I was also blessed with friends who were immensely supportive and enthusiastic about my book, including Akiko Kato, Ayumi Miyamoto, Que Chi Luu, Fadzhila Cooke, Hitoko Okamoto, Kyoko Kanda, Lesley Carnus, Miki Takizawa, Sei Watanabe, Setsuko Furuuchi, Yukako Kamashita and Yukari Suganami.

This book project began with Alastair Pennycook's generous invitation to publish my research as part of the Critical Language and Literary Studies Series at Multilingual Matters – thank you, Alastair, for being patient and keeping me inspired throughout the process. I would also like to thank the series co-editors – Ryuko Kubota, for her review of the manuscript and her mentorship over the years, and Brian Morgan, for his comments and encouragement. I am also deeply indebted to Aneta Pavlenko for her thoughtful review of an earlier version of this manuscript. Anna Roderick, Laura Longworth, Sarah Williams and Tommi Grover at Multilingual Matters also provided me with tremendous support, particularly at the final stage of publishing my very first book. Many thanks to Yukari Ichijo for capturing the lively spirit of my participants so well on the front cover.

Language fails me in expressing my gratitude to my former doctoral supervisor and website collaborator at *Language on the Move*, the ever-inspiring Ingrid Piller. She revealed a better thesis, a better book, than I could ever imagine possible. *Language Learning, Gender and Desire* is, and will always be, our conversation on the move.

Many dziękuję and ありがとうございます to my family, especially Marcin, the biggest supporter of my work and *Language on the Move*.

Finally, I cannot thank enough all the women who generously shared their time and thoughts with me for over those memorable five years in Sydney. かまちゃん、やっと本になりました。Here is the book I promised.

Transcription Conventions

Most of the data for this study comes from interviews and field notes which were conducted mainly in Japanese. These data were transcribed in Japanese first and translated into English by the researcher. In order to preserve the authenticity of interactional exchanges, the original Japanese data are presented first, followed by my English translation, in most of the quotes in this book. Transcription conventions used in this study are based on Piller (2002) as follows:

Japanese Transcription

。	clause final
、	short pause
～	extended ending typical of Japanese
…	long pause
!	sentence-level emphasis
?	tag question or question intonation
シドニー	original emphatic stress for particular words
@	laughter
@シドニー@	the statement between the two @ is made laughingly
[…]	analyst's omission
「幸せ」	change in voice quality when another voice is imitated or quoted
((sitting down))	non-verbal activity noticed by the researcher
[	beginning of overlap
]	end of overlap

English Transcription

.	clause final
…	short pause
!	sentence-level emphasis
¿	tag question or question intonation
CAPS	original emphasis stress
@	laughter
@laughter@	the statement between the two @ is made laughingly
[…]	analyst's omission
"happy"	change in voice quality when another voice is imitated or quoted
((sitting down))	non-verbal activity noticed by the researcher
[	beginning of overlap
]	end of overlap

Types of Data

Type of data and date of data collection can be found in the brackets at the end of each English quote. For instance, (f17april04chizuko) indicates that the specific quote is drawn from the field note written on 17 April 2004, about Chizuko. Other types of data are represented as follows:

e	emails
i	interview
m	MSN messenger
t	telephone conversation

Series Editors' Preface

The latest book in our series takes us on a fascinating, though sometimes troubling, journey into the lives, loves and laughs of a group of Japanese women studying English in Australia. The focus here, however, is not on those standard tropes of English language learning and teaching abroad – the struggles to adapt to local linguistic and cultural norms, for example, or the motivations for such study – but rather on the interlocking domains of language, gender, race and desire – the relations between a sexualised language industry and the trajectories these women follow through the classrooms and bedrooms of English language learning. By making the question of desire central, Takahashi does far more than provide us with an enticing ethnography of language learning; this is also about language, power, race, and gender.

A number of books in this series have focused, not surprisingly, on gender. One of the basic goals of *Critical Language and Literacy Studies* has been to relate questions of language diversity to wider issues of power and inequality. We wanted to move away from the assumption in some studies of multilingualism that there is something inherently critical in the study of linguistic and cultural diversity: This common way of framing the issue aims to critique the centripetal biases of monolingual nation states, language policies and education systems, and instead to describe and promote the centrifugal forces of linguistic diversity across the world. While this matters, of course, it was our argument that support for diversity in itself does not constitute an adequate critical project. This series was not therefore conceived around normative critical approaches to linguistic diversity (focusing on the assumed benefits of multilingualism, for example, or orienting towards language maintenance), but instead aimed to open up questions of linguistic diversity in relation to broader political concerns. We wanted to focus on the complex tensions among diversity, gender, race, class, migration, sexual orientation and so on. Our goal was to bring different critical perspectives (with a focus on power and new ways of thinking about language) to studies of multilingualism. Gender – often interwoven with other concerns – has therefore played an important role in several of the books in this series.

Gender takes on a different configuration, depending on the focus of the book. Gender is not simply a 'social category' into which we can map people in binary fashion (the tick-the-box approach to gender of some social sciences) but rather a constellation of attributes, prejudices, inequalities, hopes, desires, preferences, styles, duties, discourses, forms of work, forms of abuse. Gender also intersects with other social identifications including race, ethnicity, and nationality, For Kamada (2010), for example, we see the relationship between racial descriptions of being mixed, 'double' or 'half', the significance of life stage (these are adolescent girls) and gender. Kamada's interest is in the ways in which these girls 'discursively construct their *hybrid* identities within the context of Japan.' (p. 4). Gender here is a constructed space that allows and disallows a range of behaviours, styles and identifications. Positioned on the one hand by discourses that construct them as not fully Japanese yet also exotically different, these adolescent girls find ways to trade on their novel status as children of mixed background, to move across identities, to take up positions within new discourses within Japan.

Ros Appleby's (2010) book on English language teaching in international development also makes questions of gender central. As she points out, although female teachers dominate the language teaching professions, little work has explored their perceptions and experiences as gendered professionals. Bringing gender, race and language in development together, Appleby maps out the difficult and treacherous territory these women have to negotiate, enjoying the benefits of salaries, comforts and lifestyle that accrue to those on the right side of the development divide, while also being threatened, harassed and subject to all those patronizing and misogynist behaviours that can be the daily life of working women.

Gender is also central to Julia Menard-Warwick's (2009) book on Mexican immigrants (to cities in California). As she shows, women's and men's experiences of English language learning may be very different because of several interconnected contexts of inequality: local articulations of patriarchy, sexual harassments, child-care concerns, and so on. In spite of these struggles against such entrenched gendered norms, Menard-Warwick argues that gender in immigrant communities nonetheless shows much greater fluidity and dynamism than is often assumed, with more options than mere adherence or resistance to static norms.

Similar questions of class, poverty, access and literacy are the central concerns of Gregorio Hernandez-Zamora's (2010) study of impoverished Mexicans squeezed between colonial, patriarchal and religious ideologies as they struggle to transform their lives through literacy. Two of the women in his study, 'long-term housewives and mothers with limited formal education', Alma and Sofia, struggle against 'male dominance, domestic captivity, and a paralyzing sense of powerlessness. But they both developed a strong sense of agency that fueled their decision to reach out and engage in social activities and groups that afforded powerful discourse resources, new roles of competence, and interaction with *intellectual sponsors.*' (p. 56). For these women, there had been no space for written language activities among the survival activities (raising children, working) of their daily lives. As they eventually gained access to classes and literacy, their gendered lives slowly changed.

Gender also appears as an important theme in Higgins' (2009) work on English in East Africa. In her discussion of beauty pageants, and the roles English and Swahili play in constituting the discourses around traditions, global modernity, and cultural hybridity, she highlights the tensions in changing norms around images of beauty and gender roles. Gender is also highly significant in Higgins and Norton's (2010) edited book on language and HIV/AIDS. And here gender refers not only to women (as is all too often the case in discussions of gender, men remain a discrete, unmarked, ungendered category) but also to men and sexuality. One of the crucial connections in this book is the way in which gender, sex, sexuality and HIV are locally understood through particular discourses of abstinence, patriarchy, condom use, health-related visual images and so on.

Through most, if not all, of the books in this series, we see the particularity of the struggles many women face: not just poverty but patriarchy too, not just racial definitions of hybridity, but gendered images of mixed ethnicity, not just the contradictions and difficulties of teaching English in development contexts but the added positioning of being a White woman in such contexts, not just struggles to deal with HIV/AIDS, but the many local attitudes to sexuality, disclosure and education. And as with all good critical work, we also get stories of hope, resistance and change. Rather than gendered inequalities defining lives, we also see the solidarities of women's groups, the possibilities against the odds of gaining access to literacy, the ways in which young women can turn discourses to their advantage. Gender, then, emerges as a complex range of positions, prejudices and possibilities.

Kimie Takahashi's book brings a new and important dimension to this, the issue of desire. The question of why Japanese women learn English is not here the narrow one of motivation, acculturation, or betterment that have received deserved critiques for a number of years (Norton, 2000), but rather broader questions of language ideologies (cf. Seargeant, 2009) and what English means in Japan (Kubota, 2011; Kubota & McKay, 2009). Centrally, however, we see here the relation between desire for English and sexual desire, perhaps nowhere more obvious than in the hope to get a 'native-speaker boyfriend'. Expanding on Kelsky's (2001) historical and discursive analysis of Japanese women's desire for White Western men, Takahashi sheds new light on how language learning is specifically linked to Japanese women's romantic feelings toward White English-speaking men in Australia. Takahashi traces this *akogare* (desire or longing) for Western people, cultures and artefacts from childhoods watching *Sesame Street*, adolescent years idolizing Western music and Hollywood movie stars, the engagement with English at school, encounters with Western men in Japan or Australia, media images of languages schools and study abroad programs, and on into the current lives of these women in Sydney.

Drawing on Piller's (2002) argument that relations between language learning and gender cannot be reduced to questions of social and economic power, but need instead to include issues of desire, Takahashi here develops an understanding of the complex bundles of desire that may lie behind language learning: desire for transformation, mastery, migration, romance, and profound involvement with the Other. She shows how language desire among these young Japanese women is formed at an intersection between discourses of English language learning, Western masculinity and identity transformation. Takahashi thus carefully demonstrates that this desire is not an individual, cognitive orientation but rather a socially produced passion. At the same time, while these women may appear from some perspectives as very discursively constrained, Takahashi also locates this desire within larger life trajectories in which these women play a very active role.

This book has a number of important implications. Not only does it add another part to the picture already sketched above of the many ways in which language, gender, and race are interrelated, but it also has implications for how we understand second language acquisition, motivations and life trajectories. These are Japanese women *on the move*, a focus that also aligns this book with other recent attempts to understand the importance of relating language and mobility (Blommaert, 2010; Pennycook, 2012). Mobility, argues Blommaert (2010, p. 21), 'is the great challenge: it is the dislocation of language and language events from the fixed position in time and space attributed to them by a more traditional linguistics and sociolinguistics.' While Blommaert's focus is on the need for a sociolinguistics that is attentive to the mobility of linguistic resources, to linguistic repertoires as they occur in time and space, Takahashi brings another dimension to this as we follow these women's life trajectories in and around English.

The book pioneers the emerging inquiry that not only illuminates romantic desires attached to language learning but also problematizes power, politics, and ideologies hidden behind *akogare*. The uniqueness of the author's focus and positionality shapes a significant part of the rising scholarship on the intersectionality among gender, race, language, and power, as found in such topics as masculinity and heterosexuality as unmarked norms in English language teaching (Appleby, in press; Bailey, 2007), economic exploitation of such desires by the language teaching industry (Bailey, 2006; Kubota, 2011), and the feminization of non-Western women vis-à-vis Western women in cyberspace dating (Kubota, 2008). The unveiled *akogare* of the women on the move as introduced in this book poses intriguing questions for researchers and practitioners not only in Japan and Australia but also in other global locations.

Alastair Pennycook
Ryuko Kubota
Brian Morgan

References

Appleby, R. (2010) *ELT, Gender and International Development: Myths of Progress in a Neocolonial World*. Bristol: Multilingual Matters.

Appleby, R. (in press) Desire in translation: White masculinity and TESOL. *TESOL Quarterly*. doi: 10.1002/tesq.51.

Bailey, K. (2006) Marketing the eikaiwa wonderland: Ideology, akogare, and gender alterity in English conversation school advertising in Japan. *Environment and Planning D: Society and Space* 24, 105–130.

Bailey, K. (2007) Akogare, ideology, and "Charisma Man" mythology: Reflections on ethnographic research in English language schools in Japan. *Gender, Place and Culture* 15, 585–608.

Blommaert, J. (2010) *The Sociolinguistics of Globalization*. Cambridge: Cambridge University Press.

Hernandez-Zamora, G. (2010) *Decolonizing Literacy: Mexican Lives in the Era of Global Capitalism*. Bristol: Multilingual Matters.

Higgins, C. and Norton, B. (2010). *Language and HIV/AIDS*. Bristol: Multilingual Matters.

Kamada, L. (2010) *Hybrid Identities and Adolescent Girls: Being 'Half' in Japan*. Bristol: Multilingual Matters.

Kelsky, K. (2001) *Women on the Verge: Japanese Women, Western Dreams*. Durham, NC: Duke University Press.

Kubota, R. (2008) A critical glance at romance, gender, and language teaching. *Essential Teacher* 5 (3), 28–30.

Kubota, R. (2011) Learning a foreign language as leisure and consumption: Enjoyment, desire, and the business of *eikaiwa*. *International Journal of Bilingual Education and Bilingualism* 14, 473–488.

Kubota, R. and McKay, S. (2009) Globalization and language learning in rural Japan: The role of English in the local linguistic ecology. *TESOL Quarterly* 43, 593–619.

Menard-Warwick, J. (2009) *Gendered Identities and Immigrant language learning*. Bristol: Multilingual Matters.

Norton, B. (2000) *Identity and language learning: Gender, Ethnicity and Educational Change*. Harlow: Longman

Pennycook, A. (2012) *Language and Mobility: Unexpected Places*. Bristol: Multilingual Matters.
Piller, I. (2002) *Bilingual Couples Talk: The Discursive Construction of Hybridity*. Amsterdam: Benjamins.
Seargeant, P. (2009) *The Idea of English in Japan: Ideology and the Evolution of a Global Language*. Bristol: Multilingual Matters.

1 Introduction

1.1 'No Gossip, Please. I'm a Researcher!'

In July 2001 I was an enthusiastic new doctoral student who was going to do a PhD about language anxiety and the motivation of Japanese learners of English in Sydney, Australia, and I was just beginning to collect data at a university-affiliated English language school. I first headed down to the busy school canteen to look for Japanese students during the lunch break. Although there were over 100 students having lunch and chatting in various groups, locating those from Japan was unproblematic. One after another, these young Japanese students were happy to introduce me to more Japanese students. After a few visits, I knew almost all the Japanese students at the school. This trouble-free beginning to my fieldwork was reassuring, and being Japanese was a great advantage for a researcher new to ethnography, as I was at that time.

Slowly but steadily, however, I began to feel puzzled about what I was learning from these students – particularly the female students. Back then, I was still formulating my specific research questions and, in order to do so, I asked very basic questions of both male and female Japanese students. These were: 'Why are you studying English?' 'Why did you want to come to Australia to study English?' 'How do you find learning and using English in Sydney?' The responses to these questions were noticeably different between the men and women. Male students were more or less straightforward and practical: English was necessary to get into an Australian university and an overseas qualification would be useful upon their return to Japan. They were concerned that lack of progress in English would be fatal to their chances of getting onto a university course.

By contrast, female students' responses were 'colourful'; they would often start with their childhood *akogare* (desire or longing) for English and

Western countries. These responses usually extended to their encounters with Western men either in Japan or in Sydney. For example, their *akogare*, many enthusiastically told me, came from watching *Sesame Street*, Hollywood movies and Western pop/rock stars. Others professed to be in love not only with Western culture and lifestyle and Western male stars, but also with the idea of one day finding a *gaijin* (foreign) boyfriend. Sitting down in the canteen, these female students would giggle as they related their experiences of meeting a *kakkoii* (good-looking) Western man on the street or at a party, and how they regretted not being able to have a proper conversation in English or to get his phone number. Ichi (all names are pseudonyms), who later became one of the main participants in this study, for example, excitedly told me in detail about her quest to form a romantic relationship with a particular Australian man. She showed me all the text messages that they had exchanged in organising a date, extensively commenting on his good looks and the coolness of his manner. I was also becoming a sort of counsellor for another female student who was in a rather difficult intercultural relationship with a Korean schoolmate. She confessed that, although she felt comfortable with him, his accented English was not authentic enough, and she was worried that this might be a bad influence on her English.

At that time, all these narratives seemed naïve to me. I considered the student's *akogare* confessions and their desire to meet Western men as irrelevant to English language learning (ELL), which was the central theme of my research. I even began to think that I needed to change my approach to the female students from that of a friendly fellow-Japanese woman to an authoritarian researcher, telling them, 'No more gossip, please. I'm a researcher!', so that they would stop gossiping about their girlish *akogare*, and instead start taking my questions more seriously. A few weeks went by without my being able to gain what I then saw as relevant data from female students. My frustration was growing. A short conversation with a female student, however, changed my perspective on the whole *akogare* discourse.

1.2 'I Need a Man!'

In August 2001, I was waiting for a Japanese student whom I had scheduled to meet in the canteen. One of the female students that I had briefly met previously came to greet me. Kaori was a university graduate in her late twenties and was planning to apply for entry into a master's program at a university, paying for tuition with her own savings from Japan. In anyone's eye, Kaori was a serious student: she socialised very little and used all her time to study English. Thus, what she said on this particular day caught me by surprise.

カオリ：	キミエさん、私男がいると思います。
Kaori:	Kimie-san, I need a man.
キミエ：	え？＠なんで？＠
Kimie:	what¿@ why¿@
カオリ：	＠前にも言ったんですけど、ここのクラスとかの前にユニの図書館で勉強してるって言ったじゃないですか。あと授業の後も。来てからそうやって自分で6ヶ月勉強してるんですよ。でも私の英語全然良くなって無くって、それでわかりました！男なんだって。英語の練習が出来るネイティブの彼が必要なんだって。
Kaori:	@I told you that I have been studying in the uni library before and after the class here. I have been studying by myself for six months since I came. but you see, my English hasn't been getting any better. I finally got it, though! it's really a man. I need a native-speaker boyfriend so that I can practice my English with him. (f13aug01kaori)

As she rushed off to her classroom, I remained in my seat, absorbing the meaning of her declaration. Did she just say she needed a man to improve her English? It was not something that I had never heard of; I knew of the popular discourse of 'pillow talk' as a means of learning a foreign/second language. In my limited imagination, however, it was entertained only amongst the *gaijin* groupie Japanese women, described as 'Yellow Cabs' in the 1980s in Japan, and Kaori certainly did not fall into this stereotypical, socially stigmatised group. Moreover, what was striking about her comment was her strong sense of conviction about it: she was not joking, but talked about 'the man' in the way that language learners might when they debate different types of learning strategies, such as the best way to memorise vocabulary.

In light of Kaori's seriousness about the need to find an English-speaking boyfriend, the romantic gossip of the Japanese women I had met suddenly also made sense to me. Indeed her comment allowed me to see what I initially thought was irrelevant gossip – that is Japanese female students' *akogare* narratives of English, the West and Western men – in a different light. At the same time, however, as a beginning PhD candidate/ethnographer, I was not sure if Japanese women's romantic idea of the West would be considered a legitimate doctoral thesis. It was in fact one of my supervisors, an experienced ethnographer, who urged me to be true to my 'ethnographic instinct' and take on the topic of *akogare* as it was emerging from the data – a fundamental principle of ethnography. As I will discuss below, reading the poststructuralist work on identity, desire and power in general and the work of three researchers, Karen Kelsky, Bonny Norton and Ingrid Piller in particular, further assured me that an ethnography of Japanese women's *akogare* in relation to second language learning (SLL) and use could be an important research endeavour.

1.3 Identity, Desire and Power

The American anthropologist Karen Kelsky (1996, 2001, 2008) investigated the phenomenon of *akogare* (desire) for, and increasing engagement with, the West among educated, internationalist, middle-class Japanese women. Although Japanese women's social status and experiences are changing, educational opportunities, social relations and the labour market in Japan are still largely characterised by rigid, traditional gender stratification (Bailey, 2002). Kelsky (2001) found that many women were attracted by the allure of the foreign realm and associated activities such as: foreign language learning (particularly English); studying overseas; working for a foreign-affiliated company, non-government organisation (NGO) or non-profit organisation (NPO); or romance with Western men. All these activities, Kelsky argues, provide 'a foreign-inflected vocabulary for a sustained critique of Japan's gender relations, as well as the means to circumvent or reject them' (Kelsky, 2001: 3).

At the same time, *akogare* for the West and Western masculinity is not a recent phenomenon. Kelsky's detailed historical account of Japanese women's *akogare* for the West includes many records of Japanese women's romantic, if not sexualised, contact with Western men since the mid-19th century, many of which attracted significant media attention and at times caused a national outcry. For instance, the *pan-pan* phenomenon (Dower, 1999) was sensationally reported by the media, when Japanese women were increasingly seen with American GIs during the Occupation period in the 1940s. The etymology of the word *pan-pan* remains unclear. Folk etymology suggests that the term originated from Japanese soldiers who clapped twice to call sex workers serving military bases in China, Korea and southeast Asia during WWII. The term was used as an insult to Japanese women who provided sexual services to foreign servicemen in the aftermath of the war (Gerteis, 2009). The Japanese Government recruited thousands of young, poor women as prostitutes for the Allied troops to protect 'good' Japanese women from them. By 1946, there were reportedly 668 registered brothels which exclusively catered for the Allied troops in Tokyo alone and approximately 8000 Japanese women worked in them (Gayn, 1946; cited in Johnson, 1988: 75). These sex workers and other women who intimately associated with the American GIs came to be called *pan-pan*, becoming symbolic figures of Japan's early years after the defeat (Leupp, 2003). It was not only their intimate contact with the foreign men that became the focus of social scrutiny; the type of English they spoke was socially ridiculed. To communicate with the American GIs, these women developed and capitalised on their English proficiency, and their English, characterised by its mixture of a prostitute's rough Japanese and a GI's unsophisticated English, was given a derogatory term, *'Panglish'*. The stigmatisation of these women and *Panglish*, however, reflects Japanese men's growing insecurity at that time as 'hundreds of thousands of men were also struggling to survive by dealing with the conqueror in the conqueror's tongue' (Dower, 1999: 135).

Several decades later, Japanese women's sexual engagement with Western men was once again at the centre of media attention; this time they were called *'Yellow Cab'*. The nickname came from yellow taxis in New York which were easy to 'get into' and 'out of', and was introduced by Ieda (1991) in her controversial 'non-fiction' book, *Yellow Cabs*. Drawing on their strong financial power (backed by the increasingly strong Yen in the midst of Japan's bubble economy), these women allegedly sought out sexual encounters with Black and White men in metropolitan cities such as New York, Tokyo and Los Angeles. It was later reported, however, that the 'yellow cab' phenomenon was largely fabricated by the author. Some consider that the male-dominated Japanese media simply used the criticism as a surveillance tool to control young Japanese women overseas (Ma, 1996; Toyota, 1994). Nevertheless, the notion of 'yellow cab' quickly spread, creating societal uproar. It was increasingly used to describe any Japanese woman who ever associated with foreign men, while at the same time stigmatising her attempt to study English in Japan or overseas. In sum, women's romantic *akogare* for the West in general and their contact with Western men in particular have been a subject of immense contestation in Japan (Kelsky, 2001).

Although I found Kelsky's work to be enormously informative, language learning was not her main focus. Questions were forming in my mind: How does *akogare* for the West and romance with Western men intersect with the ways in which Japanese women learn English? How exactly does their *akogare* for the West link up with learning English and going overseas? Once in Australia, how do Japanese women interact with English-speaking men, and would they actually go with anyone from a Western background for the sake of improving their English, as the media would have us believe? If they in fact find an English-speaking partner, could it really be good for their English, and in what way?

With my initial fieldwork, these emerging questions and Kelsky's work in mind, I revisited the literature from the field to which my research primarily belongs: second language acquisition (SLA). I found that Japanese women's *akogare* had neither been explored in the field of SLA, nor had gender been adequately theorised in relation to L2 (second language) motivation (Pavlenko & Piller, 2001). The traditional notions of motivation and identity, which SLA had to offer back in 2001, did not seem adequate for my study, either. Motivation and identity had been treated as a given, unitary and fixed entity and there had been very little regard for the effects of gender, romance or sexuality. Moreover, from a traditional SLA viewpoint, success in SLL was all about achieving linguistic competence or native-like fluency, having little to do with the role of gender and gender ideologies in the way learners consider what success is.

My work forms part of a growing trend in SLA, which had taken a social, political and gender turn in the 1990s through the work of several poststructuralist theorists (in particular, see Pavlenko et al., 2001). Poststructuralism emphasises the centrality of language to social organisation, power and subjectivity (Weedon, 1997). In this view, language is not just a tool to express human individuality, but rather is a site where possible forms of identities and social relations are produced, performed and negotiated. Poststructuralism thus moves away from the essentialised notion of identity (people 'have' a core identity) and instead embraces the view of identity as something we 'do' and something that is historically and socially constructed in and by discourse (Weedon, 1997). This implies that identities are always in the process of change across time and space, as we constantly construct, negotiate and contest who we are in relation to other social actors and social structures. Norton's (2000) work with immigrant women in Canada was a landmark in this regard. She challenged the earlier essentialist notion of identity and motivation, and advanced the concept of investment (based on the work of Bourdieu (1991)) that regards the language learner as having a complex social history and a wide range of desires. She argued that, in social contexts, language learners were not simply practising their L2 with target language speakers, 'but they were constantly organising and reorganising a sense of who they are and how they relate to the social world' (Norton, 2000: 11). As such, an investment in a L2 needs to be understood as an investment in the language learner's identity which, in turn, is fluid across time and space.

Although Norton's (2000) work was useful for my gender-focused research, her concept of L2 investment, being concerned primarily with economic and social advancement, could not fully explain the romantic and sexualised *akogare* phenomenon that I had observed up to that point. A few years later, Piller (2002) introduced the concept of language desire. Based on her ground-breaking work, *Bilingual Couples Talk*, Piller (2002: 6) argued that language learning or gender relations cannot be reduced to 'questions of economic and social power' and that 'the sheer "sex appeal" of certain languages for some people has been widely overlooked'. Based on data from the study which forms the basis of this book, Piller and Takahashi (2006) conceptualised language desire further as a bundle of desires – desire for identity transformation, for a mastery of a desired language, and/or for friendship/romance with a speaker of the desired language – all of which intersect with one another.

Piller's and Takahashi's (2006) approach to language desire was inspired by the work of Cameron and Kulick (2003a, 2003b, 2005) and Kulick (2003), which have brought a new level of interest to the notion of desire in the study of language and sexuality (Ahearn, 2003; Bucholtz & Hall, 2004; Eckert, 2002; Kang, 2003; Kiesling, 2002; Rumsey, 2003; Valentine, 2003). Although desire is widely considered in Western academia as originating in unconscious, inner processes (the key tenant of psychoanalysis), Cameron and Kulick (2003) argue that 'desires are not simply private, internal phenomena but are produced and expressed – or not expressed – in social interaction, using shared and conventionalized linguistic resources' (Cameron & Kulick, 2003: 125). Based on the work of Deleuze and Guattari (1996), Cameron and Kulick (2003) also stress that desire is not necessarily always bound up with sexuality, and that it does not have a single origin but has multiple sources and workings.

The notion of language desire (Piller & Takahashi, 2006) is a response to their call that the study of language and desire need to go beyond theories of 'inner states' to explorations into the ways in which a variety of desires are discursively constructed and enacted (Cameron & Kulick, 2003). In this book, therefore, I seek to explore the dialectic relationship between public discourses and subjective agency in shaping Japanese women's private desires and how these desires mediate their approaches to learning and using the desired language.

In addition to the dialectic relationship between the public and private domains of desire, power relations are also central to the notion of language desire. This is in line with Foucault's (1978) assertion that desire is always an expression of power: 'where there is desire, the power relation is already present' (Foucault, 1978: 81). Following Foucault (1980), we consider power as multidirectional, (re)produced and negotiated at the intersection of desire and identity (Piller & Takahashi, 2010a; Takahashi, 2012). As such, the workings of power might even 'include the inculcation of desires that lead individuals to modify their own bodies and personalities' (Piller & Takahashi, 2006: 61). When people become so in thrall to the allure of a certain language and its promised benefits (for discussions on the promise of English, see Park, 2011; Pennycook, 2007), they are likely to make a significant investment, be it financial, emotional or physical, in learning the desired language, and continue to do so even if the cost of learning the language is obviously much greater than the benefits it brings (Piller *et al.*, 2010). Therefore, one important analytical consideration lies in the fact that language desire may work against the individuals, particularly if the expected outcomes are not met (Lukes, 1974). Convinced that the construction and embodiment of desire, language and power relations can be understood only in the context in which they occur, Piller (2002) called for a further context-specific investigation into the notion. My research was a response to this call, with an empirical inquiry into Japanese women's *akogare* for the West and the English language and how it intersects with Japanese women's life trajectories. Based on the findings which will be presented in the following chapters, I will offer in Chapter 7 a fully elaborated conceptualisation of language desire, that is processes of its construction and effects, and their intersection with SLL, identity transformation, migration, power and gendered life choices.

Having decided to adopt Piller's notion of language desire as a framework, I sought to explore Japanese women's *akogare* for English and its intersection with their identity and linguistic practices, through the following guiding questions. First, it was important to locate the origin of their *akogare* for English. I wanted to know what kinds of image and attitude Japanese women have towards English, how these attitudes emerged and in what ways their *akogare* intersected with their identities before they left Japan for Australia. Second, even though ELL hype has been a persistent characteristic of Japan for a number of years, obviously not all Japanese can afford to, or even desire to, venture overseas. What did it mean, then, for these women, to act on their desire for English and decide to study overseas? What were the factors involved in choosing Australia, particularly when other English-speaking countries, such as the US and the UK, have dominated the imagery of the West among Japanese? Third, with the understanding of the origin of their *akogare* and the meaning of *ryugaku* in the pre-departure phase, I sought to understand how their *akogare* and identities intersected with the processes of learning and using English once they arrived and began their 'new' life in Sydney. In particular, the inquiry focuses on their views on the 'best' way to learn English and on the meaning of 'success' and 'failure' in language learning, while observing their linguistic practices in their daily lives. The resulting long-term ethnographic engagement allowed me to observe the factors that seemed to structure their opportunities to practise English and the ways in which their *akogare* and identities were played out.

These were the questions that I set out to answer. My ethnographic data collection was based on interaction with five primary participants and several secondary informants. In addition to field notes, telephone conversations, email exchanges and interviews, I collected a wide range of public discourses on women's experiences in relation to SLL and *ryugaku*. To explore the dialectic relationship between the macro- and micro-domain of *akogare* discourses, I combined ethnographic data with public discourses prevalent in the media and other public arenas (see Section 1.4 below for a further discussion on the data collection).

Towards the end of my data collection, I started to notice another widespread phenomenon among my participants. From mid-2004 onwards they began talking about leaving Australia, but they expressed remarkable reluctance to return to Japan. I realised that this phenomenon had not been addressed in the literatures in the field of SLA and international migration studies. SLA theory at that time did not see desire for language learning as being linked with migration desires, while international migration theory considered international students as temporary residents who invariably return to their country of origin (Ono & Piper, 2004). In this respect my participants' narratives yielded a great deal of contradictory evidence. I thus decided to document their narratives on 'departure' in order to explore the impact that *ryugaku* may have had on their identity, sense of belonging and future career trajectories.

Based on the guiding questions above, I sought to obtain an in-depth picture of Japanese women's *akogare* or, more specifically, their gendered practices and outcomes of SLL, and the impact of these phenomena on their lives before, during and after their *ryugaku* experiences in Australia.

I started this research with the understanding of the value of English and *ryugaku* in Japan, which I will discuss in the next section.

1.4 English Language Education and *Ryugaku*

As in many non-English-speaking countries engaged in processes of recent globalisation (Niño-Murcia, 2003; Park, 2009; Piller *et al.*, 2010; Prendergast, 2008), English fever in Japan has been phenomenal. Since the 1970s, English has been the icon of a government-led effort towards achieving the *'kokusaika'* (internationalisation) of technology, education, business, commerce, transportation and communication (Kubota, 2002). The bubble economy of the 1980s saw a mushrooming of hundreds of thousands of *eikaiwa* (English conversation schools) throughout the country (Bailey, 2002; Kubota, 2011). Their commercial success was largely due to their ability to provide what school English education could not offer: small classes, native-speaker teachers, conversation-based teaching methods and flexible timetables. Studies by Bailey (2002) and Kobayashi (2002) have also shown that Japanese female students have more positive attitudes towards the English language than their male counterparts and that more women than men study English at university and private schools. Much of the English language industry in Japan has indeed been supported by young Japanese women (see also Chapter 5).

Furthermore, during the bubble economy period, young Japanese women (i.e. teens to 30-year-olds) began going overseas to study English on both a short- and long-term basis. In particular, short-term ESL (English as a Second Language) study programs in the United States became popular among middle-class Japanese women. The scope of these programs ranged from serious academic endeavour and attempts by individuals to test their progress in English after several years of *eikaiwa* training, to a modified version of a short-term vacation before marriage (Seo, 1992). According to Miya (1997), the term 'OL (short for "office lady") *ryugaku*' was invented to refer to two types of feminised study overseas. The first type, the 'career-up *ryugaku*' OLs, would resign from their jobs and enrol in a certificate course (most popularly a secretarial course) at a college or a vocational school overseas in the hope that their English skills and international exposure would gain them employment at a foreign-affiliated company in Japan. The other type was the 'little adventure *ryugaku*'. Dissatisfied with their OL jobs, women in this category would often resign in order to enrol in short-term ESL courses overseas, either to change their life-course or to enjoy their last years of freedom before marriage.

The United States has dominated Japanese people's imagination of *ryugaku* for decades (Dower, 1999; Kelsky, 2001; Leupp, 2003). However, Australia also began to attract Asian students in the 1980s (Australian Education International, 2000), and the number of young Japanese students coming to Australia increased in the 1990s. By the time I began my research, Japanese women had become a significant part of the growing Australian market for global international students. During my research, the number of Japanese students coming to study in Australia increased from 13,424 in 1996 to 18,987 in 2003, and female students (6239 out of 10,220) significantly outnumbered their male counterparts (3981) in Australia in 2000 (AEI, 2000). One of the earliest to recognise this phenomenon was Atsumi (1992):

> The prevalence of females in this age group [i.e. 15–29] indicates certain characteristics of Japanese society. ... Some of these young women may come to Australia after finishing high school or some tertiary education or after working for a few years in Japan, wishing to learn English and/ or taste life abroad. (Atsumi, 1992: 17)

The way in which Japanese women outnumber men in overseas educational enrolment was an unparalleled phenomenon in Asia (Ichimoto, 2000).

The pattern of Japanese women's motivations for studying English in Australia stated above contradicts the general belief that Asian students undertake overseas education courses for economic or career reasons. Earlier studies of Japanese female overseas students conducted by Andressen and Kumagai (1996), Habu (2000), Matsui (1995) and Ichimoto (2000: 2) found that women who left to go overseas were not primarily driven by career-related future prospects, but rather, 'in their pursuit of greater freedom and self-development, to relax, to escape from social pressures and to look for an alternative way of living that can free women from the constraints of life in Japan'. As mentioned earlier, although some Japanese women's engagement with English language studies and *ryugaku* may be motivated by economic factors, the literature suggests that hopes of economic advantage are not necessarily the only or even the primary factor (see also Kim, 2011).

The studies and statistics cited above suggested some important links between the situation of women in Japan and the study of the English language and *ryugaku*. At the same time, there had been a lack of empirical inquiry about their romantic *akogare* and how it manifests in their day-to-day experience in learning and using the English language in Australia. Once they arrive, for example, how do they negotiate access to practise English and how does this change over time? How are they positioned by the local people with whom they come into contact and how does this affect the way they see themselves and socialise in Sydney? Are there commonalities between those types of individuals with whom Japanese women interact while overseas? If *ryugaku* is not primarily driven by economic factors, what do they consider as success or failure in their *ryugaku* and English-learning experiences, and how does that affect the way they position themselves in society? My research for this book aimed to provide context-based insights into these questions, and there was one research method that particularly suited my purpose.

1.5 An Ethnographic Affair in Sydney

I began this research aiming to explore Japanese students' experiences of learning English in Sydney. To achieve this aim, I chose an ethnographic approach to data collection and analysis. As discussed earlier, the data from my initial fieldwork led me to narrow the overall theme to Japanese women's *akogare* discourse and, from then on, I collected micro-domain data, that is 23 informal interviews, ranging from anywhere between one and four hours, with five Japanese women, as well as a longitudinal observation of them and some other women in a wide range of social contexts in Sydney between July 2001 and early 2005.

In the early stages of the research, I explained to them that I would like to observe their lifestyle and their socialisation in Sydney. Due to the fact that the main participants were not located in a physically coherent space such as a school or workplace, interaction with them varied depending on their availability and their willingness to share their private space with me. Gradually, I began to be invited to their social occasions such as having a coffee/dinner/drink, often with their other Japanese friends, going to parties/pubs, going shopping, studying for exams, accompanying them on dates, visiting other friends, cleaning or moving houses and so on. We were also contacting each other increasingly via email, telephone and text message. My identity as a Japanese woman of a similar age who understood their language was key to this relative ease of access into their private lives: I was less of a researcher than a 'friend' who happened to be interested in their lives in Sydney.

The five primary participants of the study, in order of joining the research, were Ichi (21), Yuka (22), Yoko (29), Eika (30) and Chizuko (39) (these are all pseudonyms and the number in brackets is their age at the time of joining my research). All had come to Sydney with the explicit purpose of improving their English and all began their lives in Sydney as ESL students, apart from Eika, who arrived on a working holiday visa and started taking English lessons several months later. Their status changed over the duration of their stay as they became involved in other forms of tertiary education. Table 1 is a summary of some basic information about the five women, and a detailed description of each participant is provided in Section 1.6.

I also spoke with several other individuals, the secondary participants, to supplement the data from the five primary participants. They were Japanese women from similar backgrounds to the main participants, the participants' friends and romantic partners and some key players in the education industry (see Appendix 1).

Given the main theme of the research, *akogare* for English, the data obtained from them centred on their reasons for and experiences of learning and using English. More specifically, I sought to collect and analyse the following references from my participants:

(1) *akogare* narratives such as preferences for types of English, music, movies, countries, nationalities, friendship, romance and sex;
(2) comments about ELL, including learning strategies, opportunities to practise and use English, who participants aspired to socialise with, who they actually socialised with and how they felt about themselves and their interlocutors in these particular interactions; and
(3) their views on the relationship between their future and English.

Table 1.1 Key information about the primary participants

Name	Arrival date	Date of joining study (age)	Departure from AUS	Time spent in AUS (years)	Education in Japan	Prior work in Japan
Ichi	May 2001 (21)	July 2001 (21)	Jul 2005	4.2	Women's college	None
Yuka	Aug 1996 (17)	Feb 2002 (22)	Jul 2005	9.1	Junior high school	None
Yoko	Jan 2002 (29)	Apr 2002 (29)	Sep 2004	2.8	Women's college	Public servant (9 years)
Eika	Mar 2003 (30)	Apr 2003 (30)	May 2005	2.2	Vocational college	Office worker (9 years)
Chizuko	July 1999 (36)	Oct 2003 (39)	–	12 in 2011	High school	Sports instructor (15 years)

A large part of the research for this book also involved analysing macro-domain data, that is the media discourses that circulated in Japan and Australia during the period of data collection and analysis. Media materials such as advertisements, television programmes and websites play a significant role in producing certain social realities (J. Chang, 2004; Kress & van-Leeuwen, 1996; Piller, 2003, 2011a; Piller & Takahashi, 2006). Previous studies on Japanese women's *akogare* (Bailey, 2002; Kelsky, 2001) made it clear to me that media discourses such as women's magazines, comics, advertisements, websites and English textbooks would provide valuable data for my investigation into the discursive construction of desire and identity in an ELL context. I collected advertisements from English schools/courses, English textbooks and various types of magazine including women's magazines and ELL magazines. Almost all of my participants said they knew of or had purchased some of these magazines at some point in their lives. As the following chapters demonstrate, the critical discourse analysis of such macro-data contributed to my understanding of its intersection with the micro-domain data, that is my participants' *akogare* narratives.

As with any ethnographic studies, my study is partial, analysed and narrated through my way of seeing, and with my analytical skills and limitations. I am aware, for example, that the experiences of this small group of Japanese women in Sydney can never be representative of all Japanese women of their generation or of those who desire to study English. Some readers might also wonder if my own position as a Japanese woman who has been living overseas might have biased my analysis. As Prendergast (2008: 22) points out, I consider ethnography as 'more about the fact that experiences of reality and the expressions of these experiences differ than it is about uncovering a universal truth'. I also do not see any point in claiming that my research was objective or unbiased (Foley & Valenzuela, 2005). Instead, I see myself as a primary instrument or 'co-performer' (Madison, 2005: 22) in constructing and interpreting realities and meanings with my participants. In this book I have written myself and my own experience into my analysis, where such an account has served to enhance the understanding of the discursive construction and the embodiment of *akogare* and the negotiation of power relations *in situ*.

Ultimately, the goal of my critical ethnography of Japanese women's *akogare* is oriented towards social change. To pursue such a goal, critical ethnographers, as Madison (2005: 5) suggests, need to explore possibilities 'that may challenge institutions, regimes of knowledge and social practices that limit choices, constrain meaning and denigrate identities and communities'. This was on my mind at all times during my five-year ethnographic affair with my participants in multicultural Sydney.

Sydney, where I carried out the majority of my fieldwork, is located in New South Wales (NSW), one of the six states of Australia. NSW is the most populous state, containing 7.2 million of the total Australian population of 22.1 million (Australian Bureau of Statistics, 2010a). Sydney is the capital city of NSW and is the largest city in Australia, with a population of over 4.5 million, and is located on the eastern coast of the country (Australian Bureau of Statistics, 2010b). The Sydney 2000 Olympic Games was instrumental in showcasing the city to the world, and over 5.6 million international tourists visited the Sydney metropolitan area in 2005 (City of Sydney, 2005).

While Australia's national language is English, today there are over 200 languages spoken in the country and some 3.1 million people, more than 16% of the total population, speak a language other than English at home (Australian Bureau of Statistics, 2008; see Clyne, 2005, for his analysis of Australia's multilingualism). The cultures of Sydney range from those of early post-WWII immigrants from Greece and Italy, to much later and much larger waves of immigrants from China, Vietnam and other parts of Asia, South America, Africa, Eastern Europe and the Middle East. In inner Sydney, where the most of my fieldwork took place, the linguistic diversity is even more pronounced: some 41.3% of its residents were born overseas and 31.8% of Sydneysiders speak a language other than English as their sole language at home (Australian Bureau of Statistics, 2010c). The most common languages other than English spoken at home in inner Sydney include Greek (3.1%), Mandarin (2.6%), Cantonese (2.5%), Italian (1.5%) and Vietnamese (1.5%).

This linguistic diversity in inner Sydney owes significantly to the large number of international students studying at universities, private colleges and English schools. During the five years I spent with my participants in the city, it was common to see Asian students, including those from Japan, chatting outside their campus buildings or working in restaurants, cafes, hotels and grocery shops where conversations were carried on in a wide variety of languages. My participants and I were becoming part of Sydney's linguistic landscape – as they embarked on their *ryugaku* or working-holiday programmes, and I on my ethnography of language desire.

In the next section I will finally introduce my main participants, five Japanese women on the move.

1.6 Japanese Women on the Move

My five main participants arrived in Australia at different times, under different circumstances, with different desires and aspirations. This section provides a short biography of each participant in terms of their hometown, family, education and work experience, including their trajectories of *akogare* for English and the West prior to their move to Australia.

1.6.1 Ichi

Ichi was born in 1978 and was brought up in a small country town in Mie Prefecture. Her initial *akogare* for the West and English emerged while attending a local Christian secondary school. In particular, Ichi experienced romantic feelings for an Australian teacher of English at the school, with whom her mother still keeps in touch. Impressed with Ichi's enthusiasm for learning English, teachers at her school organised a special conversation class with the Australian teacher for Ichi and her like-minded schoolfriends. A short-term study abroad programme to Australia was also arranged for them during one summer holiday in their second year, and this trip convinced her that she wanted to study at university in Sydney one day. After Ichi graduated from a women's college with a diploma in American History, she had difficulty finding a job that satisfied her ideal (i.e. a workplace with equal opportunities for men and women). Ichi believed that an overseas qualification as a teacher would boost her career prospects, and she convinced her parents to fund her undergraduate study in Australia.

I met Ichi in July 2001, and she was one of the first Japanese students I met at the English language school during the exploratory stage of my research.

1.6.2 Yuka

Yuka was born in 1978 in a country town in Gifu Prefecture. She led an ordinary childhood until she fell victim to group bullying in her first year at junior high school. Not knowing what had caused her to become so unpopular among her classmates and unable to gain help from other students or teachers, it became extremely painful for her to attend school. Finally she stopped going to school in the middle of her second year, becoming a *hikikomori*, or social recluse. An old family friend who was a *ryugaku* consultant understood the problem and suggested that going overseas might give her a chance to start afresh. Yuka found this suggestion attractive: she had always wanted to go overseas, and the idea of moving away from all her problems and of relocating to a foreign country where no one knew her past was tremendously appealing. Yuka's parents had been very enthusiastic about her education, and English was one of her favourite subjects until she dropped out of school. Although her English was quite limited at that time, her excitement in moving overseas outweighed this linguistic concern. Yuka's parents were also happy to take any opportunity to help their teenage *hikikomori* daughter restart her life.

I met Yuka in the middle of 2001 through a mutual Japanese friend. When she began a university course in early 2002, Yuka started to visit my office occasionally. In February 2002 I invited her to be part of my study as Yuka had different qualifications from the other participants: she had been in Australia longer than most of the participants in my study, and the circumstances under which she came to Australia were somewhat unique, while at the same time the issue of Japanese *hikikomori* youth was increasingly reported in the media both in Japan and overseas.

1.6.3 Yoko

Yoko was born in 1972 in a small town in Shizuoka Prefecture. In her final year at high school she followed her parents' suggestion of studying Nutrition at a women's college, as she did not have any specific goal at that point in her life. Upon graduation from the women's college, she became a public servant with the town council, an occupation that her parents thought was stable and respectable. She met her husband at work and they married in 1998. After joining the town council, Yoko began to take English lessons together with a friend at a small English conversation school, where she met a variety of people. At that time, her husband was having extramarital affairs with one of their colleagues. Yoko began investing more and more time and energy into learning English and watching many Hollywood movies, as her married life increasingly fell apart. Her marriage finally broke down in October 2001. In her small town, where many people knew about his affair and their subsequent divorce, she felt that there was no privacy in her life. She was frustrated about the fact that she was seen as a miserable divorcee and, after much consideration, she decided to go on *ryugaku* to Australia, to start a new life.

I met Yoko in April 2002, only a few months after her arrival in Sydney. I had known her Japanese host family, the Tanakas, who introduced me to Yoko as a potential informant. During our first meeting in a café, Yoko told me about her experiences during the divorce, and I was interested in learning more about her because none of my other participants had been married.

1.6.4 Eika

Eika was born in 1971 in Tokyo. During her secondary school years, she became interested in learning English and about American culture. Her first exposure to a foreign country was through a short-term English *ryugaku* to Arizona during one summer holiday. Since then, Eika had been 'hooked' on both the US and English, and had always imagined herself going back there for tertiary education. It was thus natural for her to go on to study English in a college after finishing high school. However, after graduating from college in Tokyo, her parents refused to let her study in the US because of security concerns. Without her parent's financial support, she had no choice but to postpone her *ryugaku*, and sought to become financially capable of paying for the *ryugaku* herself. For the next nine years, Eika worked for a major corporation in Tokyo. Eika considered herself to be a 'career woman', with an extensive social network and financial freedom. Her earnings were relatively high, and living with her parents also helped save money towards her *ryugaku* plan. In her final year at work, her job became increasingly international, creating the need to communicate with clients and colleagues from several Asian countries such as Korea and China, in English. According to Eika, this increased her access to English at work, which in turn resurrected her desire for the language and *ryugaku*.

Although her passion for English remained while she was working, her interest in attending university faded. Thus, when choosing a *ryugaku* destination, she no longer saw the US, the country of her *akogare*, attractive; she would have been unable to work there on a student visa. She did not want to go to the UK because of its poor weather, nor to Canada with its cold climate. Eika chose Australia mainly because it offered a one-year working holiday visa, which allowed her both to study and work, and partly because Australia was well known for its warm climate all year round.

I had known Eika through my social network in Japan. When she arrived in Sydney in March 2003, she was happy to participate in my study and provided critical feedback on my ongoing analysis throughout the study.

1.6.5 Chizuko

Chizuko was born and grew up in a rural area in Gifu Prefecture. When she was a young child there were no shops or cafes in her neighbourhood, and she spent her entire childhood running around, picking fruit and vegetables with her friends on a small mountain behind her house. Growing up in this remote country village, she became mesmerised by television images of Western countries and their 'sophisticated' cultures. In her childhood it became her dream to one day move out of the rural area into the outside world. Chizuko developed a great deal of *akogare* for Westerners and the English language during her teenage years. For instance, when she heard the rumour that the high school in the next town had an American exchange student, she jumped on the train and went to the school just to see and take photos of the American. While Chizuko was studying at a two-year college, she often spent time with foreign teachers of English who resided within the college. She enjoyed socialising with the Western teachers even though she could hardly speak or understand English at that time.

In her early twenties, Chizuko moved to Tokyo in order to experience an exciting metropolitan lifestyle. She became an aerobics instructor, which was her dream job at that time. She met an Australian man though her extensive social network of drinking friends. According to Chizuko, he was the man of her dreams, who showered her with romantic presents and sweet words. Although they were planning to get married, they decided to end their relationship due, from her point of view, to her limited English, which made it impossible for the pair to discuss important matters. Some years later Chizuko found out that he had married someone else. Devastated about the news and unable to forget about him, she decided to go overseas. Chizuko's choice of *ryugaku* destination was Australia, as she had positive images of the country because of her ex-boyfriend and her Australian friends. On the day she decided to move overseas, Chizuko signed on for a three-month English study programme and immediately began preparing for her first *ryugaku*.

In mid-2003, Chizuko moved in with Yoko's former Japanese host family, the Tanakas. I was introduced to her by the host family.

1.7 Summary

In this introductory chapter I revisited the process through which the research focus for this book, *akogare* (Kelsky, 2001), and the theoretical orientation, language desire (Piller, 2002), had emerged. Being a novice ethnographer with an untrained eye for what was relevant, the early stages of the research were chaotic and at times frustrating, and the later fieldwork also continued to pose a number of challenges. There was, for example, an overwhelming volume of information generously provided by the participants, a common problem qualitative researchers face (Miles & Huberman, 1994). The key to the management and analysis of ethnographic data was to categorise and analyse data as they came in, identifying emerging themes and developing relevant categories, and then to organise the data according to these themes and categories as I collected more data while fine-tuning the research questions. This circularity is one of the advantages of qualitative research because 'it forces the researcher to permanently reflect on the whole research process and on particular steps in light of the other steps' (Flick, 2002: 43). My research questions were formed and refined in this manner. As you will see below, although each chapter deals with a particular issue, they also closely intersect with each other, illuminating *akogare* as it was central to the embodied trajectory of the five women – from their teenage years and *ryugaku* preparation in Japan (Chapters 2 and 3), to their arrival and stay in Australia (Chapters 4 and 5), and finally to the day of their departure for yet another new beginning in their transnational lives (Chapter 6).

In sum, *Language Learning, Gender and Desire* offers a critical exploration of Japanese women's *akogare* on the terrain of globalisation, a new discourse of empowerment and social inclusion for all women on the move out there.

2 Language Desire

2.1 Introduction

In this chapter I will explore media discourses of ELL and their constitutive effect on Japanese women's *akogare* for English, the West and romance with Western men. In Section 2.2, we will look at multiple media discourses of language desire. Firstly, we will look at the ways in which media discourses of ELL construct and promote certain identities for English language teachers in Japan, and explore how such teachers are portrayed as an effective strategy for learning English. Secondly, I will examine the promotional materials from an English language school to illuminate how sexual innuendos between a Japanese woman and a White man constitute the media discourse of language desire. Thirdly, I will discuss the discourse of *renai* (relationship) English as it regularly emerged during my fieldwork. In Section 2.3, I will explore how media discourses were played out in my participants' *akogare* narratives, demonstrating that, for these women, the idea of the West and Western men became romanticised and increasingly linked with ELL during adolescence.

2.2 Media Discourses of Language Desire

The education industry and the media in Japan target the most enthusiastic consumers of English – young Japanese women (Piller et al., 2010). According to Odagiri (2004), as many as 80% of women in their twenties were found to be interested in learning English. There are other implications, too; in the mid-1990s, Tsuda (1995: 156–157) reported that the *eikaiwa* (English conversation) industry in Japan comprised half the international market, reaching approximately 1 trillion Yen [approximately AUS$11.48 billion].

Major sources for these large revenues come from ELL magazines, tapes, videos and textbooks for radio and TV programmes on English and English proficiency tests (Tsuda, 1995). According to J Net 21 (2005), the number of *eikaiwa* schools in Japan in 2003 (at that time of the research) totalled 3118, producing revenues of 129 billion Yen [approximately AUS$1.48 billion].

ELL has become a business strategy for magazine publishers. In numerous women's magazines, ELL-related articles are regularly featured, and advertisements for *eikaiwa* schools and *ryugaku* agents abound (Kelsky, 2001). According to Kimura – a media development manager of ALC, a major publishing house that specialises in publishing works on language learning and teaching and *ryugaku* – a special feature on an English-related topic often leads to an increase in sales (Odagiri, 2004: 5).

This section presents an analysis of ELL media discourses in Japan. The main aim of the analysis is to show ways in which media discourse constitutes, promotes and reinforces Japanese women's language desire. It does so by endorsing and connecting three discursive spaces: English, the West and Western masculinity, as desirable means of creating a new lifestyle and identity. Firstly, I will demonstrate how White male native speakers of English are sold as ideal English teachers in media discourse. Secondly, the promotional strategies of Gaba, a popular English language school, is analysed in order to further examine the ways in which romance with a White Western man is linked with ELL. Thirdly, I explore media discourses of *renai* English in depth.

2.2.1 The White native-speaker male as an ideal English teacher

At the beginning of Chapter 1 I discussed Kaori's comment, 'I need a man', as an eye-opening incident at an early stage of the research. It sparked my initial interest in the link between ELL and romance with an English-speaking, Western man, and I wanted to locate where such a link was made. I first turned to the media. In examining women's magazines, for example, one of the first things I noticed was that many of the English teachers depicted in advertisements and other ELL-related articles were smiling White men wearing suits and ties. Although female teachers were not totally absent, the intended usage of Western female teachers seemed to differ considerably from that of Western male teachers. For instance, as Bailey (2002: 297) reports, in *eikaiwa* advertisements, on the one hand, Western women were often depicted as 'professional' so as to appeal to Japanese female clients who seek to enhance their professional lives through English. On the other hand, it seemed that *eikaiwa* English schools and publishers were well aware of the market value of White men, and by using them tried to appeal to

Japanese women's romantic *akogare* for English and with romantic involvement with such men. At the same time, these magazines defined and promoted the meaning of English learning for Japanese women by stating and disseminating a view of what is proper and successful, and therefore desirable for female learners of English. In particular, such media discourse seemed to construct an English-teacher identity in terms of 'good-looking' White Western men, conflating them with success in ELL and romance.

For instance, in a special edition of *an-an* (Magazine House, 2002a: 37) on learning English, male teachers are constantly presented as desirable and effective in teaching English to Japanese women. One article from this edition of *an-an* presents a portrait feature of five *ikemen* (good-looking) teachers representative of their English conversation school. All the *ikemen* teachers in their neat suits are White males, presumably native speakers of English. The camera shot is 'close-personal' (including only head and shoulders), minimising the space between the viewer and the *ikemen* teachers (Kress & van Leeuwen, 1996). In the article above, the editor implies that good-looking male teachers are conducive to language learning by stating:

> せっかく英語を習うんだったら、'次回も会うのが楽しみ' そんな気分になる先生に担当してほしい・・・。
> Having made the decision to learn English, you want to be taught by a teacher that makes you think 'I look forward to the next lesson'. (Magazine House, 2002a: 37).

The text below each photo of the *ikemen* teachers focuses on their positive personal traits rather than their educational background or teaching career. Although the text was produced by the editor and not by the teacher himself, the content closely resembles that of dating advertisements. For instance, the description of Kevin Black of the Gaba English conversation school reads as follows:

> 「Gabaマンツーマン英会話」ケヴィン・ブラック先生日本の歴史と、温泉が大好きで、箱根に足繁く通っているらしい。「生徒さんによって教え方を変えるのが僕のやり方。英語に対する恐怖心を取り除く事も意識しています。」カラオケに行くのが好きで、なんと、ケミストリーなどのJポップの歌を日本語で歌うのだとか。びっくり。
> [Gaba Mantsuman English conversation] Teacher Kevin Black. Kevin frequently visits Hakone (one of the most famous hot spring towns in the Western part of Japan) as he loves Japanese history and hot springs. 'My policy is to change my teaching method depending on my students. I try to get rid of their fear of using English.' He likes going to karaoke and

what's more, he likes singing Japanese pop songs like those of *Chemistry*. It's a surprise. (Magazine House, 2002a: 37)

Coupland (1996) shows that those who place personal advertisements often represent themselves by referring to a list of attributes from the following sets: gender, age, location, appearance, personality/behaviour traits, interests, career/solvency/status, generational/marital status and ethnicity (in order of frequency of mention). In the example above, characteristics of the teacher including gender (male), location (language school), appearance ('good-looking' White male) and career (English teacher) are self-evident from the photo and the theme of the article. The text constructs Kevin Black not only as an *ikemen* teacher, but also as a likable and approachable man by mentioning his positive 'personal' traits and behaviours (he likes Japanese culture, history, hot springs and music; he goes to Hakone and sings karaoke), none of which is directly related to language teaching. Desire for the teacher is created not primarily for his teaching qualifications or educational background (neither of which is mentioned in the text) but for his personal qualities as a good-looking Western man, interested in the culture of the targeted consumers of ELL. In this example of media discourse, ELL and romance with Western men become mutually constitutive.

The image of White men as good-looking teachers of English can be found in women's comics, too. The characters in these comics are usually said to resemble Westerners to begin with (Kelsky, 2001), and this Westernisation of cartoon characters both reflects and intensifies Japanese women's *akogare* for blue-eyed, blond-haired Western men with long legs and arms and small faces. For instance, in this highly erotic love comic, entitled, '彼はシーフ (He is a thief)', written by Yokota (2004), a young 'good-looking' Australian man, Josh, is not only presented as a typical 'ladies-first' and all-knowing gentleman, but also as a private teacher of English and love. In one scene (see Figure 2.1), a young Japanese girl, Meg, tries to apologise for mistaking Josh for a thief at Cairns International Airport. In the first speech bubble, Meg says shyly: 'I'm sorry ... I mistook you えーと(umm) a thief.' Then in the second speech bubble, Josh accepts Meg's apology by saying with a shy smile, 'No problem but ...'. As the 'but' indicates, he then goes on to correct a grammatical error by stating in the third speech bubble: 'I mistook you FOR a thief.' In the fourth thought-speech bubble, Meg's face closes in as she says to herself, '添さく(Correction)'. Although a grammatical correction can threaten loss of face (Ellis, 1994), the air between them is overwhelmingly romantic with the soft tones of several pentagonal patterns in the background.

The story leads to Josh's erotic act of 'stealing' her sexually on the beach in Cairns (once again, he is a thief) and ends on a happy note with

Figure 2.1 'He is a thief' (Yokota, 2004: 144)

Meg's decision not to pursue tertiary education in Japan and instead to study in Australia. Her romance with Josh dramatically transforms Meg's life trajectory and identity, from that of an ordinary Japanese university student in Japan to a *ryugaku* student in Australia with a *gaijin* boyfriend who is good looking, sexy and an empathetic teacher of English.

Kelsky (2001: 145) notes that White men 'appear in women's media as sensitive, refined and without sexism' and 'they are *redi fasuto jentoruman* (ladies-first gentlemen)'. As exemplified above, a similar tendency is evident in the case of the *ikemen* teachers in the *an-an* magazine and Josh in the women's comic. In reality, however, it is likely that the behaviour of such Western men is motivated differently in different contexts; these men would behave differently in an EFL business context from a non-business context. In the former, the Western teachers are presumably paid and trained for the emotional work of being gentlemanly to their students. However, the media tend to blur the boundary between the teachers who are being paid to 'perform' and the general populace of White men who have no material inducement to act in a gentlemanly fashion.

In addition, the media discourse of Western men as good-looking teachers of English places Japanese women in contradictory positions. On the one hand, the discourse promotes the value of Western men as desirable and effective English teachers, marrying ELL with interracial romance. Young Japanese women – the targeted readers – are turned into the desirous consumers of Western masculinity and of English as an international language. On the other hand, the discourse also functions to construct these women as powerful consumers of such commodities or, in other words, grants them the power to choose, buy or reject such commodities on the basis of criteria such as race, nationality, eye-colour, hairstyle, fashion sense and so on. As will be further illustrated below, the women's power of consumption has an effect on the practices of the media and the ELL industry, whose existence depends largely on Japanese women's participation as consumers.

2.2.2 Promotional materials: The case of Gaba

There are several genres of promotional materials for *eikaiwa* schools in Japan (Bailey, 2002). Chang (2004) argues that examination of such media discourse is a useful tool in revealing the mechanism of language ideology in a specific context. Although media discourse analyses of ELL advertisements in Japan have been rare in the field of SLA, increasing attention has been paid to *eikaiwa* advertisement as a gendering practice in anthropology (Kelsky, 2001), geography (Bailey, 2002) and critical applied linguistics (Tsuda, 2000).

Researchers such as Bailey (2002), Kelsky (2001), Ma (1996) and Tsuda (2000), report that the creation of romantic and sexual chemistry with White men has been one of the most frequent strategies used by English language schools in Japan. In their view, *eikaiwa* advertisements play on Japanese women's romantic and sexualised *akogare* for White masculinity. Of course, the use of sexual innuendos in advertising is an ancient practice. 'Sex sells' has been the entrenched truism in advertising in many capitalist societies (Piller, 2010), and certainly Japan is not an exception (Russell, 1998). In his research on the *eikaiwa* industry in Japan, Bailey found that the eroticisation of Western instructors was obvious only in Japanese female accounts. He identified the primary difference between *eikaiwa* advertisements and others in Japan as:

> the extent to which the promised discovery of new selfhood – *atarashii jibun* – is bound up in an Occidentalist West through the practice and customs of mythicized English language learning and how they rely on the presence of the White male signifier. (Bailey, 2002: 275).

His point is best exemplified in the promotional materials produced by Gaba. Gaba was identified as one of the most rapidly expanding *eikaiwa* chains in Japan in the mid-2000s (Shuukan Diamond, 2005) and its commercial success, at least initially, owed a great deal to an earlier campaign which drew on, and further strengthened, the link between ELL and romance with White Western men. In his study of gendered participation in the *eikaiwa* industry, Bailey (2002) had his informants (Japanese female students studying English in Japan) look at several advertisements from major English-conversation schools in Japan and asked them for their opinions. He reports that Gaba's was identified as 'the most sexualized of all advertisements' (Bailey, 2002: 286).

Although Bailey's analysis of Gaba's advertisement is insightful, what is not mentioned is that this highly sexually charged advertisement was not a 'one-off' attempt by the school. In fact, Gaba made a concerted attempt to commodify *mantsuman* (one-to-one) lessons as a romanticised and sexualised product by making strategic use of various media and promotional materials. In particular, its advertisements and home page contents were designed to appeal to Japanese women's desire for 'private' and 'intimate' times with White men in a fashionable space.

According to Odagiri (2004: 5), 70% of Gaba's 60,000 registered students were women in their twenties and thirties. When Gaba was established in 1995, the *mantsuman* lesson was promoted as the distinguishing feature of its classes. Previously, group lessons had been the norm in the *eikaiwa*: private lessons were thought of as expensive, and the thought of spending one hour alone with a native-speaker teacher may well have been considered uncomfortable for shy students. Gaba's *mantsuman* lesson challenged these stereotypes. In terms of the lesson fee, Gaba's *mantsuman* was not inexpensive. For instance, a regular *mantsuman* student pays approximately 8,285 Yen [approximately AU$100.00] per lesson, while other *eikaiwa* schools offer 2000 Yen private lessons [approximately AU$23.00]. However, the ways in which *mantsuman* lessons were packaged and promoted in advertisements on the Gaba home page evidently boosted the attractiveness of the programme.

As mentioned earlier, Gaba's advertisement was identified as the most sexualised in Bailey's (2002) study. His female informants saw the Japanese woman in the advertisement as having control over the White male teacher, and their relationship was sexualised through the use of the handcuffs. Her knowing smile (as opposed to the White man's non-smiling face) and her pull on the handcuffs were signifiers of power, which led the researcher to conclude that this advertisement 'inverted the customary gendering of such images in such a way as to empower the female *eikaiwa* clients' (Bailey, 2002: 286).

Gaba's later advertisement took a similar approach and further mystifies its romanticised product of *mantsuman* lessons. In this monochromatic composition, a young Japanese woman and a tall man stand face-to-face on a small boat in a dark, mysterious cave. The man is pictured from behind and so his facial features are invisible. However, because of his height and the fact that GABA ads always pair an Asian woman with a White man, it is safe to assume that most viewers will understand the man to be White. What is most striking about the Japanese woman is the way she is positioned as the holder of power. For instance, she holds the oar (a symbolic act of power similar to the handcuff pull) which signifies control and agency, while the man remains faceless: his identity is to be determined by the viewer, that is the female client. Back-lit by a soft glow, she emerges as the focus of the advertisement. This light can also be interpreted as signifying the hope of a brighter future which is connected with her intimate relationship with the White man.

What makes this advertisement different from the first is the emphasis on the sense of privacy and intimacy with the White man. Unlike the portrait style of the first advertisement, the camera shot in the second is long, distancing the viewer from the two people in the frame (Kress & van Leeuwen, 1996). This creates a sense of isolation from the ordinary and mundane world for the viewer, while intimacy between the couple is visually and instantaneously created. The *mantsuman* promotion emphasises and guarantees this sense of intimacy with a White man by transporting the client and her White male teacher to the world of fantasy.

In this advertisement, the catchphrase is also designed to promote desire and a need for intimacy with an English-speaking Western man; it reads: '二人だから、あなたは話したくなる (Because there are only two of you, you will want to talk)'. According to Kress and van Leeuwen (1996: 43), unequal relations of power are established by the text postulating the needs and wants of the reader, even though there is no channel of negotiative reciprocity between them and the text. The catchphrase states and defines what the readers should want and how they should behave. Opportunities to spend time in private with the White man are posed as a major motivation for female clients to learn English and, in doing so, position Japanese women as desirers of English-speaking Western men.

The online photo demonstration of a *mantsuman* lesson on Gaba's homepage (www.gaba.co.jp) illustrates the exact process of the lesson. It leaves very little to the reader's imagination. The first frame depicts the introduction phase in which the instructor greets his student. The second frame shows the beginning of the *mantsuman* lesson. The third indicates the middle of the lesson and the fourth shows the role-play method of the lesson. Finally, the last frame shows how the lesson ends. Throughout the demonstration sequence, the student (a young Japanese female) and the instructor (a tall

White male) are seen interacting in complete privacy with one another. The social space between them is very close and the instructor's full attention is on the student throughout the lesson. There is a physical contact (holding hands) in the fourth frame of the sequence. However, as can be seen in the photo, the contact is depicted as not being overly sexual or threatening, but rather as an honourable or romantic gesture as both instructor and the student smile at each other. As the student waves goodbye to the instructor, the last frame creates the sense that it is the student who, in leaving her instructor, positions herself as the powerful, satisfied customer who can choose to purchase the intimacy with the instructor.

As in the case of the discourse of *ikemen* teachers, Gaba's promotional materials simultaneously position their targeted customers, that is young Japanese women, as being desirous of White masculinity and as the consumers of Western men and English as commodities. It is clear that Gaba actively participates in the construction of the media discourse of *renai* English, which capitalises on and promotes language desire among Japanese women.

2.2.3 Understanding David Beckham: *'Renai* English'

Now, let me introduce you to a related media discourse called, *'renai* English'. My interest in this topic came from a conversation with Yoko:

ヨウコ： 君江さん、英語でセクシーってどうやってやるんですかね？
Yoko: Kimie-san, how do you *do sexy* in English? (f1aug02yoko).

This topic emerged one day as she was telling me how she was often unable to 'chat up' a *gaijin* man in a pub – that is despite her obvious eagerness for intimacy, even if that included a 'one-night stand'. To improve her chances, Yoko began paying close attention to learning 'sexy' phrases in English and the seductive body language of Hollywood actresses in the movies that she saw. During the fieldwork, I often saw her practising romantic and provocative lines and 'sexy' movements such as looking over her shoulder while winking and puckering her lips, all of which reminded me of Marilyn Monroe's classic 'sexy' look. Yoko was not alone in this respect. I found that most of my primary participants considered playing romantic and sexy English rather challenging and often looked to Hollywood movies as sources of information and inspiration.

In fact, the media and the ELL industry in Japan have provided materials for the specific purpose of establishing and maintaining romantic and sexual relationships with foreign men in English for a long while. Women's magazines and websites sometimes feature English lessons entitled *'Renai* English', and there is a wide range of textbooks that teach so-called romantic English phrases and vocabulary. The ESP genre of publications, such as English for business, travel and academic purposes, have a much more prominent presence in the ELL industry. *Renai* English as an ESP genre has received very little scholarly attention to date (but see Kubota, 2008; Piller, 2011a; Piller & Takahashi, 2006, 2010a). As is demonstrated below, *renai* English provides a rich site for gaining insights into the intersection between gender, sexuality and power in relation to ELL in the Japanese context.

Based on data collected for the research, I identified three common characteristics of the *renai* English discourse:

(a) ELL linked with romantic relationships with *gaijin* men;
(b) Hollywood movies as legitimate sources for learning and teaching English; and
(c) the portrayal of Western style romance and sex as romantic and desirable.

Renai English offers multiple and contradictory identities for Japanese women (i.e. the targeted consumers) and their possible romantic partners (i.e. White Western native-speaking men).

In most cases, the discourse of *renai* English promotes the idea that success in learning English equals success in romance with Western men. For example, *Virgin English* was published for the ELL women's market by *ALC* in 2004, with a unique sales proposition that women can beautify themselves through becoming proficient in English. Oonoki, the media development manager of *ALC* mentioned earlier, explains:

英語というツールが身につくと内面に自信がわく。それが「美しさ」となる。
When one acquires English as a tool, she becomes more confident inside. That creates 'beauty'. (Odagiri, 2004: 5)

In this magazine, success in ELL is routinely linked with romantic relationships with Western men. However, by that the magazine does not mean to signify just any Western man, but encourages the readers to find *ikemen gaijins* (good-looking foreigners). One section of the magazine offers various linguistic strategies for developing relationships with *ikemen gaijin* and for rejecting *damenzu gaijin* (useless/ugly foreigners) (Virgin English, 2004: 48–51). Thus, readers can learn not only romantic English phrases (see below) but are also exposed to the categorisation of 'good *gaijin* men' and 'bad *gaijin* men'. The most typical *ikemen gaijin* men are Hollywood stars and Western sports stars.

In the Japanese media space, *renai* English is presented as the necessary means of attaining imaginary romance with Hollywood stars and international sports players. For instance, David Beckham, a British soccer player, has become an icon of glamorous Western masculinity for many Japanese women since the sensational media coverage of his on-field exploits during the World Cup in 2002. Beckham appeared in an edition of *an-an* as part of its theme focused on 'methods for mastering English' (Magazine House, 2003) (see http://www.zassi.net/detail.cgi?gouno=4113, last accessed on 23 October 2012). One of the headlines on the cover page of this issue suggests to Japanese women that it is important that they understand Beckham in English:

英語できちんと理解しよう！ベッカムが語った本音
Let's understand what Beckham is really talking about in English!

This headline suggests that knowledge of English is the only proper vehicle for understanding Beckham, who is represented as the epitome of desirable White masculinity.

Another significant feature of the *renai* English discourse is the promotion of Western women's identity as a key to success in English. To communicate effectively in a romantic context, Japanese women are urged to imagine themselves within the linguistic and romantic identities of Western women. Typically, female celebrities from television and Hollywood are set up as desirable models. Women's magazines often run articles featuring lines delivered by famous female stars in movies. For instance, the aforementioned *Virgin English* (2004) features ways to 'learn love and sex through movies' (Virgin English, 2004: 52–57). Provocative phrases from Hollywood movies are suggested such as:

- 'I will have poetry in my life, and adventure and love above all.' (Gwyneth Paltrow in *Shakespeare in Love*, 1998);
- 'You know what's going to happen? I am gonna fall in love with you. Because I always do.' (Marilyn Monroe in *The Prince and the Showgirl*, 1957);
- 'Oh yeah, right there.' (Meg Ryan in *When Harry Met Sally*, 1989);
- 'To hell with Brett, you know? I've got a vibrator.' (Cameron Diaz in *There's Something About Mary*, 1998); and
- 'We had a great weekend, Leo. And that's that. Now, it's Sunday. And it's over.' (Meg Ryan in *Kate and Leopold*, 2001).

These lines, printed in pink, are presented as effective and sexy, and each phrase is recommended differently depending on the type of romantic outcome desired. All of these actresses are White native speakers of English and the readers are advised that the effective way to memorise these lines is to imagine themselves as one of these White actresses.

Furthermore, the discourse of Hollywood movies and TV programmes as *renai* English promotes Western fictional models of romantic heterosexuality as desirable. A clear example comes from the growing popularity of *Sex and the City* (*SATC*) as ELL materials. *SATC* is a popular American TV programme that took Japan by storm. Its four main characters are in their thirties, all good-looking, fashionable and successful career women, whose vivid and sensational girl-talk centres on romance, sex and life choices.

The Japanese official website for *SATC* (http://dvd.paramount.jp/satc/quote/quo01800.php, accessed 18 July 2011) presents it not only as a hit TV programme, but also endorses its fictional models of Western heterosexual romance and links them with ELL. The website carries five subsections including: (1) news; (2) how to enjoy the programme; (3) cast; (4) quotes of *renai* conversational English; and (5) the episode. In the section on quotes of *renai* conversational English, provocative and 'useful' *SATC* phrases and expressions are periodically introduced and explained by a native English-speaking teacher from Gaba. The bottom section features a native-speaker instructor, Jonathan. The first two sentences of the advertisement read:

> せっかく英語を身につけるなら、SATCの4人みたいに洗練された会話ができるようになりたいもの。そこでオススメなのが Gabaマンツーマン英会話。ネイティブスピーカーの講師とのマンツーマンレッスンだから、ナチュラルで洗練された英会話のセンスをしっかり身につけられるのが Gabaの魅力。
> If you are going to learn English, you want to be able to carry on a sophisticated conversation like the four women from *SATC*. That's why I recommend Gaba's *mantsuman* English conversation course. An attractive point of the *mantsuman* lesson is that you can learn natural and sophisticated English usage through one-on-one lessons with a native-speaker instructor.

These women's lifestyles are obviously fictional. Yet, in this advertisement, the English used by them and their lifestyles (particularly the romantic and sexual aspects of their lives) are positioned and promoted as 'sophisticated' models to be adopted by Japanese women learning English. The text conflates ELL with learning about a fictional model of contemporary Western romance.

In most of the *renai* English textbooks examined, there were similar tendencies to endorse the allegedly Western style of communication and romance (Piller & Takahashi, 2010a; Piller *et al.*, 2010). Ootomo's (2004) '恋愛イングリッシュ：簡単なフレーズで話せる (*Renai English: Speak English with Simple Phrases)'*, one of the *renai* English textbooks I collected during my research, provides a good example. The author, Sanae Ootomo, is a freelance writer specialising in (British) ELL. One of the fundamental tenets of her textbook (Ootomo, 2004: 11) is, as she asserts in the first section, improvement in English proficiency through the power of love. Ootomo states:

> 外国人に恋をすると英語がうまくなるのは本当です。
> It is true that English improves when you fall in love with a foreigner (Ootomo, 2004: 11).

Ootomo's *'Renai* English' consists of 160 pages and is divided into five sections:

(1) improving English proficiency through the power of *renai*;
(2) simple dialogues that connect romance and conversation;
(3) improving English and *renai* through 180 basic phrases;
(4) practical *renai* English – the use of 180 phrases; and
(5) sending cards and emails.

The first section is comprised of several short essays in which Ootomo makes the case for the link between romantic relationships with foreigners and success and enjoyment in ELL. The second section introduces simple English sentences covering issues ranging from dating to marriage. In this section, 30 topics are covered. On the left-hand page, a theme (e.g. talking about oneself, expressing love) and a grammatical form (e.g. do/did you ...?) are introduced; the author's short comment on the theme is provided on the right-hand page. In the third section, examples of conversational exchanges between a Japanese woman and a foreign man are provided. The last section contains several examples of how to write to a foreign man (e.g. birthday cards, thank you cards, emails and text messages).

In her *renai* English textbook, the illustration of the student and her boyfriend indicates that the reader is assumed to be a young woman while her boyfriend is presented as a White native speaker of English (see Figure 2.2). Typically, her examples are situational and phrase based, accompanied by explanations and advice from the author. One example from her textbook demonstrates the ways in which gender, linguistic and sexual identities are constructed and offered to Japanese women.

The example in Figure 2.3 comes from Lesson 20 in the third section entitled: 'Talking about yourself' (Ootomo, 2004: 94–95). The grammatical point to be covered for the lesson is the use of the words 'I've/I haven't ~' The first example is the sentence: 'I've just started my period', which is suggested by

Language Desire 33

Figure 2.2 Illustration of a man and a woman

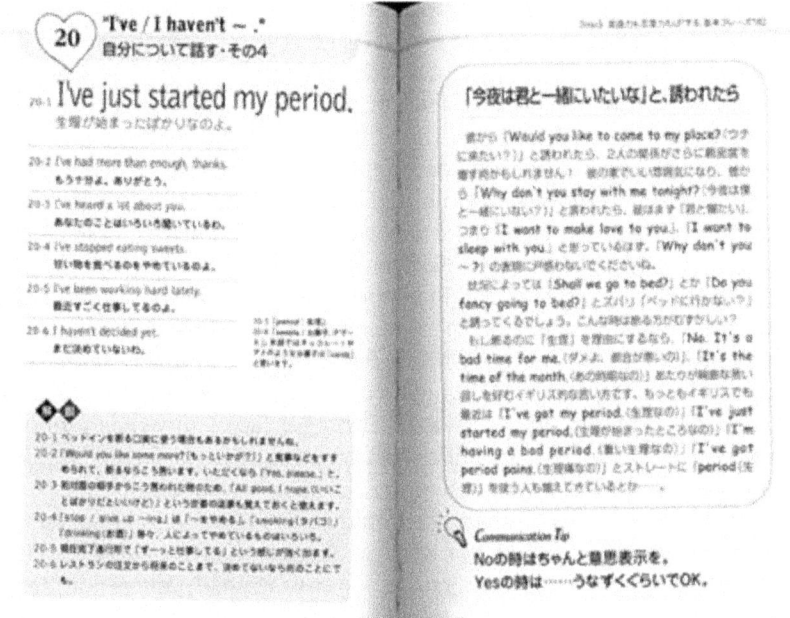

Figure 2.3 Lesson 20 from *Renai English* (Ootomo, 2004: 94–95)

Ootomo as a possible excuse for turning down a sexual invitation by a boyfriend/man. On the right-hand side of the section is a box carrying advice on how to answer when a man says, 'I want to be with you tonight'. In the advice box, Ootomo suggests that it could be time for your relationship to become intimate if 'your boyfriend' asks, 'Would you like to come to my place?'. Ootomo goes on to suggest that if things are getting 'moody' at your boyfriend's place and he asks, 'Why don't you stay with me tonight?', he really means 'I want to make love to you' or 'I want to sleep with you'. Ootomo also warns the reader, 'Don't get fooled by the "why don't you ~" expression'. Ootomo says that sometimes men can be more direct and ask, 'Shall we go to bed?' or 'Do you fancy going to bed?', and then goes on to offer some 'advice' on how to turn down the offer/suggestion such as: 'If you are going to use your period as an excuse, you can use roundabout British-style expressions like (a) No. It's a bad time for me; or (b) It's the time of the month.' However, she goes on: 'Recently there is an increasing number of people who use more straightforward expressions even in England such as: (a) I've just started my period; (b) I'm having a bad period; (c) I've got period pains; or just, (d) period.' In this text, the way in which British women are thought to refuse unwanted sex is constructed as a desirable model. The examples begin by being traditionally indirect but become increasingly more straightforward.

Furthermore, on the bottom of the page is the 'Communication Tip', where Ootomo gives a final piece of advice, stating: 'If you want to say no [to the suggestion of sex] express yourself firmly and properly': but 'If yes, just nodding is OK'. In this example, the author offers options that are widely advocated in the media and romance literature. The 'say no' option seems to be influenced by assertiveness training and anti-rape discourses that blame women for being afraid to refuse sexual advances and simply advise them to say 'no' clearly and loudly (see Kitzinger & Firth, 1999). More significantly, signalling the 'yes' option by nodding reproduces the idealised gendered identity of the passive Japanese woman. Ironically, this passive identity is not what the author initially claims learning English can do for them. In the introduction titled 'This is what is wonderful about a *gaijin* darling' (Ootomo, 2004: 26–27), the author claims that, although Japanese women who are expressive and direct are not popular with Japanese men, *gaijin* men often find these women desirable and attractive. Yet the subject position that the author offers in the example above sharply contradicts her argument. However, it is important to point out that this passivity is also reported in a study by Talbot (1997) on Western romance literature, who examined representations of heroes and heroines in romance fiction. She found that a romance hero is typically portrayed as a dominant man who always knows the heroine's desires and helps her admit to them. The heroine, on the other hand, is represented as a recipient of the hero's education about her secret desires. Her emotional and sexual passivity is presented as 'a natural and even desirable element of femininity' (Talbot, 1997: 119). Therefore, Ootomo's 'yes option' may not only reproduce the idealised Japanese culture-specific identity, but also reproduce this normalised heterosexuality (i.e. the sexual agents of men as active and women as passive), which circulates widely in international contexts. Additionally, the majority of other *renai* English texts collected for the present research did not offer dialogues in which women initiated sexual encounters.

2.2.4 ELL, consumerism and international heterosexual romance

An examination of women's magazines, 'ladies' comics', advertisements for English language schools and *renai* English materials shows that the meaning of and images of success in learning English are highly gendered and sexualised in the Japanese ELL market. More specifically, ELL is powerfully associated with the media discourses of international heterosexual romance that reify particular subject positions: 'sexy', provocative and demure femininity for Japanese female learners of English, and good-looking, chivalrous and powerful masculinity for male English teachers.

During my fieldwork, I had several opportunities to discuss the media discourse of *renai* English with my informants. Most of the participants showed a keen interest in purchasing *renai* textbooks, and some wanted to borrow my magazine collections. When Eika was going out with her first *gaijin* boyfriend (White Australian) in March 2003, she expressed an interest in buying such a book. Until she came to Australia, she had little knowledge of this genre of English. At that time, she thought that communicating her needs and emotions to her Australian boyfriend was constrained by her lack of English vocabulary. Discussing *renai* textbooks one day, Eika jokingly said:

エイカ： そいう本があったら買うよぜったい@@
Eika: I would definitely buy a textbook like that @@ [i.e. a textbook designed to teach how to negotiate in a romantic context] (f27march03eika)

Although *renai* English may be a fairly recent development, Hollywood movies have long made their mark on Japanese women's imagination about the West, English and heterosexual romance. In the next section, I turn to the implications of exposure to Hollywood celebrities in girlhood and adolescence for the construction of Japanese women's *akogare* for English and the West.

2.3 Dreaming of Tom Cruise and Brad Pitt

All the primary participants and many of the secondary participants reported having developed a varying degree of fascination for Westerners, particularly Hollywood celebrities and Western musicians, in their girlhood and adolescence. For example, in her first interview, Chizuko enthusiastically told me about her increasing admiration for the 'beauty of Western people' when she was growing up in a small country town (i10oct03chizuko). For example, hearing a rumour that an American exchange student had arrived at a junior high school in the next town, she took a train to go to the school just to take a photo of him, which she still cherishes in her photo album back home.

While the participants seem to have had a general admiration for the West in their childhood, it became rapidly gendered and romanticised as they entered adolescence. For instance, in their secondary school years, Eika and one secondary participant, Miri, had a romantic obsession with Tom Cruise, particularly as the star of *Top Gun* (1985). Miri believes that women of her generation (i.e. born in the 1960s or 1970s) have a soft spot for a man like Tom Cruise and she still believes that 'he is really hot' (f15aug02miri) (Takahashi, 2010a). Chizuko fell in love with Christopher Atkins who starred in *Blue Lagoon* (1980), while one of the secondary participants, Sato, devotedly listened to the 1980s Norwegian but US-based pop group, a-ha, in her junior high school years. Yoko professed to have been obsessed with the Hollywood movie star Brad Pitt since her early twenties. Although my participants' *akogare* for specific movie stars and musicians differ, the objects of these feelings are usually White Western men, from or based in the United States, and act or sing predominantly in English (see Chapter 7 for the racial implication of language desire for their socialisation in Sydney). During the participants' adolescence, their romantic *akogare* for Western celebrities became increasingly conflated with a desire for learning English, resulting in an immediate or future increase in their contact with English.

To express their admiration for movie and rock/pop stars, some of the participants wrote them fan letters in English. For instance, after seeing *Top Gun*, Eika and her classmate decided to send a fan letter to Tom Cruise. At that time their English was not advanced enough to compose such a letter but that did not deter them and they actively sought resources to achieve their goal. Initially published in the 1970s, a popular movie magazine *Screen* (Kindai Shoten) often carried articles advising Japanese fans on how to write a fan letter in English to Hollywood celebrities. Using the template letter provided in *Screen*, Eika sought help from their English schoolteacher, who proof-read and edited the letter. Eika recalls that, as they passionately wrote the letter, they began imagining the possibility of receiving a personal invitation from Tom Cruise.

エイカ:	あの時あれだったよ〜、ビックドリーマーだったよね@ あたし達書いてる時さ〜ウッキウキじゃない？　で彼［トム・クルーズ］がさ〜、日本の女子高生の情熱を知ったらひょっとしてハリウッドにご招待とかね〜考えててさ〜！@@@
Eika:	you see, we were big dreamers at that time@ when we were writing the letter. we were so excited about the whole thing and we thought if he [Tom Cruise] found out about our passion for him, from Japanese high school girls, we thought that we might get invited to Hollywood!@@@ (i4june03eika)

Although neither a personal response nor an invitation from a Hollywood star was very likely, their fantasy about meeting him was powerful enough to motivate them to rehearse their self-introduction in English.

エイカ:	でさ〜、もし本当にそういう事になっちゃったらどうする〜とか言ってて。そんな時にじゃあトムにどうやって自己紹介するみたいな？彼女とあたしさ〜@
Eika:	we were talking about what if it really happened. how should we introduce ourselves to Tom? she and I @
キミエ:	@@
Kimie:	@@
エイカ:	一緒に練習してたよ@
Eika:	we were practising together@
キミエ:	え、英語？
Kimie:	what, English?
エイカ:	うん、英語の練習
Eika:	yeah, practising English.
キミエ:	@冗談でしょ？@
Kimie:	@ are you kidding me?@
エイカ:	彼が目の前にいる想定でさ〜、「How do you do?」、「My name is Eika」［with deliberate intonation and higher pitch of her voice］@@@。本当にバカだったよね〜。あたし達さ〜@@@

Eika: imagining him in front of us, 'How do you do♂?', 'my name is Eika' [with deliberately stronger English intonation and higher pitch of her voice] @@@. we were so stupid then, really. we were. @@@ (i4june03eika)

The secondary participant, Sato, provides another case of the link between *akogare* for the West and ELL. When Sato was 13 years old, she 'fell in love' with *a-ha*, the Norwegian pop group popular in the 1980s. While she had always liked English since childhood, it then became her 'mission' to improve her English.

サト： 子供の頃から英語に慣れてはいたんだよね。タイでインターナショナルスクールに行ってたし、親が結構英語喋れたから。a-haに夢中になった後英語の事真剣に考え出して。よく@「私の彼らへの愛が英語を習うのを助けてくれる」って思ってた@

Sato: I felt comfortable with English since my childhood. I went to an international school for a year in Thailand and my parents were fluent in English. it was after I fell in love with *a-ha* that I started to think I must get serious about English. I used to think, @ 'my love for them will help me learn English!'@

キミエ： @@
Kimie: @@

サト： @そう、バカだと思うでしょ？
Sato: @yeah, don't you think it was pretty stupid♂?

キミエ： いやいや@@
Kimie: no, no @@

サト： @@でも絶対私の彼らへの愛で英語マスターできるって信じきってたもん@@
Sato: @@but I had unshakable faith that with my love for them, I would be able to master English@@ (f26feb04sato)

Most of my primary and secondary participants told me similar stories indicating how their already existing *akogare* for the West became gendered and romanticised in adolescence. These examples illustrate how emergent romantic desire for Western celebrities was the first in a series of links created between ELL and romantic attraction. In practising how to introduce themselves in English to Tom Cruise, Eika and her friend created an imaginary relationship between the actor and themselves, hence constructing gendered and national identities as young Japanese girls in love with a stern male star.

Yoko's case presents another example of ELL and Hollywood movies as a site of lifestyle and identity construction. Unlike most of the other participants who caught the 'fever' of movie stars in their adolescence, Yoko's passion for the West and English became intensified and romanticised during a turbulent marriage in her mid-twenties. Highly disillusioned with her married life, she began investing her energy and time in learning English and watching Hollywood movies, which provided her with an emotional refuge.

ヨウコ： その時の生活がすっごくいやだったんですよ。だからね、逃げてたって訳じゃないんですけど、いいなあと思うものに、こう、がーっと入っちゃう様な物に依存してたのかもしれないなって、後で思いました。映画を狂ったように見てた時期があったんですよ[…]
映画一日三本とか・・・今思うとすごいよかったと思うんですけど。色んなもの見れて。今は時間ないし。[…] でもきっと何か嫌なものから逃げてるために、「私はこんなに映画を見てるのよ」っていいたかったのかも。

Yoko: my life at that time was awful. so, it was kind of like running away from it, but I thought later that I was becoming dependent on something cool that I could become obsessed with. there was a time when I was watching movies like crazy [...] three movies a day... now that I think of it, it was good. seeing many different movies. I have no time now. [...] but maybe I wanted to say, 'I am watching so many movies', in order to run away from something awful.
(i30april02yoko)

Through the movies, she also developed a great deal of *akogare* for the concept of all things White.

キミエ： 何に対して憧れがあったの？
Kimie: what did you have *akogare* for?

ヨウコ： 白人。白人男性、白人女性、白人社会。なんていうんですか、アメリカの映画に出てくるような。典型的な感じ。
Yoko: White people. White men, White women, White society. how can I put it? like the ones that appear in American movies. a traditional image...

キミエ： どんな感じ？
Kimie: like what?

ヨウコ： ハニー、ダーリン、「行ってきま〜す」。チュ、みたいな感じ。で、学校行こうって子供も「行ってきま〜す」とか言って黄色いスクールバス乗って行くみたいな。
Yoko: honey, darling, 'see you later'. kiss, something like this. and children when going to school say, 'see you later' as they get onto a yellow school bus. (i30april02yoko)

Yoko told me that her rapidly increased *akogare* for the West resulted from an extensive exposure to Western ideals of love and family through movies at that time.

ヨウコ： 映画を見出してから特に。だから、「ああ、こういう世界があるんだな〜」って思いました。
Yoko: especially since I started to see movies. I used to think, 'wow, there is a world like this'. (i30april02yoko)

Most notably, Brad Pitt, a Hollywood celebrity, emerged as the object of Yoko's intense romantic *desire* during her movie craze. The star thus became a signifier of ideal Western masculinity and a tremendous item of symbolic capital. As will be discussed later, for Yoko, standards of desirability and worthiness of male Western interlocutors were almost always judged against those of Brad Pitt. Furthermore, Yoko's comment indicates that English is intricately linked with her desire not only for White men, but also with the image of the typical heterosexual romantic/marital relationship that circulates in the international media.

2.4 Summary

In this chapter I have presented an analysis of the media discourse of ELL in Japan and Japanese women's discourses of *akogare*. ELL in a Japanese context is closely linked with power and the discourses of race and heterosexuality. The ELL media discourses function to blur the boundary between good-looking, chivalrous White Western men as desirable English teachers and romantic partners. The example of Gaba demonstrates that the ELL media deliberately conflate ELL and romance and use that to generate further desire to consume English and White masculinity as commodities. Using examples of *ikemen* teachers and Gaba promotional goods, I argued that the media promote the consumerist mode of ELL: the type of instructors and the style and place of learning are presented as within the control of Japanese women. Thus, in this mode of ELL, contemporary femininity merges with a consumer identity; English and romance become objects of consumption.

The media discourse of *renai* English was presented as a further example in which ELL and international heterosexual romance become mutually constitutive. Such discourse endorses particular subject positions, those of 'sexy', provocative and also romantically passive femininity, which have circulated widely in the international media for some time (Marchetti, 1993; Talbot, 1997). English has become a new element in an ancient script of gender identities and heterosexual romance, which is resold to young Japanese women as something modern and sophisticated.

The final section presented an analysis of Japanese women's discourses of *akogare* in their adolescence. The majority of the primary and secondary participants reported having developed a passion for Western musicians or/and actors in their teenage years, and had dreamed of communicating their romantic desires to these celebrities. Such passion worked as a link to their increased desire for and use of English in their lives. In contradiction to the discourse of English as an emancipatory tool for women (Matsubara, 1989), my participants' examples suggested that English functions as a means to perform their typical heterosexual identity as adolescent girls desiring a Western male.

Overall, this chapter has mainly focused on women's perception of Western masculinity and, as such, leaves us with many questions about their self-perception. What does it mean, for example, when comic book pictures portray Japanese girls with unusually rounded eyes (Section 2.2.1), or what does it mean for the women to look to Caucasian Western – rather than Japanese – actresses as models of modern womanhood and romance (Section 2.2.3)? While these are open to various interpretations, what these examples demonstrate is that orientalism (Said, 1978 [1994]) is deeply ingrained in Japanese popular culture, and that it has impacted on the way women see and present themselves. Particularly since the end of WWII, to be 'modern' and thus 'attractive' has entailed erasing the 'traditional' and thus 'unattractive' Japanese traits (e.g. narrow eyes, lack of sexual assertiveness) and appropriating Western ones (e.g. large eyes, sexual assertiveness) in self-representation. English and Whiteness are sold in a way that the English language offers a means of transcending racial boundaries, and an association with Whiteness – be it through learning White women's talk about their private lives or how they conduct their romantic lives – emerges as a legitimate way of learning English.

Finally, subject positions that are offered in the media discourse of language desire are many and complex. This also raises the question of how the subject positions available to young Japanese women may in fact impact upon their actual linguistic practices in interactional contexts. I will provide some answers to this question in Chapters 4–6. However, first it is necessary to consider the ways in which my participants decided to leave Japan and go on *ryugaku* to Australia. Why did they choose to come to Australia? This is the main focus of the next chapter.

3   *Ryugaku*

3.1 Introduction

From the outset of my fieldwork, I was struck by my participants' eagerness to tell me about their *akogare* for English and *ryugaku* (study overseas). It was as though I did not even have to ask them questions. It appeared that they genuinely wanted me to understand their reasons for learning English and coming to Australia for *ryugaku*. It also seemed as if they were reassessing their choices and the realities of their situation in our dialogues. At the same time, I felt that they were looking for my acknowledgement that what they were doing in Sydney was meaningful, despite all the difficulties they were facing. Although this enthusiasm was common among my participants, their reasons for *ryugaku* varied widely. As Ahearn (2001) reminds us, 'motivations are always complex and contradictory'. Indeed, my participants' narratives of *ryugaku* life in Sydney revealed motivations and desires which were multiple, fluid, complex and at times highly conflicting.

In this chapter I will introduce you to Japanese women's narratives about *ryugaku* in Australia. Firstly I explore the ways in which the Japanese media promote certain countries as destinations of language *ryugaku* and construct the practice of *ryugaku* as a dramatic way of reinventing women's identities and lifestyles. I then examine issues surrounding my participants' decisions and experiences of *ryugaku* in Sydney.

3.2 English *Ryugaku* in the Media

In the major bookstores I visited in Tokyo, there was often a special booth set up by an English school and/or *ryugaku* agency. The agency was there to promote a wide range of services and products around English learning and *ryugaku*. Perhaps because I was walking around with a pile of English textbooks and *ryugaku* magazines for my research, I was often stopped by a female representative from one of these booths and asked if I was interested in learning English and going on *ryugaku* one day. She then proceeded to offer me a special deal and also invited me to attend their free seminar. One female representative said to me: 'If you have time *right now*, I can take you to our office, which is nearby, and help you figure out what type of *ryugaku* is suitable for you.'

Although I never took up such an offer, I wondered if their invitation to 'help figure out what type of *ryugaku* is suitable for you' could be appealing to those considering going overseas. As there are so many different ways in which *ryugaku* can be arranged, those new to this discourse might be easily confused and feel at a loss as to what the best option is. Numerous magazines and guidebooks offer a vast variety of *ryugaku* programmes, from small-scale one-week *ryugaku* to a long-term university degree *ryugaku*. They are often published by *ryugaku* agents, travel specialist publishers or publishing companies specialising in foreign language education. Women's magazines, too, often carry special articles dealing with the topic of *ryugaku* and offer wide-ranging advice to their readers.

Despite all the varieties of *ryugaku*, two common characteristics can be identified in the media discourse of language *ryugaku*. Firstly, in most *ryugaku* magazines and *ryugaku* articles in women's magazines, the choices of language (usually English) *ryugaku* destinations are often limited to five or six major English-speaking nations, almost always including the United States, United Kingdom, Canada, Australia and New Zealand. *ALC*'s comprehensive guide to ESL programmes (ALC, 2002) (see Figure 3.1) provides a typical example of the media representation of *ryugaku* destinations. The headline on the top right-hand side, referring to a *ryugaku* destination, poses the rhetorical question: 'How should I choose?' The main body has a list of six destination countries (from the top: America, Canada, Australia, New Zealand, United Kingdom and Ireland) and their characteristics in terms of ESL programmes.

What is missing from this example is that, despite its claim to be a *comprehensive* list, other English-speaking countries from the outer circle of countries in which English is widely used (Kachru, 1992) including, for example, India, Singapore, Hong Kong, the Philippines and countries in Africa, are not mentioned as destinations. The media discourse of *ryugaku* functions to legitimatise the ownership of English by the inner circle countries by ignoring the status of other countries, namely those in the outer circle. However, *ALC*'s representation is by no means an isolated example. Most *ryugaku* magazines I examined follow the same line. As will be discussed below, options that were entertained by most participants prior to their coming to

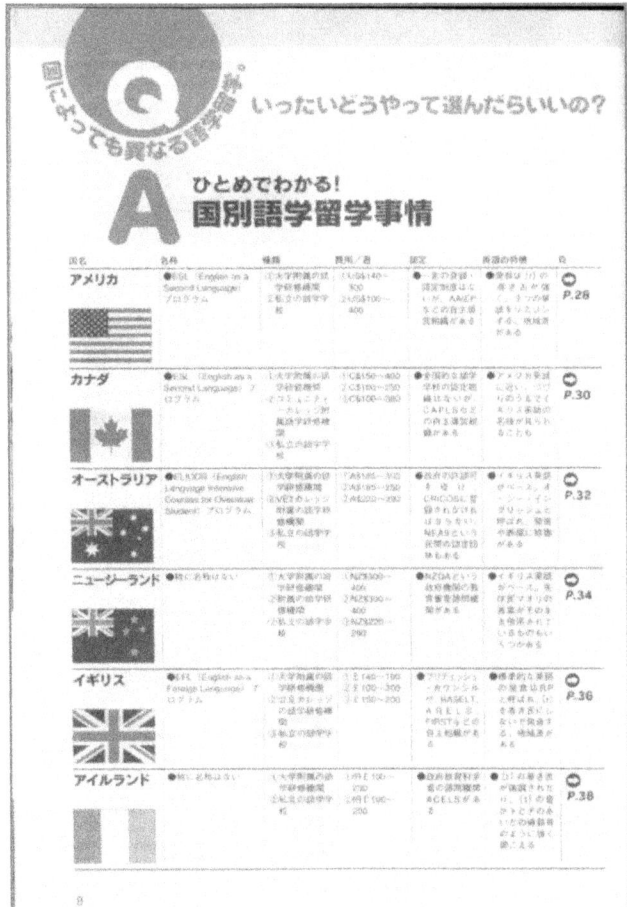

Figure 3.1 ALC's comprehensive guide to ESL programmes (ALC, 2002: 8)

Sydney were also limited to these countries, in particular, the United States, Canada, UK and Australia.

Secondly, the Japanese media typically portray *ryugaku* as a glamorous means of reinventing and empowering womanhood and kick-starting a new lifestyle. *Ryugaku* magazines often carry sensational headlines such as '海外生活で見つける新しい自分：留学で人生を変えよう in Australia (Finding a new self overseas: change your life through *ryugaku* in Australia)' (Ryugaku Journal, 2002) and 'オーストラリア＆ニュージーランド：新しい生き方始めよう (Australia and New Zealand: let's start a new life)' (Wish International, 2002).

Figure 3.2 Yappari kaigai e ikoo (Let's go overseas, 2000: 38)

The heading and the photo in the *ryugaku* magazine, 'やっぱり海外へ行こう (Let's go overseas)' (see Figure 3.2) reflects this tendency. The headline states 'For *ryugaku* and language training without regret: going overseas to find a new self', while the young woman in the close-up camera shot looks to the left with a sense of determination and hope. In the next section, we will see that my participants also considered the act of learning English overseas as a means of finding a new self and/or lifestyle.

3.3 Australia as a Destination

Kelsky (2001) points out that, despite the dominant discourse of *akogare* for the West and ELL and in spite of the large number of women choosing to study English domestically (Kobayashi, 2002), those who actually commit themselves to *ryugaku*, particularly long-term *ryugaku* programmes, are still in a minority. This suggests that there could be a wider range of factors which, together with *akogare*, may lead to the decision to go on or not to go on *ryugaku*. In fact, my participants had a tendency to narrate their particular experience of critical life events/experiences behind their final decision to act on their *akogare* for going overseas. In the following sections, I will introduce you to their personal reasons for coming to Australia to study English and/ or work, highlighting the issues surrounding their decision and their experiences of *ryugaku*. Such issues include: critical events that led to *ryugaku*; the political economy of Australia as a *ryugaku* destination; the working holiday programme; age and *ryugaku*; and images of Australia.

3.3.1 Critical events

Linde (1992: 3) points out that an individual needs to have 'a coherent, acceptable and revised life story' in order to live comfortably in the social world. In particular, when it comes to professional identities, life decisions that hold considerable significance for the individual, it becomes increasingly important to account for particular choices we make. When I first met my participants, I usually began my interview with a question: 'Why did you want to come to Australia?' From their replies it was evident that a host of complex social, economic, cultural and familial factors were at play. Put another way, their decisions to leave Japan and spend time overseas studying and working in an English-language environment were inextricably bound up in a complex host of 'push' and 'pull' factors. Nevertheless, in each case one particular factor was described as their final reason for undertaking *ryugaku* and choosing Australia as their study destination. I will explore these key events and experiences in this section.

For Yoko, her final push was narrated as her experience of divorce in her late twenties and her desire to escape gossip in a country town where 'everyone' knew of her ordeal. Her emotional turmoil was heightened by the fact that her husband and his new girlfriend worked in the same public office as she did. She found an emotional refuge in Hollywood movies (see Chapter 5) and in extramarital affairs with a Japanese-speaking American man and a second-generation Japanese–Brazilian boyfriend. However, it was not until she visited her friend in Sydney for a holiday that she was able to find a new direction in her life. To her surprise, she was able to forget tormenting thoughts about her divorce during this holiday.

ヨウコ： それで、全然[主人]思い出さなくってそこで私、あっ忘れてた！とか思って。あ、もういいやって。だから仕事ももう辞めて［…］私もずっと前から海外行って英語マスターしたいな～と思ってたんで。

| Yoko: | and I didn't think about it [the husband] at all and I thought, 'oh, I've forgotten about it!' it didn't matter anymore. I was ready to quit my job [...] I've always wanted to go overseas to master English. (i30april02yoko) |

After returning to Japan, she decided to resign from her job and move to Sydney as an international student. Thus, *ryugaku* for Yoko served as a means of rejecting her identity as a miserable divorcee and of restarting her life by reinventing herself as an international woman with fluency in English. This personal reason for *ryugaku* had a tremendous impact on the way in which she approached socialising and language learning in Sydney (we will revisit this in Chapters 7, 8 and 9).

Similarly, Chizuko considered the painful break-up with Tony, her Australian boyfriend in Tokyo, to be the main reason for her coming to Australia. In our interview, she described him as a man of every woman's *akogare* and I could sense that for her he was still a very special person, an unattainable ex-lover. Although their break-up was amicable, Tony proved to be unforgettable and, when she discovered a few years later that he had married someone else, she was devastated to the point that she decided to change her life through relocating overseas.

チズコ:	[...]「幸せ」って聞いたら「ああ、幸せだよ」って一応言って、「ああ、じゃあ、幸せにね、じゃあねバイバイ」って別れたんだけど、それでもうあたし、「海外行く！」って思って@@
Chizuko:	[...] when I asked him if he was happy, he said, 'yes, I am'. I said, 'I wish you a lot of happiness, bye' in parting, but then, I thought to myself, 'I am going overseas!' @@
キミエ:	なんで？
Kimie:	why?
チズコ:	わかんないでも、生活環境を変えたいって思ったのよ
Chizuko:	I don't know, but I wanted to change my everyday environment
キミエ:	それがショックだったんだ？
Kimie:	were you shocked?
チズコ:	そうなの、よっぽど引きずってたんじゃないの。だけど、日本にいたらトニー日本にいるし、どっかでたまたま会えるかもしれないっていうのがあったんじゃ無いの？未練がましいからさ
Chizuko:	yeah, I must have been still obsessed with him. I was hoping to run into him and this would have been possible as long as I lived in Japan. I was still attached. (i10oct03Chizuko).

As discussed in Chapter 5, Chizuko grew up fostering a great deal of *akogare* for English and Western culture. Interestingly, her break-up with Tony did not extinguish this; if anything, it promoted an even stronger desire to master English, as she saw her limited English as the main cause of the failure of their relationship:

チズコ： うん、結婚する多分予定って言うか、しようと思ったんだよね、でも、だけど最終的に、なのが、やっぱり子供の問題・・・コミュニケーションがすごいディープなところが出来ないんで・・それがネックでやっぱり別れちゃった・・・私の語学力がこ〜〜〜〜んなもんだったから・・・
Chizuko: yeah, we were kind of planning to get married, wanted to marry. but in the end, the issue of children came up ... it was impossible to communicate at deep levels ... we broke up because of it ... my proficiency was thiiiiiis low ... (i10oct03Chizuko)

Chizuko was convinced that, had she been more fluent in English, they would have taken their relationship to the next level – marriage.

キミエ： じゃあ、もしちずちゃんがもう少し英語が出来たら、トニーがもう少し [日本語できたらって・・
Kimie: then, if you had more English or he had [more Japanese,

チズコ： [そしたら結婚してたよ！
Chizuko: [we would have been married! (i10oct03Chizuko)

For Chizuko, *ryugaku* to Australia was a means, not only of changing her life circumstances, but also of transforming her identity as a deficient speaker of English, which, in her view, partly led to the end of her relationship with Tony who she adored and who she still describes as the 'most wonderful man on earth' (i10oct03Chizuko).

   For Eika, *ryugaku* to the United States had been a long-term project in which she had invested a great deal, both emotionally and financially, for over a decade. She had learnt English since her late teenage years, during which time she fantasised about going to the United States. As mentioned earlier, due to her parent's refusal to support her *ryugaku*, Eika began working to self-fund her study overseas after graduating from a college of English. However, she recalls losing a sense of direction in life after some years of working in a large company.

エイカ： だから、あの、留学がダメって言われて、取りあえず働きだした時からだよね・・・なんか目的を失っちゃったって言うの？英語が全てだ

ったじゃない？こう、それ以来自分が何をしたいかって事が全然見失っちゃってさ〜。まあ、そんなに遣り甲斐の無い仕事ではなかったけど、結局本当に自分がやりたいと思ってやってた仕事じゃなかったからさ〜。もうあれ以上はあのマンネリの仕事続けられなかったよね。

Eika: so, since the idea of *ryugaku* was rejected and I started to work … it's like I've kind of lost a sense of purpose in my life because English was everything for me. like, since then, I've lost the sight of what I really wanted to do. well, my job wasn't too bad, but it wasn't a job that I was really inspired to do. I couldn't possibly continue that mundane job. (t15april04eika)

Thus, her purpose of a working holiday in Sydney was two-fold. Firstly, she wanted to re-engage with her decade-long *akogare* project of mastering English, which she said had meant 'everything for her' since her teenage years. Secondly, Eika was unlike Yoko and Chizuko: she had no traumatic emotional experiences in Japan. Rather, Eika had a lack of direction in her life that seems to have driven her towards the option of a working holiday in Australia (the contradiction between her *akogare* for the United States and her choice of Australia is explained in section 6.3.2). Like many hundreds of thousands of Japanese women, Eika wanted to find 'something', a new direction, a new life commitment that would bring about a sense of happiness and fulfilment. She had *akogare* for the English language and the West, both of which were central to this project.

Yuka's case was part of an increasing social phenomenon within Japan (Saito, 2003). At junior high school, she became a victim of school bullying and, as a result, she had become *hikikomori*, or 'socially withdrawn' and dropped out of school at the age of 14. As a solution to this problem, a friend of her parents suggested that she spent time overseas studying English, which she had had a positive image of. She enthusiastically responded to the suggestion.

ユカ: あたし、全然日本になんていたくなかったから。でも英語は昔から好きだったから、行く行くみたいな@

Yuka: I didn't want to stay in Japan at all. I always liked English, so I was like, 'I would love to go' @ (f9march03yuka)

Her case differs from the other participants in my study in that her *akogare* for the West, and consequently White Western men, emerged after her arrival in Australia. However, Yuka's view of *ryugaku* as a powerful way of reinventing her identity and finding a brighter future was consistent with that of many of the other women.

For Ichi, her intense *akogare* for English and overseas began with her *akogare* for the Australian English teacher at her high school. *Ryugaku* became her dream after a short-term visit to Australia (this also happened to Eika and many of my secondary participants). After majoring in English at a woman's college she first considered finding a job in Japan. However, she did not want to 'live the rest of my life as an office worker' (i27july01ichi) and wanted to build a career in a field in which men and women were treated equally. Ichi thought that becoming an operator in a control tower at an airport would be an ideal job and she undertook a two-year correspondence course. However, when she failed the national exam, she finally acted on her long-term *akogare* to study at a university overseas and persuaded her parents to fund a university degree in Australia. She believed that an overseas qualification as a teacher would enable her to earn social respect in Japan and to obtain a job with greater gender equality. Therefore, *ryugaku* for Ichi was a means of resistance to an ordinary lifestyle as a young woman in Japan and also a means of gaining social capital which would enable her to fight for greater gender equality in the workplace.

Yoko, Chizuko and Yuka's cases demonstrate that English *ryugaku* served as a means by which they attempted to overcome critical life events. It gave them an opportunity to leave their local area and those people who positioned them negatively. This indicates the importance of understanding that these Japanese women did not come to Australia simply to study English, which they could have done in any case without leaving Japan. Their decisions to move to Australia were intimately bound up with their desire for identity transformation through the attainment of proficiency in an international language, English. Relocation to the fantasised West, they believed, would allow them to leave their problems behind.

However, it was not only specific negative experiences that drove Japanese women out of their homeland. General frustration with their lives was often the motivation behind *ryugaku*. For instance, as Ichi and Eika's cases demonstrate, gender inequalities in the workplace still mar the prospects of working women in Japan and, out of frustration, these women attempt to attain the career-boosting overseas qualifications and English fluency that are often promoted in media discourses in Japan. Both Ichi and Eika had had *akogare* for the English language and Western countries since their childhood. It was their disillusionment about their career prospects as women in Japan that prompted them to turn to their long-term *akogare* for *ryugaku* and ELL in order to find new lifestyles and job opportunities. This finding is consistent with the conclusions of Kelsky (2001) and Matsubara

(1989) — that highly career oriented women in Japan tend to consider overseas education and English as indispensable to the realisation of their aspirations. Although Eika and Ichi were not as highly career oriented, they were fully aware that their gender imposed constraints on their prospects in the male-dominated job market in Japan.

3.3.2 The political economy of *ryugaku* in Australia

リナ： アメリカはやっぱりテロとかで危ないかなって。高いしね、生活費とか。で、カナダとかイギリスは寒いからやだな〜って。で、よーく考えたらオーストラリアって英語圏で一番安全だし、ワーホリで行けるしね〜。

Rina: America would be too dangerous because of terrorism. the cost of living is high, too. and Canada and England would be too cold. after I really thought about it, Australia is the safest English speaking country and has the working holiday system. (f10dec03eikarina)

This comment by a secondary participant, Rina, well summarises a typical decision-making process about *ryugaku* in Australia among many of the Japanese women in my study. She had recently graduated from a two-year English college course and wanted to spend a year overseas before joining one of the major English conversation schools as a regional manager. When the participants of this study were nurturing their *akogare* for *ryugaku* in Japan, not surprisingly, the United States was their first choice, followed by the UK (largely England), Canada and then Australia. New Zealand was only occasionally mentioned, and Ireland and outer circle English-speaking countries such as Singapore, Hong Kong or India were never mentioned. This indicates the powerful influence of the prevalent media representation of the most desirable *ryugaku* countries described at the beginning of this chapter. Consistent with the media representation of *ryugaku* destinations and Matsuda's (2003) report, the concept of English *ryugaku* among my participants was always related to living in one of the inner circle English-speaking countries.

What Rina's account further shows is that Australia was seldom the participants' first choice. In other words, only a few had a passionate *akogare* for Australia prior to their departure. Most chose Australia for socioeconomic or 'practical' reasons rather than other inner circle English-speaking countries, particularly the United States. Despite its popularity in Japanese women's *ryugaku* narratives, the United States was often excluded primarily for security reasons in light of the 9/11 acts of terrorism. Moreover, the United States and the United Kingdom were rejected for their high costs of living and study, while the UK and Canada were eliminated predominantly for their poor weather: The UK was seen as 'gloomy' and Canada as 'too cold'. Although all participants raised 'mastery of English' as their first priority, Australia was their chosen destination on the basis of factors that were more related to lifestyle choices than to conditions for learning English.

In the *ryugaku* market, Australia emerged as an attractive choice thanks to its reputation for relatively low costs of living and study, its relative safety, its sunny weather and its English-speaking Western identity. This view dovetailed with the way the Australian English language industry marketed Australia as 'value for money' (Evans, 2005). Although the majority of participants knew of Australia as an immigrant-receiving country, very few raised multiculturalism or multilingualism as part of its attraction. As is discussed in the following chapters, the majority of Japanese women in my study preferred socialising with White native speakers of English and often expressed ambivalent feelings about associating with non-White, non-native speakers of English.

Australia was the first choice for both Ichi and Chizuko. What they had in common was that, for both, their first close encounter with Australia was highly gendered. Ichi's first encounter with Australia was through an Australian male teacher of English at her high school, for whom she developed a romantic *akogare* which was later translated into an urge to visit Australia.

キミエ： へ〜あこがれてたんだ〜？
Kimie: I see, you had *akogare* for him?
イチ： うん、すっごくかっこよかったよね。それで、オーストラリア行きたいな〜って思ったんだもん。
Ichi: yeah, he was so good-looking. that's what made me want to go to Australia. (f29oct03ichi)

In her high school years, Ichi had in fact visited Sydney on a one-month English homestay *ryugaku*. During the visit, she 'fell in love' with Australia and became determined to return for further study. Among all the participants, Ichi probably had the most positive view of Australia and strongest emotional connection with the Australian people and culture, that is, with the dominant Anglo-Saxon facet of Australia (I will discuss this further in Chapter 7).

Similarly, Chizuko's first encounter with Australia was through Tony, her first *gaijin* Australian boyfriend, in Tokyo in the early 1990s. As mentioned earlier, their three-year relationship ended due to a 'language problem' (i10oct03Chizuko). Even after the break-up which 'made the air look grey' (i10oct03Chizuko), Australia was a 'natural' choice for Chizuko.

チズコ： やっぱりトニーはすっごいいい人だったからね〜。今思ってもできた人だったんだなって。で、他のオージーの友達とかもすごくいい人達だったから、オーストラリアだったら間違いないって思ったんだよね
Chizuko: Tony was a wonderful person. even in hindsight, he was such a good person. and other Australian friends were nice people, too, so I thought that I couldn't go wrong with Australia.
(t5may04Chizuko)

Situations like those of Ichi and Chizuko were rare among my participants, both primary and secondary. The USA and American English dominated *akogare* narratives of ELL and *ryugaku* in both media discourses and those of the participants in my study, for many of whom, even after their arrival in Sydney, the United States remained the dominant point of reference or a standard against which their Australian experiences were measured. Among other things, they talked at length about the difference between Australian English and American English. In their narratives, Australian English was often framed as something 'cute' or 'strange', constructing the language as inferior to its American counterpart. However, as their stay extended, images of the United States and American English began to change: even for Yoko, the most passionate admirer of the USA.

There was one significant factor that made Australia more attractive than the United States for some participants. My data suggests that Australia would not have been chosen if it were not for its working holiday programme. Based on an agreement negotiated among eight governments (the eight countries participating in the working holiday visa programme at that time of the study were Australia, New Zealand, Canada, Korea, France, Germany, UK and Japan (Japan Association for Working Holiday Makers, 2006), this programme allows citizens under the age of 30 to travel, study and work for one year in any of the participating countries. As in the case of English *ryugaku*, working holidays were also a highly gendered practice (at least among the Japanese participating in the programme). According to one staff member of the Japan Association for Working Holiday Makers (JAWHM) (t7april-04JAWHM), since the programme began in 1980, over 70% of Japanese working holidaymakers have been women. According to the staff, taking a working holiday is impossible for Japanese men after they begin their business careers.

スタッフ： 男の子は、［ワーキングホリデー］大学中に行くんですよ。それがベストなんですよね。どうしてかっていうと、大学だったら戻れるでし

ょ？でも、一度仕事しちゃって、辞めて行くっていうと、大変なんですよ、社会的に。浪人になっちゃうじゃないでうか。だから、一度就職したら滅多にワーホリでは行きませんよ。仕事に戻れませんから。

Staff: boys go [on working holiday] during university. that's the best for them because they could go back to university, couldn't they? but, it is a lot of trouble if they are already working and decide to quit work in order to go [on working holiday]. they would become *roonin* (unemployed). so once they get employed, they don't go on working holiday. they won't be able to go back to their job. (t7april04JAWHM)

In contrast, women have less hesitation about leaving their jobs and embarking on a working holiday overseas as they consider the programme to be a means of advancing their careers.

スタッフ： だいたい、ワーホリは圧倒的に女性が多いですね。7・3の割合。女の子は仕事辞めていくんですよ、キャリアアップとかで。

Staff: fundamentally, working holiday makers are overwhelmingly women. 70–30%. Women usually quit their job to go in order to boost their career. (t7april04JAWHM)

Eika was one of those women who saw a working holiday programme as a more suitable choice than a short-term English *ryugaku*. Although she had had a strong *akogare* for the United States since her adolescence, she was deterred by the fact that the United States did not allow international students to work. Mastery of English was her main motivation for overseas travel, but it was not the only one. Indeed, her choice of a working holiday in Australia over an English *ryugaku* in the United States was formed on the basis of her multifaceted desires.

エイカ： あたしは、オーストラリアに英語をもう一度やりに来たんだけど、それと同時に、自分の人生の中で本当にやりたい事を探しに来たってのもあるじゃない？だからまあ、最初の一年は英語の勉強したり、ボランティアの仕事したりいろいろやってみて、で、もし、大学行きたいなら行きたいで、後仕事でなんか、やりたい事見つけたりしたら二年目ぐらいいてもいいかなって。

Eika: I came to Australia to study English again, but another purpose is to find something that I can get passionate about in my life. so for the first one year, I am going to do many things like studying English and doing volunteer work. and if I want to go

to university or find a type of job that I want to try out, then I
might consider staying here for another year. (f31march03eika)

Her choice of Australia for her working holiday also reflected her belief that
ELL would be a long-term project. In contrast to most of my other participants, she believed that mastering English would require a considerable
amount of time and effort and that it would not be simply a matter of a few
months' study. Furthermore, her decision to undertake a working holiday
was associated with her identity choice; she did not want to be just a student
of English. Eika had been working since she was 20 and had considerable
savings in Japan which lasted during her entire stay in Sydney. Maintaining
this worker identity thus was of great importance in her choice of taking a
working holiday rather than an English *ryugaku*.

エイカ： やっぱりさ〜、英語ちゃんとやるなら、何ヶ月とかじゃだめじゃん？だ
から、ワーホリで一年かけて、ね〜、お金稼ぎながらさ〜、仕事で英
語も使えるだろうし。仕事ゲットできればの話だけどね@
Eika: really, if I really want to learn English, a few months wouldn't
do. so working holiday is great as I can stay here for one year
while earning money and practising English at work at the same
time. that is if I can get a job @ (f31march03eika)

What was interesting about Eika's working holiday narrative was 'age'. She
set the age of 30 as a personal time limit to 'get out of Japan' and give herself 'one last chance' to fulfil her decade-long *akogare* for mastering English
in a Western country. As in the case of Eika, age emerged as one of the most
complex issues intersecting with Japanese women's discourse of *ryugaku*
and ELL.

3.3.2 Age

男友達： おまえさ〜、もう23だろ？女なんだからその年齢で留学なんか
しても無意味だよ。
Male friend: hey, you, you are already 23, aren't you? there is no point
for a woman of your age in going on *ryugaku*. (Tokyo, 1992)

In 1992, one of my male ex-classmates began talking to me at my farewell
party in Tokyo. His comment above was directed at me, when I was about to
leave Japan for Australia where I intended to undertake a three-year undergraduate degree in psychology. He told me that I would not succeed because
I was an 'old woman', urging me to start thinking about marriage with my

then boyfriend. A female classmate, after listening to our conversation for a while, erupted in anger and literally took him outside the restaurant to 'sort him out'. This incident is still vividly present in my mind. Until then, I did not consider my age, let alone my being a woman, as having been an issue in my decision to study overseas. However, his comment suddenly linked age, gender and ELL in a problematic way. During my undergraduate years in Australia, I remember recalling his comment occasionally, wondering if I was really too old to master English and succeed at a university where I had to study in my second language. When I experienced difficulties, his comments often crept back in my head and I would think to myself: 'Perhaps I am too old to learn English. I should have married instead of coming to Australia.'

For many of my 'older' participants, age was central to their decision to study English overseas, too. Age was particularly a serious issue when it came to a long-term *ryugaku* or/and working holiday. For instance, one secondary participant, 30-year-old Haru, who in her mid-twenties had been a working holidaymaker in Sydney and who had recently returned to live with her Australian boyfriend, said that she considered it too late to go overseas and attempt to master English.

ハル： やっぱり30近くになってくると、出にくくなるんですよ。いまさら英語やってどうすんだみたいな。
Haru: getting close to 30, it becomes difficult to get out. it's like, what's the point in studying English now? (f17march04haru)

Since her teenage years, Haru had always had *akogare* for mastering English. Although age did not appear to be an issue during her working holiday, she was ambivalent about going overseas again and attempting to seriously learn English after turning 30. Because of her age, her decision to finally return to Australia took a great deal of consideration, time and emotional struggle.

Like me, Yoko never considered age as an issue until it was pointed out by someone else – in her case, her mother. When she decided to go on a short-term English *ryugaku*, she was 29 years old and newly divorced. Anxious to escape the aftermath of her divorce, and with her longstanding *akogare* for becoming like the actress Cameron Diaz (in terms both of English fluency and physical appearance), there was no space left in her mind to worry about her age.

ヨウコ： 全然年なんて気にしてませんでしたよ。もう、早くあの町が出たかったのと、絶対キャメロンの様になれるんだってワクワクしてましたから@@

Yoko: I was never worried about my age. I just wanted to get out of town and was so full of hope that I was finally going to be like Cameron Diaz@@ (t5may04yoko)

However, her concerned mother was not happy. She tried to dissuade Yoko on several occasions. In her mother's view, an English *ryugaku* at the age of 29 was not the right option for her daughter, who needed to reconstruct her life after the divorce.

ヨウコ： ああ、でも、母親には言われましたよね。「もう29で、英語なんて勉強しに行ってどうするの。」みたいな
Yoko: yeah, but, my mother said to me, 'what are you going to do, studying English at 29?' (t5may04yoko)

For other participants, age was the very factor that pushed them out. They felt the urge to get out of Japan 'before it was too late'. For instance, when Chizuko finally decided to go on *ryugaku*, she was 36 years old. She said that she felt 今 '出ない'と、一生出られないなって言う危機感 (an overwhelming sense that I may not be able to 'get out' if I don't do it now (i10oct03Chizuko).

Age was also a crucial issue for Eika. The age limit of 30 years for participants in the working holiday programme forced her to decide to abandon her career and pursue her youthful *akogare* for mastering English (Department of Immigration and Citizenship, 2010b).

エイカ： 30歳までにワーホリのビザとって、31歳のバースデーまでにオーストラリアに入国しないといけないわけよ。だから、本当に今行かなかったらもう一生出れないような気がしてさ〜。行きたい行きたいって言ってたけど、こう、重い腰だったわけじゃない、10年以上も？年齢制限があって、逆によかったみたいなね。
Eika: I had to get a working holiday visa before I turned 30 and enter Australia before my 31st birthday. at that time, I felt that if I don't leave now, I will never ever leave for the rest of my life. I always wanted to go overseas, but was unable to decide for over the last ten years. it was good that there was an age requirement. (f31march03eika)

Eika's decade-long hesitation about going on *ryugaku* relates to another significant part of the discourse of age and *ryugaku*: the problem of finding employment on return to Japan. Even though that consideration did not stop my participants from coming to Australia, many told me that they gave it much thought before leaving Japan. Quitting her job of nine years at the age of 29, Eika felt unsure about her re-employment prospects on her return to Japan. She hoped that her (initial) plan of taking a one-year working holiday in Australia would somehow enhance the prospect of a new career which would involve her English skills (which she expected to improve during the year in Sydney). Despite the English skills she possessed before she left Japan, she was pessimistic about finding employment in the 'tight' Japanese job market for women, particularly for those in their thirties. The same concern was expressed by many other older participants; while wanting to find a job using English on their return to Japan, very few knew exactly how they could do this, especially now that they were older than 30.

In comparison, age did not emerge as an issue in the younger participants' narratives. For instance, Yuka was 17 and Ichi 21 years old when they arrived in Sydney. In their narratives, age was not mentioned as a factor that might have pushed them out of Japan or made them hesitate about going overseas to study English. As mentioned earlier, Ichi used *ryugaku* as a strategy to improve her career prospects in Japan, while the issue of employment upon return to Japan was never raised in Yuka's narrative about her motivation for English *ryugaku*. In Chapter 9 I will discuss how the participants' views about their age and employment changed during their stay in Sydney. In spite of the macro-discourse of English *ryugaku* as a career tool for women, and of Ichi's prior expectations, *ryugaku* experiences and language skills did not necessarily always work as an absolute advantage for employment, even for younger participants.

These data indicate that the discourse of ELL and *ryugaku* cannot be understood without reference to the local discourse about Japanese women's life courses and their age. Haru, Eika and Yoko were all single women in their late twenties and their age was central to their decision-making processes with reference to studying English overseas. These older participants had to deal with emotional struggles about whether they were too old to learn English or invest in a *ryugaku* to change their life course. On the one hand, I found that the discourse of English as emancipatory for all women was indeed prevalent (particularly in the media as discussed earlier). On the other hand, 'older' (i.e. those approaching or having already passed 30) Japanese participants had to justify their decisions to themselves as much as to anyone else. They also had to negotiate the disapproval of those who disagreed with their move outside the expected life course of a Japanese woman. Despite the macro-discourse of English and *ryugaku* as a career booster for women, Japanese women's micro-discourse indicates that their commitment to learning English for career purposes intersects closely with the local discourse of age and the job market for women in Japan. In sum, for many Japanese women, English *ryugaku* is never only about gaining linguistic knowledge or obtaining 'cross-cultural' experiences. It is also intimately linked with the traditional discourse of women's life cycles (e.g. education, career and marriage) and age, which in turn powerfully informs who they desire to socialise with in Sydney, an issue I will return to in Chapter 7.

3.3.3 Images of Australia and *ryugaku* life

Very few participants in my study made Australia their first choice of a *ryugaku* destination. For many, Australia represented a 'compromise' with the more desirable United States. Nevertheless, the majority of my informants report having had a positive image of Australia prior to their arriving here. For instance, a secondary participant, Tokiko, who decided to come to Australia for the socioeconomic and lifestyle reasons mentioned earlier, said that she had a positive image of Australia.

トキコ： オージーは、暖かくって、フレンドリーで、解放的って言うイメージあったよね
Tokiko: I had the image of Aussies as warm, friendly and easy-going. (t8may04tokiko)

Prior to their departure for Australia, my participants typically imagined they would experience everyday life 'surrounded by friendly Aussies' and believed that would provide a 'natural' way of learning English. Yoko's account prior to her arrival in Sydney testifies to this.

ヨウコ： オーストラリアに来る前に、シドニーのどっかのカフェで美しい白人の友達に囲まれてる自分を想像してましたもん@@、**流暢**な英語で話したり笑ったりして@@
Yoko: before coming to Australia, I used to imagine myself surrounded by many beautiful White friends in a café, somewhere in Sydney @@, chatting and chuckling with them in my FLUENT English @@ (i30april02)

As is evident in her comment, she imagined that the Australian community would mostly consist of *hakujin* (White people) and her ideas on this score were typical of most of my participants; very few participants knew about Australia's multiculturalism/multilingualism prior to their arrival or raised it as an attraction for Australia as a *ryugaku* destination. In fact, many of the women expressed surprise about Sydney's multiculturalism, or more precisely, its Asianisation. This 'discovery' was often framed as a 'disappointment' in typical phrases such as, 'I'm so surprised that there are so many Asians in

Sydney. It's not so different from being in Japan'. What they wanted to experience through *ryugaku* in Australia was immersion in an imagined community of White Australians and they felt that the large number of Asians (who look just like Japanese) in Sydney did not contribute to this aspect of their *ryugaku* project.

However, my participants' view of the Asian population in Sydney was not static. In fact different stories were told at different points during their stay (I will discuss this issue in more detail in Chapters 7 and 9); at times they expressed positive identification with Asians at varying levels of social participation. For instance, discouraged by a distant Australian flatmate, Eika chose her next shared-accommodation partner partly on the basis of her Asian identity (see Section 8.3.2).

Furthermore, Yoko's remark illustrates a common idea about *ryugaku*, a belief that participants would pick up English 'naturally' while socialising with local people, and therefore become fluent in a short time. For instance, prior to departure, Ichi's friend told her to socialise with Australians as much as she could and that mastery of English 'usually' required approximately three months (the time-bound concept of progress in English will be discussed further in Chapter 7). Prior to arrival in Sydney, the majority of the participants seemed to subscribe to the idea that success in ELL was dependent on access to native speakers of English, an issue I will explore in the next chapter.

3.4 Summary

In this chapter I have examined the notion of *ryugaku* for Japanese women. In the first section I argued that the media discourse of language *ryugaku* functions to give legitimacy to major Western English-speaking countries as desirable destinations. We have seen that media discourses in Japan promote language *ryugaku* as a means of reinventing women's identity and creating prospects for a glamorous lifestyle and future career. In the second section I examined my participants' narratives about their decision to go on language *ryugaku* to Australia. For Yoko, Chizuko and Yuka, English *ryugaku* offered them not only a geographical and emotional break from the social space that imposed unfavourable subject positions, but also a wider range of identity options. For Eika and Ichi, in contrast, *ryugaku* was closely linked with their occupational possibilities which, in turn, were connected to a sense of commitment and fulfilment and an ideal of gender equality.

On the whole, their decisions to come to Australia were not simply based on their *akogare* for English and living overseas (as discussed in Chapter 5), but intersected with a host of other social, cultural, economic and logistic factors, including age, education, family agreement, career, economic background of the family and types of visas available to them. Their *ryugaku* was not simply linguistically and educationally motivated and was not all fantasy and romance, but required a great deal of money and consideration. Therefore, the process involved making choices and revising them on a long-term basis from a variety of subject positions (e.g. that of a woman, a daughter, a worker, a divorcee), and also required them to think and behave as consumers, who gathered pamphlets, visited *ryugaku* agencies and negotiated prices for tuition fees to help them as they decided about investing their resources (e.g. time, money) in *ryugaku*.

Insights into the ways in which Japanese micro- and macro-discourses shaped my participants' decisions to study English in Australia were instrumental in understanding their discourse about socialisation with a variety of speakers of English. The next chapter presents findings on these issues.

4 Desired Interlocutors

4.1 Introduction

A wide range of macro- and micro-discourses constituting Japanese women's *akogare* for English in a Japanese context has been discussed in the previous chapters. In Chapter 2 we looked at media discourses of language desire in which English, the West and the Western men were linked and promoted. The previous chapter introduced the discourse of *ryugaku* as a means of identity and lifestyle transformation for Japanese women, discussing the process by which my participants decided to come to Australia to study English.

In fact, insights into my participants' discourses of English *ryugaku* in Australia helped me understand two important things; first, what they considered as 'learning' and 'success' in ELL and, second, who they found as 'desirable' and 'undesirable' interlocutors in their everyday lives in Sydney. In this chapter I will discuss the discourse of 'desired interlocutors'. Firstly, I will introduce you to my participants' narratives relating to the gap between their imagined lifestyle and ELL, and the reality of their experiences that set in after a certain period of time in Sydney. Secondly, I will discuss the discourse of Western native-speaker men as ultimate linguistic resources and teaching aids. In conclusion, I report on my participants' ideas of what makes men desirable or undesirable interlocutors.

4.2 Desires, Images and Realities

The participants' views on ELL and success in *ryugaku* varied. My data suggest, however, that there was a widely held belief that socialisation with Australians/native speakers of English was key to learning English in the *ryugaku* context. This is hardly surprising, given the fact that language study overseas has been marketed to create this image in Japan and other countries (Freed, 1995; Tsuda, 1995). Very few would argue against this general theory of language learning.

In the context of my study, however, I found it interesting that access to and social acceptance by Australians/native-speakers, in the form of friendship or romance, emerged as a measure of success in *ryugaku* itself. The participants, particularly Yoko, Eika and Ichi, enthusiastically talked about their desire to 'get in', 'get accepted in', 'become part of' and 'stay in' *'hakujin no sekai/shakai* (White people's world/society)'; they also talked about their ultimate inability to achieve these aims. Particularly in the early part of their *ryugaku* days in Sydney, their everyday thoughts seemed preoccupied with finding opportunities to use English with Australians/native speakers of English. Most of the participants who attended an English school in Sydney told me that Asian students at school often exchanged notes as to how to meet Australian native speakers and make friends with them (agency in meeting locals is further discussed in Chapter 8. For the case of Taiwanese international students in Sydney, see C.-L. Chang, 2011).

In my observation, Japanese students who managed to make friends with Australians or other English speakers displayed a certain sense of pride and confidence. For instance, when Ichi started a university foundation course in the end of 2001, she was thrilled about the fact that she was the only Japanese student on the course and that there was an increasing number of Australian acquaintances in her life. Japanese students who seemed well immersed in Australian society were often looked up to as successful ESL learner/users by other Japanese students; the former often becoming the object of respect and, at times, of envy and jealousy by the latter.

One reason for this became clear from my observations: while in Australia my participants got the dawning realisation that gaining access to the wider Australian society was not as 'natural' or 'easy' as they had imagined. It was often the case that their prior image of 'everyday life surrounded by friendly Aussies' quickly lost its validity after their arrival in Sydney. Yoko, Eika and many secondary participants were profoundly disappointed by their inability to socialise with Australians/native speakers. They complained that their lack of knowledge of English grammar made speaking difficult, if not impossible, and also that their 'untrained ear' made it difficult for them to understand what was being said, particularly in 'Aussie English'. They often felt guilty about their inability to understand and make friends with Australians/native speakers. For instance, in the beginning of her stay in Australia, Eika blamed her difficulties in interacting with Australians/native speakers on her limited English and not being outgoing enough.

エイカ： だって、私はそういう風には怒れないな。会話に入れないのは自分がね、もっと、積極的にいかないのがいけない訳でしょ？自分がもっと英語に磨きをかけないといけないんじゃん[…] 人の事言ってたら切りが無いしさ。

Eika: I can't get angry at them, you know, because the reason why I can't join in a conversation is because I am not outgoing enough. I just have to get better at English […] there is no end to blaming others, you see. (f4july03eika)

Although they continued to be self-critical, over time my participants also began expressing dissatisfaction with Australians/native speakers who rejected, ignored and ridiculed them, making social interactions not only unsuccessful but also unpleasant. All of my participants believed, albeit to varying degrees, that their racial identity was the main factor and that being Asian was associated with deficiency in English. Even one of the most pro-Australian, Yoko, often told me that:

ヨウコ： なんか、オージーはアジア人の事見下している所がありますよね。なんか、変な英語喋るみたいな。

Yoko: I think Aussies look down on Asians. they think Asians speak strange English. (f3april03yoko)

As a result, their image of Australians started to shift from that of 'friendly people' to 'rude and inconsiderate people'. Having worked with Australians in a restaurant, Tokiko told me that, in sharp contrast to her prior positive image of Australians, she increasingly found them to be 'cold and conservative' and 'unprofessional at work' (t7may04tokiko). Eika, too, experienced unpleasant encounters with Australians soon after her arrival in Sydney. For instance, when she was booking a taxi on the phone, the operator rudely hung up on her when she twice failed to understand a question. Although Eika initially blamed herself for this kind of incident, after repeated offensive encounters she came to reject 'friendly Aussies' as a myth:

エイカ： 日豪プレスの留学コーナーとかに、「フレンドリーなオージーと学ぼう」みたいな事良く書いてあるじゃん。何言っちゃってんのって感じだよね。オージーがフレンドリーなんて全然思わないよ。アタシにしてみればマレーシア人の方が全然フレンドリーだよね。

Eika: the *ryugaku* section in *Nichigo Press* often says, 'study with friendly Aussies'. what are they talking about? @@ I don't think Aussies are friendly at all. for me, Malaysians are much friendlier. (t9may04eika)

Actual experiences of being 'surrounded' by English and White Australians did not always correspond to the participants' previous images either. In fact, socialisation with Australians/native speakers often involved contesting their social and linguistic identities and many reported a sense of isolation, frustration and anger in interactional contexts. For instance, Yuka lost her positive attitude towards Australians, particularly White Australians, soon after she began a university degree in 2002. Yuka told me that she used to admire White people when she had just arrived in Sydney and tried very hard to learn English in order to make friends with them. But once she started studying at university, she felt unable to fit in with the White Australian classmates in her Faculty. She continuously felt discriminated against, and considered her racial and linguistic identity as the main reason. Yuka told me:

ユカ： いつも私の事英語が出来ないんだろうって感じで、[学部の白人生徒からの] 扱いが最低。例えば、リサとコーヒー飲んでるじゃないですか、で他の生徒が来て一緒に座るじゃないですか。目の前に座っているのにも関わらず、無視ですよ、私が英語喋れないって決め付けてる感じで。

Yuka: they [White students in her Faculty] always look at me as if I can't speak English at all and treat me like shit. for example, I am having a coffee with Lisa on campus and other students might come and sit with us. although they may be sitting right in front of me, they would just ignore me, assuming that I can't speak English. (f4nov03yukaichi)

It is impossible to judge whether or not her interpretation of White students' behaviour was correct. Her numerous complaints about White Australians indicate that race (Whites versus Asians) had become one of the most salient issues in Yuka's life, and negative interactional experiences were often interpreted as racially motivated. Furthermore, half way through her university degree Yuka developed the belief that she could not get along with 'monos', that is monolingual speakers of English whom she considered narrow-minded and unsophisticated with a limited worldview. As a result, her social circle increasingly consisted of international students who were multilingual and multicultural.

Similarly, Ichi often felt isolated at social gatherings with Australians/native speakers. She had always lived with Australian homestay families or in university dormitories, and she was thus constantly surrounded by Australians/native speakers throughout her stay in Sydney. While this was what she wanted to have in her *ryugaku* life, being 'constantly' unable to participate in conversations made her feel lonely and unworthy. In contrast to

Yuka, who increasingly saw White Australians as arrogant, Ichi, because of her self-perceived lack of vocabulary, poor understanding skills and limited knowledge of Australia, saw herself as the main cause of her failure to establish friendships. She was initially adamant that she would rather go out with Australians and feel lonely than socialise with Japanese people. However, a growing awareness of racial and linguistic discrimination against Asians in Sydney made her 'selective' about who she wanted to socialise with over time.

My participants were constantly in a dilemma. On the one hand, many continued to have a desire (although in varying degrees) to socialise with native-speaker Australians, as association with them seemed indispensable to success in their language *ryugaku* project. On the other hand, my participants discovered over time that the desire for social interaction with Australian native speakers was not necessarily mutual. They increasingly felt that it was impossible to be accepted into Sydney's wider society due to both their limited English (Yoko, Eika, Ichi and Chizuko in particular) and the wildly circulating racial subordination of Asians by White people (Yuka, Yoko and Eika in particular).

Those such as Ichi who chose to follow through their *akogare* for immersing themselves in the local Australian environment continued to experience this dilemma. Others, such as Eika, Yuka and Chizuko, after trying hard to be accepted by Australians but finding it difficult to do so, began socialising more with other Japanese or Asians who were easier to make friends with (see Chapter 8). For instance, while Chizuko, who worked and lived with Japanese people, expressed concern about her Japanese language environment and lack of opportunity to practise English with Australians/native speakers, she did not allow this to dictate her social life in Sydney. She was happy that she had caring Japanese flatmates and a wide social circle even though it consisted solely of Japanese/Asian friends. Yet others, like Yoko and Tokiko, tried to balance the 'Japanese world' and the 'Western world', often by living or working with Australians but socialising with other Japanese or Asian people in their private lives (also see Chapter 8). Over time, the discourse of native speakers as desirable friends shifted, and was even contested by some of the participants, Yuka in particular, who had stayed in Sydney for a long period of time.

In the next section, I will introduce you to a particular discourse of ELL that emerged against this background.

4.3 Western Men = ELL Success

The majority of my participants experienced bitter disappointment about their inability to interact with Australians/native speakers in English. Many bought additional grammar textbooks in Sydney or asked their parents in Japan to send Japanese textbooks on English grammar. At home, they would diligently watch TV and listen to the radio in order to 'train' their ear to Australian English. However, these conventional learning strategies proved to be not only ineffective, but were dull. In addition, their attempts to use and practise English in public were often met with indifference or unfriendly treatment by Australians/native speakers. Yoko, Eika and Ichi regularly complained about their excruciatingly slow progress and the gap between their prior imagination of *ryugaku* life and the reality of their experience. Half way through her university degree course, Yuka no longer thought it worthwhile to socialise with Australians for the sake of improving her English as she had done in her early days in Sydney.

At the same time, at school and in their social circles of friends, they were increasingly exposed to success stories of other women who became rapidly fluent in English due to their romantic relationships with native-speaker boyfriends. What emerged in this context was the discourse of romance with a Western man as the best means of achieving success in ELL. The case of Kaori described in Chapter1 provided the initial lead on this discourse. Inspired by her Japanese cousin who married an Australian man, Kaori became convinced that getting a native-speaker boyfriend would solve her frustration over her slow progress in English. Eika reached the same conclusion at one point during her stay. She found the conventional means of using textbooks, watching TV, listening to the radio and so on mind-numbing and unhelpful.

エイカ： 　で、思ったんだよね〜、もしこう、コンスタントに英語をね、ちゃんと喋れる機会を作るとしたら・・・男だっ！て。ネイティブの彼が必要かなってさ。

Eika: 　I thought, if I need to create a more constant opportunity to actually speak English ... a man! I need a native speaker boyfriend. (f22oct03eika)

Furthermore, one TAFE college student, who had lived in Sydney for three years, passionately claimed that not having an Australian boyfriend was the fundamental reason for her lack of success in ELL (m28mar04eika-friend). The specific advantages of a native-speaker partner for ELL are summed up by Rina as follows:

リナ： 　だって友達といるのと全然過ごす時間が違うから。毎日会ってるから話すことも違うし。例えば、時間があるから、いろんな事を細かいところまで話すでしょ。でも友達とだといっぱい話す事あるけど、

	時間が無いって感じで。で、友達とグループでいると、聞き役にな
	っちゃうんですよ。でも彼といると、いやでも話さないといけない
	し＠＠それに彼が自分の事好きだって知ってると安心して話せる
	し。彼は話を聞くのが上手いんですよ、だからもっと話したくなっち
	ゃう感じ。
Rina:	the amount of time spent together is so different from being with friends. we talk about different things because we meet every day. for example, because we have plenty of time, we talk about many things in details. but with friends, you have so much to catch up on in so little time, so you can't talk in details. and when I am with my friends in a group, I become a listener. but when I am with my boyfriend, I have to talk even if I don't want to@@ besides I feel relaxed speaking English with him because I know that he likes me. he is a great listener, too, which makes me want to talk more. (f10dec03rina)

The significant aspect of her comment above seems to be that women have more power to negotiate their self-importance in the context of emotional/sexual relationships. Similarly, for Eika, the knowledge that her Australian boyfriend romantically and sexually desired her led to a sense of importance, reassurance and bravery.

| **エイカ:** | やっぱり、この彼が自分を好きだって知ってると有利だよね。なんか うわてに出れるって言うの。相手がさ、自分に特別な感情があるって 知ってるともっと自分の事話したくなるよね。で英語でやるのもそん なに怖くないみたいな。 |
| **Eika:** | I think it's really advantageous when you know that this man likes you. you kind of have the upper hand. when you know that he has a special interest in you, you kind of feel like talking more about yourself and taking risks in English doesn't seem as threatening. (f17mar03eika) |

Many other participants in my study agreed with Rina and Eika. While they often found it daunting to interact in a group situation, they were able to relax more in a one-on-one context in which they were able to position themselves and be positioned as objects of desire.

However, Western men were much more than just a linguistic resource: they were also a symbol of Western romance and chivalry. In fact, quite a few participants expressed their *akogare* for Western terms of endearment, confessing that they had always wanted to be called 'darling', 'honey' and 'sweetheart'.

イチ： 西洋の人はよく「ダーリン」とか「スイーティー」とか「ベイブ」とか言うやん[...]昔からそういうの弱いんよ@@@でね、二回目のデートの時にショーンがディナー作ってくれたんよ。で買いもん行ったとき、あの、彼を呼んだんよ、「ヘイ、ショーン」って、そしたら彼、「yes, darling↗」って、そういうのすっごい憧れてたから、なんか、彼の女になったんやなって感じしたわ@@@

Ichi: Westerners often say 'darling,' 'sweetie' and 'babe' [...] I have a soft spot for these words @@@ well, on the second date, Sean cooked dinner for me. when we went shopping and I called out to him, like, 'hey Sean,' he said to me, 'yes, darling↗' I have had so much *akogare* for it. it really made me feel like I was his girl @@@ (i30sep03ichi)

Such terms gave the Japanese women a transformational experience from their 'Asian/Japanese world' to the 'Western world'. My informants believed the romantic nuances of these terms were lacking in the Japanese language, and therefore being called 'darling' was experienced as a discursive and emotional entry into the Western world of their *akogare*. Eika recalls feeling drawn into another world when called 'honey' by her Australian boyfriend.

エイカ： 最初はびっくりしたよ。「これかウエスタンの世界！」みたいな感じでね。始めはびっくりしてちょっとむず痒かったとおもうよ、でちょっと他人事だった感じがする。でも嬉しかったよ確かにね、ああ、アジア人じゃないヒトと恋愛してるんだなって。日本語ではないニュアンスでしょ？だから違う世界に来ちゃったなっと思ったし。うれしかったのは響きだよ。ダーリンの言葉の響き。

Eika: at first, I was surprised. I thought 'wow, this is the Western world!' in the beginning, it was ticklish and felt like it was happening to someone else. but, I was happy and it made me feel that I was really with a non-Asian man. the Japanese language does not have the same nuance and so it made me feel like I had been drawn into a different world. what made me happy about it most really was the sound ... the sound of darling. (m28mar04eika)

However, this popular discourse which positions Western men as the ultimate method of ELL among Japanese women can be problematic in several ways, as the case of Yoko demonstrates. Yoko was attracted to the idea of learning English from a White native-speaker boyfriend because by this means she would simultaneously attain two types of highly valued capital: White masculinity and success in English. This association became particularly salient when Yoko's Korean ESL friend bluntly told her that her English was not good enough to work with native speakers and that she could not recommend Yoko to her company. Positioned as a deficient speaker of English by another non-native speaker of English, she was deeply humiliated and angry. This incident prompted her to re-examine her approach to learning English.

ヨウコ： 私思ったのは、本当に英語をマスターするのに努力してるなって。勉強ちゃんとしてきましたし、オーストラリア人二人と住んでるし、オーストラリア人と仕事もしてるし、いつも話す努力してるんですよ。なんか、全部やったなって、やってないのは何なんだろうって考えるようになって。
Yoko: I thought, I have been trying really hard to master English. I've been studying hard, I live with two Australians, I work with Australians, I am trying to speak English all the time. I started to think, 'I've done everything ... what is it that I am not doing?' (f19mar03yoko)

She concluded that romance with a native speaker would solve her problems and that intimacy with a White acquaintance, Phil, was the only way to bring an end to her ongoing agony about her limited English.

ヨウコ： それで思ったんですよ。あ、男だ、恋愛だって。ボーイフレンドいないから。フィルと、もっとこう親密なレベルで付き合ったらもっともっと英語が伸びるんじゃないかって思ったんですよ　((泣きながら))。
Yoko: then I thought that it was a man, or a relationship. I don't have a boyfriend. I thought that if I went out with him at a more intimate level, my English would be much better ((sobbing)). (f19mar03yoko)

She did not follow through this idea, but her thinking provides important insights into how language desire, which is strategically promoted for commercial purposes (see Chapter 5), could also induce romantic and sexual choices.

As Yoko's case demonstrates, the gendered discourse of Western men as an ELL method and the actual choices my participants made were not necessarily consistent. In fact, the majority of my participants approached their interlocutors in a much more complex way. In the next section, I turn to several factors that powerfully constructed the desirability of male interlocutors.

4.4 Desirability of Interlocutors

According to Ma (1996: 92), many young Japanese women have what she labels as a 'Western chivalry fantasy': *gaijin* men are all *yasashii* (kind and gentle). Ma (1996: 92) and others (Tsuda, 2000) allege that such fantasies are applied 'indiscriminately to every *gaijin* man [who women] meet'. This misogynistic discourse often positions female ESL students as women who desire and try to interact 'indiscriminately' with every *gaijin* man for the sake of learning English and gaining power.

My field notes suggest, however, that the *akogare* discourse is not nearly that simple. Although many of my participants did fantasise about having a *gaijin* partner and learning English from him, they were never the uncritical, passive recipients that Tsuda (1995, 2000) suggests. My participants regularly and critically talked about the men they met, measuring, judging and evaluating their desirability as a friend, a romantic partner, a linguistic resource, or all of these. There were three key factors that emerged repeatedly as powerfully inflating or deflating the desirability of their interlocutors: race, linguistic background and looks. I will discuss each of these in turn.

4.4.1 Race

As expected, race occupied a special space in my participants' narratives, in that Whites often emerged as the most romantically and linguistically desired race. White men were the main object of romantic and sexual *akogare* for Chizuko, Yoko and Ichi (this was also true of Yuka when she had just arrived in Sydney) and, as such, Whiteness triggered positive emotional and linguistic responses. For instance, Chizuko had the image of a Western man as a 'prince' and confessed that Whiteness was so alluring that it affected her speech style and voice pitch.

チズコ： やっぱり白人だよ。だって子供の頃からの憧れだから白人以外考えられないよね。@もうそんな事言ってる歳じゃないんだけど、いまだに白人と話すと興奮しちゃうもん@@、なんか自分でかわいく喋っちゃったり、声が高くなっちゃったりするのわかるんだよね@@@

Chizuko: I like White men. well, it's my childhood *akogare*, so I can't think of any other option but White. @ I know that I am too old to fancy them like this, but I still tend to get excited when I talk with White men @@ and I find myself speaking more cutely and using higher pitch of my voice @@@ (t15mar04chi)

During the fieldwork in 2004, Chizuko was particularly fond of one White Australian man, Aaron. She enthusiastically visited his work (a pub) as a customer and frequently made contact with him, suggesting get-togethers. Similarly, Ichi was attracted to White men and frequently went out 'man-hunting' with her Australian girlfriend at weekends. When she got her first boyfriend in late 2003, his race and nationality as a White British national were a cause of celebration even for her mother.

イチ： おかあさん彼の事喜んでるんだよね@@@
Ichi: my mother is really happy with him @@@

キミエ： @@@
Kimie: @@@

イチ： どっから来たの〜って。UKからだよって言ったら、すっごい喜んじゃって、「わ〜じゃあ、イギリス人じゃない！」とか言って@@
Ichi: she asked me where he came from. I told her that he was from UK and she was so excited, like, 'wow, **he is ENGLISH**!' @@

キミエ： @@@
Kimie: @@@

イチ： まあ、典型的な白人イギリス人だよって言ったら、よかったねって言ってくれてさ@@
Ichi: she was excited for me when I told her that he is a classic White English man @@ (i21nov03ichi)

While Japanese women's *akogare* for Whiteness had a positive effect on their agency to seek out interactional opportunities, it also meant that they considered non-White males, particularly Asian males, as an unattractive choice as a romantic partner or a linguistic resource even if they were native speakers of English. When the main purpose of a social gathering was to find a romantic partner, this tendency was clear. Yoko, for instance, stated that an opportunity to mix with Asian Australian men at a BBQ party, even if they were all native speakers of English, was a waste of time.

キミエ： で、パーティーどうだったの？
Kimie: so, how was the party?

ヨウコ： ちょっと聞いてくださいよ〜、BBQパーティーにはいっぱいオーストラリア人来るって友達が言ってたっていったじゃないですか？で、すっごく楽しみにしてたんですよ。でも、あの、まあ沢山人は、ああ、ほとんどはあたしの友達のフラットメイトの友達だったんですけど、もう、みんなアジアンオーストラリアンだったんですよ！まあ、みんなネイティブか英語ぺらぺらな人達ばっかりだったんですけど、いや〜、きみえさん、あたしはこういう男達と遊んでいる暇は無いなって。本当によーくわかりましたよ、ああ、あたしは白人の彼が欲しいんだって。

Yoko: listen, I told you that my friend told me that there would be many Australians at the BBQ party↲ so I was really looking forward to it. but, well, there were a lot of people, mostly my friend's flatmate's friends and they were all Asian Australian! they were all native speakers or spoke English really well. Kimie-san, I am not here to waste my time mixing with men like these guys. I really realised that I want a White boyfriend. (f25july02yoko)

Sometimes my participants' fascination with White men was stronger than with their native-speaker identity. Yoko and Chizuko often told me that they found their White European classmates (non-native English speakers) attractive and they often daydreamed about making friends with them (even if they were not native speakers of English). By contrast, none of my participants expressed interest in associating with Asian men (even if they were native speakers of English) and, in fact, some participants avoided contact with them.

The social realities of many Asian ESL students, however, constrained their access to White Australian society because of the linguistic and racial boundaries (Butorac, 2011; C-L. Chang, 2011). Thus, their most accessible language practice partners or friends were more often than not their fellow Japanese or other Asian ESL students. Many of my informants were ambivalent about their default friendship with Asian individuals, often feeling 'guilty' or 'ashamed' of the fact that most of their friends were Asian with poor, accented English. For example, when Ichi was living in a university dormitory, the majority of the residents were White Australians. While very few were friendly to Ichi, several Asians residents attempted to make friends with her. One of them, an Indian international student, was particularly interested in Ichi and asked her out on several occasions. Ichi's reaction was mixed. She did not care for friendship with the Indian man as he was neither Australian (White) nor a native speaker of English. Furthermore, one female resident warned Ichi that the Indian man only wanted to take her to bed.

However, he was one of the very few people willing to socialise with her, and she continued to feel ambivalent about this friendship until he moved out of the dormitory.

While Whiteness seems to be a norm in my participants' realities and fantasies, not all White men were automatically desired either as a possible friends/partners or even as a linguistic resource. For instance, Eika had an adverse reaction when her friend's White Australian flatmate, David, tried to befriend her. In her circle of friends, David was known as an eccentric (e.g. he was an ex-alcoholic, unsuccessful hypnotherapist and scammer, living on social security) with a fetish for Asian sex workers. Eika's Japanese friend told her earlier that David went to a prostitute whenever he had extra money and, at that time of data collection, David openly talked about his sexual craze for Asian women. When she encountered him on the street, she refused to engage in a conversation with him.

エイカ： やばかったよ！電話番号聞かれたとき、「気持ち悪い！」みたいな ＠ もうそこから逃げ出したくって、車に引かれそうになっちゃったよ、はやくまきたかったからさ＠＠＠
Eika: it was so close! I was like 'yuck!' when he asked me for my phone number @ I just wanted to get out of there, so I almost got run over by a car because I was desperate to lose him @@@ (f15march04eika)

Even though Eika was looking for native-speaker friends at that time, she did not hesitate to reject David either as a friend or as a partner with whom to practise English. Another informant, Yuka, over the years that she had been living in Sydney, came to dislike White men. At the beginning of her stay, she developed *akogare* for White men and the first four males for whom she had romantic feelings were all Whites (one Canadian and three Australian males). As none of her romances with them turned out to be satisfactory, and as she was increasingly troubled by experiences of racial discrimination by White Australians, her *akogare* for White men gradually diminished. Also, her preference was noticeably shifting towards Chinese men from 2003. Her interest in learning Chinese as her third language intensified after her first short trip to China in 2003, during which she met a Chinese man with whom she developed and maintained an online friendship for two years. Since then, she had been attracted to Chinese men who were bilingual speakers of Chinese and English.

In sum, while Whiteness emerged as the norm in my participants' narratives, some of their practices suggest their ambivalence towards, and even rejection of, the idea of White men as ideal interlocutors.

4.4.2 The native

For all participants, linguistic identity was also central to their emotional responses and interactional choices. In their daily narratives, they almost always positioned themselves as non-native speakers with limited English and undesirable accents, while seeing (White) native speakers as the desirable interlocutors with authentic linguistic resources. Thus, development of friendships/romances with a 'ネイティブ (native, a term commonly used among the Japanese to mean native speakers of English)' was talked about as the most effective way to learn English and as a way into the 'Western world'. The native-speaker identity not only enhanced the romantic desirability of White men, but could make an otherwise unlikely romantic relationship/sexual encounter a possibility. For instance, within her first 10 days in Sydney, Eika, a 30-year-old ex-career woman, became romantically involved with a 20-year-old Australian university student. She identified herself as a 'slow starter' in romance and called this relationship 'unthinkable' in Japan because of the 10-year age gap, his student status and their limited future prospects for marriage. She explained that what made him attractive was the purity of his English.

エイカ： 彼ネイティブなわけだから自分の英語にはいいよね。それに、英語だといやらしさが無い。表現がストレートでそんなに素直に感情を表現されるとなんか気持ちいいみたいな。いつも彼が言ってるような事をもし日本語で言われたらなんか変な感じだよね。でも英語だと嫌な感じがしないみたいな。だから好きだよね。

Eika: [...] he is a native speaker, so he is good for my English. besides, in English, there is no sleaziness. his expression is always straight and it is very comfortable with such honest expression of his feelings. if he had to say some of the stuff he always tells me in Japanese, it'd have been kind of weird. but in English, there are no negative feelings to it. so I like it. (f27mar03eika)

According to Pavlenko (2005, 2006, 2008), bi/multilinguals often have a preferred language in which to express certain emotions, including romantic feelings. In her web questionnaire study with 1454 bi- and multilinguals, Pavlenko reports that some of the participants felt more comfortable in doing emotional work, such as flirting, endearing or declaring love, in a language they had learned as adults rather than in their native languages. English as an additional language was the most popular choice: they found it easier to say 'I love you' in English than in their native language (examples were from

Finnish, Chinese and Russian native speakers of English as an additional language), where such expression was reportedly rare or atypical (Pavlenko, 2005: 136). Eika's case above provides a further insight into the relationship between bilinguals' language choice and emotions. Her comment suggests that, in English, it also becomes easier to *receive* romantic affection: Eika's partner's love expressed in English is experienced as honest, straight and never sleazy, and she enjoys being a receiver of his romantic attention in English, which would have been 'weird' in her native Japanese language. This discourse is clearly embedded at the intersection between the global stronghold of romantic Hollywood movies and the valorisation of Western romance and romantic expressions in English in the media (Chapter 2) on the one hand, and the devalorisation of Japanese expressions of love and romance (Kelsky, 2001) on the other. In fact, according to one marriage consulting company in Japan (Zwei, 2006), a direct expression of love was the number-one reason why Japanese women were likely to choose foreign rather than Japanese men.

However, although Whiteness and being a native speaker were commonly considered as a single package by my participants, the value of the 'native' outweighed that of the Whiteness in some contexts. For instance, despite her openly claimed fetish for White men, Yoko's first boyfriend, John, was a Chinese Australian. For her, the fact that her boyfriend was a native English speaker and a typical exemplar of Australian monolinguality outweighed his Asian-ness.

ヨウコ： まあ、白人男がどうのこうのとずっと言ってましたけど、結局アジア人捕まえちゃいました。ちょっと計算違いでしたよね。でも、彼ネイティブなんで、どうにかなると思います＠＠

Yoko: I was going on and on about White men for a long time, but in the end, I got an Asian. it's a bit of a miscalculation, but really he is a native speaker, so I will survive @@ (f21dec03yoko)

His native-speaker identity was what encouraged Yoko to get romantically involved with him in the first place and then to remain in their rocky relationship despite their quickly fading romantic attraction for each other. As her ambivalent comment above, 'I will survive', implies, however, John's racial heritage was continuously talked about as a problem. Any aspect of John that enhanced his legitimacy as an 'Australian' native speaker was celebrated and accentuated in her narrative of their relationship. For instance, his monolinguality, which signified Australian-ness to Yoko, was repeatedly stressed in our conversations.

ヨウコ： 彼はアジア人なんですけど、ネイティブじゃないですか。彼の曾お
じいさんがオーストラリアにきて、彼のお父さんもお母さんもチャイ
ニーズ喋れないんですよ。ジョンもチャイニーズ全然喋れないし。
だから、本当に中身はオージーなんですよね。ある日、彼が仕事場の
コリーグに「G'day mate」っていってるのきいたんですよ。あたし
それで感動しちゃって、ああ、彼って本当にオージーなんだーって思
いました。

Yoko: he is Asian, but, he is a native speaker of English. his great
grandfather came to Australia, so neither his father nor his
mother can speak Chinese. John can't speak Chinese at all
either. so he is really an Aussie inside. the other day, I heard him
say, 'G'day mate' to his colleagues at work. that really impressed
me and got me to realize again that he was a real Aussie.
(f21dec03yoko)

For those participants who developed a romantic relationship with non-native speakers of English (Chizuko, Rina and Kaori), the linguistic identity was often phrased as a 'problem'. Given the fact that they considered their own English as limited and in need of improvement, their partners' linguistic deficiencies were believed to contribute to difficulties in their cross-cultural communication and romance. Kaori had a negative view of her Brazilian boyfriend's limited English as well as the tendency of both to depend on reading 'body languages' rather than trying to speak 'decent English' (f1april04kaori). Rina had had a few non-native speaker boyfriends (Japanese, Chinese and Korean) during her one-year working holiday in Sydney. Her first boyfriend's (Japanese) English was more limited than her own and, despite their attempt to use English with each other, his slow speech and frequent silences frustrated Rina so much that it led to their break-up. Although her second partner, a Chinese man, sounded fluent at first, Rina increasingly found his grammatical mistakes and poor pronunciation irritating. Her third boyfriend from Korea had similar problems and, on the basis of these experiences with the non-native speaker boyfriends, she concluded:

リナ： 最終的に言葉がちゃんとしてないと付き合えないなって。お互い分か
り合えないでしょ？心を広くせなあかんのにイラってしてしまう所が
あって、勝手だと思うんだけど、少なくとも自分よりは上であって欲し
いなって。

Rina: you can't go out with someone if you can't speak the language
properly. you can't understand each other. I know that I have to
be open minded and I know that I am selfish, but I want my
partner to be better than me at least. (f10dec03rina)

Her fourth boyfriend was a White native-speaker Australian man, and she was happy with the amount and quality of interaction in English she experienced with her attentive partner (see her comment in Section 7.3).

4.4.3 'Sleazy' bilingual men

Another salient aspect of the linguistic backgrounds of Western men that powerfully mediated the participants' desire to interact with them was their fluency in Japanese. Most participants had better access to men who had connections with Japan. In this context, being bilingual in Japanese and English and their interest in befriending Japanese people (especially women) were considered as advantages for a time. Soon after her arrival, Eika considered bilingual interlocutors to be a window of opportunity for friendship/romance.

エイカ: 日本語喋れる人たちってアジアが好きってことだから、まあ、いいんじゃないのみたいな。日本のいい所とか知ってるし興味をもってもらえるのってすごく新鮮なわけ。自分をまだ英語で完璧に出せないから、普通興味を持ってもらうのって大変なわけよ。でも向こうが日本とか日本語に興味があればやっぱりおのずとね、最初から態度がフレンドリーだよね。

Eika: I like people who can speak Japanese because it means that they like Asia. They know good things about Japan and it is refreshing to know that someone is interested in me. I can't express myself fully in English yet, so it's usually a struggle to get guys interested in me. if they are interested in Japan and learning Japanese, their attitude towards me is naturally much more friendly from the beginning of our meeting. (t16mar03eika)

Her comment indicates Eika's growing anxiety over her Asian and non-native speaker identity in Sydney. Since her arrival in early 2003, she had experienced indifference from native-speaker Australians on a number of occasions, and had been exposed to the racialised discourse which stigmatises Asian non-native speakers as second-class and deficient speakers of English. Thus, the attentions and friendliness of bilingual men helped restore Eika's self-image, not only as a competent ESL speaker, but also as an attractive woman, in the same way as she had seen herself in Japan.

However, in contrast to this positive image of bilingual Western men, Eika's romance with her bilingual ex-boyfriend revealed a constant struggle, particularly in relation to their language choice in their private time. As their relationship developed, her boyfriend increasingly spoke more

Japanese than English. According to Eika, while he was attentive when she spoke Japanese, he paid very little attention when she started to talk in English. Eika felt guilty about speaking Japanese with him, seeing that mastering English was the main objective of her living in Sydney and leaving behind her career and comfortable environment in Japan. She saw using Japanese on a daily basis as a betrayal of her determination to improve her English.

This frustration came from her view of her relationship partly as an ELL opportunity and her belief that he should accommodate her needs and concerns. As mentioned earlier, his 'pure' image was attractive to her, and was constructed by his straightforward expression in English rather than through his Japanese expression. Despite her protests, their common language largely remained Japanese. Even before their romance ended, Eika already had formed a new desire – for a monolingual *gaijin* boyfriend.

エイカ： もう、次の彼は絶対に日本語知らない人にする！
Eika: the next time I get a boyfriend, I don't want him to know Japanese! (f19june03eika)

In a similar vein, many of the women in my study expressed their reservations about the use of Japanese in their romantic or sexual experiences. For instance, when Ichi had a brief relationship with a bilingual Australian man, English was their common language. However, his occasional use of Japanese during sexual encounters provoked an emotional aversion.

イチ： やつがベッドで日本語使ったんよ〜、もう信じられんぐらいいややったわ〜。「すっごく濡れてるね！」って日本語で言ったんよ((顔をしかめながらイライラした口調で))。もう最低やったわ！
Ichi: you know he was using Japanese in bed and it was such a turn-off! he said to me, 'wow you are so wet!' in Japanese ((with a frown on her face and frustration in her voice)). it was so disgusting! (f31july02ichi)

When I asked my other informants about their views on this matter, most agreed with Ichi. For instance, Mie, who openly abhors flirtatious bilingual Western men, refused to teach Japanese to her monolingual Australian boyfriend for the fear that it would contaminate her image of him as 'a pure Western man'.

ミエ： なんか英語だけ喋れる方がいいかなって。イメージ悪くなるし、変なアクセントで話して欲しくないみたいな。そういうのイヤだよね。

Mie: I thought that it was better he spoke only English. it would destroy his good image and I don't want him to speak awful accented Japanese. it would really turn me off. (f7oct03mie)

The downsides to bilingual Western men were not only purely linguistic in nature. In the minds of many Japanese women I spoke with, any level of fluency in Japanese by non-Japanese men (particularly White men) immediately suggested sexual flirtatiousness and looseness, and such men were frequently labelled as 'ルーザー (losers)' (f2april04tokiko). My participants tended to raise their guard during encounters with Japanese-speaking *gaijin* men, or simply to avoid any contact with them. As pointed out earlier, there is a widespread sexist stereotype of Japanese women as having a blind *akogare* for Western men and as sleeping with just anyone who is White and speaks English. It is constitutive of the widespread sexist discourse of Japanese women's sexual easiness with White men about which a travel writer, Nishimoto (2005) writes the following. On his personal website, he does so by equating Japanese women's attempt at ELL with having sex with *gaijins*.

> [...] まとめておくと、日本人女性が外国人男性と喜んでセックスする理由は、現代日本社会のあり方が嫌でそれからどこへでもいいから脱出したいという願望の表れなんだ。こう考えると、現代日本人女性が、英語を学ぶのが大好き、英語学校大盛況、英語教師はセックスし放題、という現象が簡単に説明できる。英語はとにかく日本脱出のための、一つの武器なのだから。そして、英語を学ぶのと同じレベルで、外人男性とのセックスも成立する。外人とセックスするは、外人と英語をで話をするのと同じ事で、日本脱出への第一歩だ。しかも、セックスは英語を勉強するほど難しくない。というか、ちょう簡単なんだよ。
> [...] In sum, the reason why Japanese women are so willing to have sex with *gaijin* men is their abhorrence against Japanese society and emergent desire to escape. This easily explains contemporary Japanese women's passion for learning English, popularity of English schools and English teachers' unlimited access to sex. Sex with *gaijins* is the same as speaking English with *gaijins* and is one step towards escaping Japan. What is more, sex is not as difficult as studying English. It is in fact so easy.

In my participants' understanding, too, *gaijin* men who were fluent, particularly in feminised Japanese, were considered to be among those who target 'stupid' Japanese women who in turn are lured to the men's bilingualism because they themselves cannot speak English but are in love with the idea of intimacy with White men. Therefore a link is made between their fluency in Japanese and an identity as a sexual predator of easy and linguistically deficient Japanese women.

ヨウコ： 日本語話せる外人に会うとすぐに、「いやあ、この人ジャパニーズキラーだから気をつけないと」って思いますもん。日本人女性好きでいてくれるのはいいんですけどね。でも、なんか、かんたんにセックスやっちゃうとかいうイメージもたれてると思うと嫌になっちゃうんですよね。だから、そういう人と会うと、もうふら～っていなくなっちゃいます。わざわざそういう人達と会いたいと思いませんね。
そういう人たちと友達になるのって簡単だとは思いますけど。

Yoko: when I meet *gaijin* men who can speak Japanese, I immediately think, 'ok, this guy must be a "Japanese lady killer"' and that I have to be careful. I guess it's kind of nice that they like Japanese women. but it is their image of Japanese women as sexually 'easy' which turns me off. so when I meet one, I just walk away; I don't go out of my way to meet guys like them, even though it may be easier to be friends with them. (t17mar04yoko)

Furthermore, Western men's ability to speak Japanese was often equated with their sexist arrogance towards Japanese women. The 24-year-old Yuka complained that there was a constant struggle between her and a bilingual Australian man, Jack, in her circle of friends. In Yuka's view, Jack was attracted to Japanese girls only because he saw them as passive, obedient and convenient. When they first met, Jack immediately positioned Yuka as a submissive Japanese 'girl' with little fluency in English. However, at the time of data collection, Yuka had lived in Sydney for seven years and was one of the most fluent and confident speakers of English among my informants, and her proficiency in English, independence and outspokenness caused constant tension between herself and Jack.

ユカ： 自分がいつも遊んでる日本人の女の子達ってバカばっかりだし英語喋れないから、あたしが英語喋れるって信じられないんですよ。だから彼あたしの事いやなんですよ、だって英語喋れるし言いたい事だって言えちゃうから。最初に会った時なんて、本当にバカで英語の喋れない日本人の女みたいな感じで。あたしが英語喋れるって判ったらびっくりして信じられないって感じ@@

Yuka: he can't believe that I CAN speak English because most of the girls he goes out with are stupid and can't speak English. that's why he can't stand me because I CAN speak English and CAN express my opinions. when we first met, his attitude to me was obvious; he treated me as if I was a dumb Japanese girl who can't speak a word of English. when he found out that I was able to speak English, he looked stunned and could not believe it @@ (t15mar04yuka)

It is important to note that, among my informants, Yuka had the least *akogare*, if not mistrust, for White men, due to her disastrous relationship with a married and uncommunicative Australian man four years previously. Rather than letting Jack silence her, Yuka became even more vocal in English.

ユカ: 絶対黙りませんよ、彼が日本語で話し掛けてきても、いつも英語で返して、どう思ってるか言ってやるんです。

Yuka: I never shut up, you know, even if he speaks to me in Japanese, I always talk back to him in English and give him piece of my mind. (f6mar04yuka)

Moreover, these bilingual men were not even considered as a way into Australian society, as many of them exclusively socialised with Japanese women in Sydney.

ヨウコ: あのぉ、そういう人達って日本人とばっかりつるむじゃないですか。そういう人のパーティーとか行くと日本人ばっかりなんで何これって感じで。だいたい昔の女は日本人だったりもするんですよ。だからね、英語が目的だしそういう日本語話す外人とつるんでもしょうがないって思いません？

Yoko: you know, these guys only hang out with Japanese people. you go to their party and it will be full of Japanese people and I feel like, what the hell? most of their ex-girlfriends are Japanese, too. so what's the point in getting to know Japanese speaking *gaijin*s when my goal is to improve English? (t17mar04yoko)

Despite easy access to bilingual Western men, Yuka, Yoko and many other secondary informants tended to avoid contact with them. This not only signalled their refusal to be positioned as easy and linguistically deficient Japanese women, but also their positioning of these men as cheap, unintelligent and unworthy of their attention.

4.4.4 Looks: The myth of *kakkoii* White men

Other than native-speaker status, the factors that made men desirable as interlocutors for my participants were their physical appearance and other personal attributes such as age, height, physique, hairstyle, teeth and even clothing. Some participants mentioned that, while at the beginning of their stay in Sydney they believed that White Western men were generally good looking, as time went by they began to realise that not all were attractive. For instance, Tokiko expressed her regret about choosing Australia because she found that its White men were not as good looking as she had imagined prior to her arrival in Sydney.

トキコ：　来る前は白人みんなかっこいいと思ってたよ。でもオーストラリアに来てがっかり。一年かけてそうでもないという事に気が付いて、ああカナダに行けばよかったなって思ったよ。

Tokiko: before coming to Australia, I thought that all White men were good-looking. but I was so disappointed when I came to Australia. it took me one year to realise that that's not the case and that's why I thought that I should have gone to Canada. (f2april04tokiko)

This tendency to believe that Western men are all handsome was a common joke among some of my participants and other Japanese female acquaintances. For example, when one participant was considering going out with a White Australian man, her Japanese friend laughingly told her that Japanese women who had just arrived in Sydney for working holidays would go crazy for him, but not those who had been here for more than a year.

Indeed, my informants gradually became more selective as to who they considered as desirable interlocutors. They sought, as well as actively avoided, contact with certain types of men. Physical, romantic and sexual attractions were indeed significant factors in mediating their emotional reactions and interactional patterns. For instance, Chizuko met a White Australian lawyer through an advertisement for language exchange partners. On their first meeting, he was well mannered, attentive to what she was saying, paid for their expensive dinner, expressed his eagerness to see her on a regular basis, and offered to drive her in his stylish car to her friend's place after their meeting. It turned out, however, that they had a misunderstanding: his personal ad was for a romantic partner, not a language exchange partner. Chizuko briefly considered continuing to see him for the sake of her English. Finally, however, she chose not to see him again.

キミエ：	彼のどこがだめだったわけ？
Kimie:	what's the problem with the guy?
チズコ：	いや〜、実は、全然タイプじゃなかったんだよね。全然いい男じゃないわけよ@@
Chizuko:	well, to be honest, he is not my type. he is not good-looking at all @@
キミエ：	@オヤジ？@@
Kimie:	@ an old man? @@
チズコ：	いや@彼私より若いしいい感じだったよ。金持ってるし頭いいし、で、会いたがってたし。でもそれがダメだったのよ。彼は私のことガールフレンド的に見てたわけでしょ、それで私としては全然彼魅力的じゃなかったのよね。初めて会った時に「このヒトと寝れるかな？」って思ったら答えはNO。彼とベッドに行ってる自分が想像できなかったもん@
Chizuko:	no @ he is younger than me and very nice. rich and smart and keen to see me. but, THAT was the problem. he saw me as a potential girlfriend and I . . . didn't find him attractive. When I first met him, I asked myself, 'can I sleep with this man?' and the answer was NO. I couldn't imagine myself going to bed with him @
キミエ：	@最初に会った時に？@もうベッドにいけるかいけないか考えてたの？@@
Kimie:	@ during your first meeting? @You were thinking about whether or not you could go to bed with him? @@
チズコ：	@@@そうそう、あたしってそうなのよ@@@やっぱり出来そうじゃない人とはそういうふうに遊べないのよね。
Chizuko:	@@@ yeah, yeah, I am like that, you know @@ it's important that I find him sexually do-able or it's impossible for me to even keep hanging out with someone. (t15mar04chi)

Chizuko's case highlights one aspect of second-language learners: English proficiency is not necessarily always the top priority for even those who are most committed to attaining it. Furthermore, in a romantically charged context like this, her comment highlights that race (Whiteness) was not necessarily always the first priority, despite her claim to have a fetish for White men. In this particular instance, Chizuko felt uncomfortable with a man who was romantically interested in her because he did not fit her personal discourse of good-looking, prince-like *gaijin*. For Chizuko, a 40-year-old single woman with hopes of marriage and family in mind, romance was a serious business which could be at times more vital than English proficiency. Although, of course, being White and a native speaker appealed to her (at least she considered seeing him again as a practice partner), in this romantically charged context it was far more important that she found him sexually attractive as a man rather than as a linguistic resource. A 31-year-old TAFE student, Tokiko, agrees.

トキコ： だって外人の男と遊ぶか付き合うんだったらやっぱりかっこいい方がいいわけよ。見かけってすっごい大切じゃない？日本人とだったらさ〜簡単に分かり合えるじゃん。でも外人とだと難しいじゃない言葉の壁があるからさ。だってほとんど無理だと思うもん彼らが本当にどんな感じなのかって英語でさ、で、そういうのってすっごく疲れるじゃん。だからせめてかっこよければさ、まあ、がんばって喋ろうかなって気にはなるのよね@@

Tokiko: well, if I am to hang out with or go out with *gaijin* men, it's better that they are good-looking. looks are very important, aren't they¿ with Japanese people, we can easily understand each other, but with *gaijin* men, it's hard because of the language barrier. it is almost impossible to get to know who they really are in English and it's very tiring to have to do that. so if they are good-looking, then, at least that will give you some incentive to talk to them @@ (f2april-04tokiko)

Tokiko said that she had different ways of interacting with Western men in pubs. When an unattractive man spoke to her, she would answer his questions very reluctantly and, to show her disinterest, she would not ask questions of her own.

トキコ： だいたい「how are you¿」って話しかけてくるじゃない。「not….bad….」って感じで絶対聞き返さない@@普通は聞き返すじゃない、新しい人に会った時とか？「and you¿」みたいな@@でもかっこいい人だったら、いろんな質問して会話を伸ばすみたいな@@@もっと笑顔とかもでるかも。嫌な奴？@@

Tokiko: their typical way of starting a conversation is, 'how are you¿' I would say 'not … bad …' but I never ask them back @@ you usually ask back, don't you when you meet new people¿ like 'and you¿' @@ but when it's a good-looking guy, I will ask all sorts of questions, trying to extend our conversation @@@ I think I tend to smile more, too. am I mean¿ @@ (f2april04tokiko)

Another example comes from an encounter between Yoko and a 41-year-old White Australian man whom she met through an online singles' website. Before their first date she was untroubled, if not positive, about his age of 41, as she associated it with Brad Pitt.

ヨウコ： 　４１は結構いってるなって思ったんですよね。
　　　　　でも、「あれ、ブラッド・ピットって４１歳だ」って！＠
Yoko:　I thought that 41 was a little bit old. but I though, hey, Brad Pitt is also 41 years old! @

キミエ： 　彼の歳にしては、そんなに悪くないよね？
Kimie:　he doesn't look too bad for his age, ha？

ヨウコ： 　＠そう、でブラッド・ピットみたいな感じの若い人を期待してたんですよ＠＠
Yoko:　@ yeah, so I kind of expected him to look as young as Brad Pitt @@ (f25feb03yoko)

On their first date, however, Yoko was horrified by his looks. Unlike other Australian men that she had met, Yoko's date was attentive, trying to make her feel comfortable and showing no sign of impatience with her self-identified 'limited' English. However, during the conversation, she grew increasingly conscious of his 'aging' looks.

ヨウコ： 　こんな事をいったら失礼なんですけど、でも、「やだ、彼すっごいふけてるし、肌も気持ち悪い！」って思い出しちゃったんですよね＠＠＠ オンラインの写真ではオッケーだったんですけど、同い年にしては全然ブラット・ピットみたいじゃなかったし！彼といちゃいちゃしたりするのって全然想像できませんでした。
Yoko:　I know it's awful to say this, but I started to think, 'oh my god, he looks so old and his skin is so yucky!'@@@ he was ok in the online photo, but he wasn't at all like Brad Pitt despite their same age! I couldn't possibly imagine doing anything intimate with this guy. (f25feb03yoko)

When they were parting at the end of the evening, he unexpectedly kissed her on the lips. Yoko was horrified. The following day, she emailed him to say she had no wish to see him again, and withdrew her personal information and photo from the singles' website.

It is important to point out that not all participants were after good-looking men. In fact, some were embarrassed about interacting with physically attractive men and, as a result, they were unable to interact as well as they might with less physically attractive men. For instance, Rina told me that she did not enjoy talking with handsome men.

リナ： 緊張して英語喋れなくなっちゃったんですよね。私カッコ良い人だめなんです。 特に、こう、クールでかっこいい人。
Rina: I get too nervous to speak English. I don't like handsome men. especially good-looking men who are cool. (f10dec03rina)

These findings suggest an interesting trend. As discussed earlier, the Japanese media's glorified representation of Western men (especially EFL teachers, Hollywood stars and sports heroes) has long contributed to the identity construction of White men as attractive, sophisticated and courteous. The majority of my participants, too, had an expectation prior to their departure from Japan that 'all White men would be *kakkoii* (good-looking)' (f2april04tokiko). After spending some time in Sydney, many of them concluded that the idea that '*gaijin* men are all *kakkoii*' was a myth and they then simply regarded physically unattractive *gaijin* males as unworthy of their attention. The physical, romantic and sexual attractiveness of male interlocutors had become powerful measures of their worthiness or desirability, not only as friends and romantic partners, but also as linguistic resources for many Japanese women. Nevertheless, as Rina's last comment indicates, physical attractiveness could also inhibit some participants' attempts to interact with White native speakers as much as they motivated other participants to do so.

4.5 Summary

This chapter has presented the gendered discourse of Western men as the ultimate 'method' to achieve success in ELL. While participants considered access to the wider Australian society to be the key to success in *ryugaku*, they found such access difficult to attain. Most participants expressed increasingly bitter disappointment about their inability to gain interactional opportunities at the beginning of their stay. As time went by, they were all exposed to different forms of racial and/or linguistic discrimination by those with whom they initially wanted to associate – native-speaker Australians.

Against this backdrop, what emerged was a new appreciation of native-speaker men as the ultimate linguistic resource and teaching aid. This was closely linked with another discourse of White Western men as desirable romantic partners, which was consistent with the media representation of White men in Japan we saw earlier. However, the desirability of interlocutors was more complex than simply the racial and linguistic identities of male speakers. I discussed several factors (i.e. bilingualism, social status and the physical appearance of men) that seemed to intersect with the ways in which the women found them attractive enough (or not) to engage in interaction.

In the field of SLA, there have been tendencies to assume that second-language learners would naturally and at all times desire contact with native speakers for the sake of improving their English and expanding their social networks. For example, concepts such as acculturation (Schumann, 1978), integrative motivation (Gardner, 1985) and willingness to communicate (Macintyre *et al.*, 2002) are based on the assumption that it is natural for language learners to want to have contact with native speakers: if they fail in this regard, they are likely to have little success in language learning. More recent works on motivation have drawn on developments in self research, such as the psychological theory of possible selves (Markus & Nurius, 1986). Drawing on this theory, for instance, Dörnyei (2005) proposed the L2 motivational self system to which the notion of *ideal self* (e.g. personal hopes and aspirations) and *ought-to-be self* (e.g. sense of duty and obligations) are central. It is argued that, if proficiency in the target language is part and parcel of both *ideal* and *ought-to-be selves*, L2 learners are likely to be motivated to learn the language 'because of our psychological desire to reduce the discrepancy between our current and possible future selves' (Dörnyei & Ushioda, 2009: 4). As I have shown in this chapter, however, even if desire for proficiency in English and participation in Australian society at large predominated in the Japanese women's *ideal* and *ought-to-be selves*, or even if they wanted to reduce the discrepancy between their current and ideal selves, they faced multiple challenges, such as racism, sexism and linguistic discrimination in their daily lives, against which it became increasingly difficult to uphold their initial willingness to interact or pursue their dreams of becoming fluent in English. My analysis has thus shown that motivation in language learning cannot be reduced to a psychological desire; instead, motivation is never free of social, ideological and material constraints that play out in the specific context.

5 Agency

5.1 Introduction

The previous chapter presented the gendered discourse of ELL among my participants. Such gendered notions of ELL were not, of course, the whole story of my participants' *ryugaku* and working holiday experiences. During their residence in Sydney, they demonstrated a wide range of agency in creating an effective social environment for themselves. It extended to such matters as *how* (strategies), *where, with whom* (communities) and *how much* (desired levels of achievement) they wanted to learn and use English. At the same time, many participants became increasingly aware of the social structures and power relations that limited their participation in Australian society.

According to Ahearn (2001), there has been a move away from the conceptualisation of the term 'agency' as a synonym for 'free will exercised by completely autonomous individuals' (Ahearn, 2001: 115) to the view of agency as 'socioculturally mediated capacity to act' (Ahearn, 2001: 112). Pennycook (2001) argues that this shift has also begun to take place in SLA. A number of SLA theorists (Lantolf & Pavlenko, 2001; McKay & Wong, 1996; Norton & Toohey, 2001; Pavlenko & Piller, 2001), particularly from the poststructuralist framework, have sought to reconceptualise the notion of agency and have paid increasing attention to its link to the processes of, and its contribution to, success in SLL. The basic assumption within the poststructuralist framework is that learners are agents who actively seek to construct and negotiate their own learning options (Pavlenko & Piller, 2001). At the same time, most poststructuralist theorists acknowledge that agency never works outside power structures (Canagarajah, 1993; Pavlenko & Piller, 2001; Pennycook, 2001). Pennycook notes that learners' decisions and actions are socially and historically constructed by a wide range of macro- and micro-discourses and, therefore, the theorising of agency requires 'complex thinking about social class, gender, ideology, power, resistance, human agency' (Pennycook, 2001: 120). Following Pavlenko and Piller (2001), who consider agency as 'co-constructed learning options as predicated on language ideologies and power structures within a particular society' (Pavlenko & Piller, 2001: 29), this chapter highlights the ways in which my participants exercised agency and how it intersected with their *akogare*, identities and SLL during their stay in Sydney. In particular, I focus on two social spaces that appeared to be crucial to them: home and work.

Firstly, I present an analysis of the media discourse of *ryugaku* lifestyle, followed by an analysis of participants' choices of accommodation in Sydney and their experiences of living in such environments. Secondly, I examine the media discourse of employment and *ryugaku* and describe my participants' experiences of work as an ELL opportunity.

5.2 Home as an ELL Opportunity

This section introduces the micro- and macro-discourses of home as an ELL opportunity, presenting an analysis of the media discourse of *ryugaku* lifestyle. This is followed by an examination of my participants' agency in creating home environments that were both conducive to their attempts to learn English and accommodating to their non-ELL needs.

5.2.1 Media discourses of home during *ryugaku*

Homestay or shared accommodation with native speakers of English is constitutive of the glamour of *ryugaku* and the working holiday. *Ryugaku* magazines typically carry sections promoting homestay as an ideal and safe method of living overseas for those serious about practising English and learning about the local culture. Homestay families (and other local people) depicted in these magazines are often White, and presumed to be native speakers of English, as exemplified in the section of *Wish International* (2002). *Wish's* winter edition, entitled 'Australia & New Zealand: Let's Start a New Way of Life', features five young Japanese individuals (four females and one male) studying in Australia or on working holidays in New Zealand (Wish International, 2002: 21–41). For example, 20-year-old Noriko Aoki lives with an Australian host family in Sydney and has private lessons with her host mother who she in fact calls 'mother'. The mother is a Caucasian British-born Australian in her fifties, living in a spacious and immaculate house in a Sydney suburb. Of six photographs featuring Noriko, three depict the mother and Noriko interacting closely. Each photograph constructs multiple identities for the mother including: (1) an attentive listener/advisor, (2) a cheerful and warm mother/carer, and (3) a wise teacher, while projecting Noriko as a young learner who enjoys/needs the mother's multifaceted attention.

Another section (34–37) from the same *ryugaku* magazine features a 31 year-old working holidaymaker, Sachie Komatsuzawa, pictured with her female Brazilian and male New Zealander flatmates. Depicting the subjects with wide smiles, and Sachie and the Brazilian woman arm-in-arm, the photograph creates an impression of three young individuals having a close and fun friendship where they enjoy each other's company. The photograph focuses on the Brazilian woman as a central figure while the New Zealand man, who looks directly at the audience, exudes a sense of confidence and control. In comparison, Sachie is situated on the left-hand side with her face in profile, appearing to suggest her willingness to defer to the other two. Similar representations of Japanese *ryugaku* students can be found in many other *ryugaku* magazines.

Such media representations suggest particular social and power relations between the Japanese students and their host families and share mates. Through photos and autobiographical essays (see examples below), subject positions that are offered for the young Japanese women are those of guests, outsiders and learners of English, while Westerners are depicted as either caring hosts, insiders or capable speakers of English. Aoki's accompanying essay further demonstrates this construction of identities and power relations. In her essay (Wish International, 2002: 30), Aoki represents herself as:

- a student who desires to learn authentic English (e.g. 一度でもいいから、生の英語に触れてみたい (I want to be exposed to authentic English);
- a speaker of limited English in need of care by a generous host family (e.g. ファミリーは優しくって、私は全然英語を喋れないけど、とってもゆっくり話してくれるし、私の話そうとする事を一生懸命聞いてくれます (Although I cannot speak English at all, the family is generous and speaks very slowly to me and tries to understand what I try to tell them); and
- in need of the mother's care (e.g. 最初は英語だけの生活にとまどったけれど、マザーのやさしさに、緊張もほぐれていきました。体が弱って、気持ちも弱くなってしまったときはつらかったけれど、それもマザーのいたわりによって、のりこえることができました (In the beginning, I was at a loss in the English only environment, but, thanks to the mother's generosity, my anxiety decreased. When I became weak physically and emotionally, it was very hard. But thanks to the mother's care, I was able to overcome it.)

Such representations of a Japanese student and a (White) native English-speaking host family are portrayed as the norm of *ryugaku* and the best means of ELL. Indeed, for many of my participants, finding and choosing the 'right people' to live with during their *ryugaku* or working holiday in Sydney was perceived to be the key to success in both ELL and the overall *ryugaku* experience. However, although the choice of living with local Australians was popular among my participants, their decisions about who they lived with constantly intersected with a wide range of changing needs, conditions and belief systems, as we will see below.

5.2.2 Home

Choice of a temporary home in Sydney was one of the main concerns for all my participants. They believed that living with Australian native speakers of English would give them access to authentic English and local knowledge through everyday interactions. All participants had lived with either Australian homestay families (Ichi, Chizuko and Yuka) or with Australian flatmates (Yoko and Eika) at one stage or another during their stay in Sydney. In fact, most of them had changed their accommodation several times; my participants were long-term stayers whose aims were multiple and changed over time. Although their narratives of 'home' in Sydney were often phrased in relation to their learning and using English, their ideas of the ideal home environment constantly changed at the intersection of new needs and desires, as is clear from the cases of Eika, Chizuko and Yuka.

Eika lived in three different places during her stay in Sydney. After living with me for the first month of her stay, she rented a studio apartment and lived by herself for six months. This was largely motivated by her wish to create a private space with her then Australian boyfriend who was leaving Australia shortly. After he left, however, she felt that living by herself limited her opportunities to use English, and she decided to find share accommodation with local Australians. She moved in with Bill, a white Australian man in his early sixties who grew up in Sydney and owned a house in a quiet suburb in Sydney. Although Bill appeared to be an ideal share-mate, she felt utterly unable to relate to him from the moment she moved in. She was increasingly aware that there were few shared social practices between them at home and, as time went by, she seemed less and less motivated to interact with him. After several weeks, she even began avoiding contact with him in the house. Thus she was happy to move out when Bill's previous housemate returned from overseas.

Her next flatmate, Jackie, was a Hong Kong Australian office worker in a multinational company. Jackie rented a large two-bedroom apartment in Chinatown near Sydney's CBD and Eika moved in with her just before starting a TAFE diploma course on human resource management in February

2004. Jackie was full of social and academic commitments outside work and had many Chinese friends who visited her home frequently. From early on, Eika seemed comfortable with Jackie, who was genuinely interested in getting to know her and often suggested cooking dinner together at home. Gradually they made friends with each other's friends (Eika's Japanese friends and Jackie's Chinese friends) and their apartment became a trilingual communal space (English, Japanese and Chinese) for several Asian women in their twenties and thirties. In this community, Eika was able to perform her cherished identity as a charming and witty woman, an option that was not available at Bill's place.

Eika's different degrees of desire for interaction with Bill and Jackie can be best understood in terms of negotiation of identities, that is her ability to position herself in a certain way and be accepted by the other. To begin with, she predominantly regarded Bill as a landlord, not as a housemate on an equal footing to whom she could casually suggest a drink or dinner. My field notes suggest that most of their interaction was restricted to logistics around the house (such as cleaning, rent and garbage clearance), positioning and distancing Eika as a tenant who lived in 'his' house. During the four months she stayed, there was little development in their predominant identities as landlord and tenant.

On the other hand, Jackie and Eika negotiated their identities in a way that contributed to a sense of respect and empowerment for Eika. Although Jackie was regarded as the main tenant of the apartment and owned all the furniture and household appliances, this did not seem to translate into unequal power relations. From the beginning, Jackie showed her curiosity about Eika's past experiences and her views on life. In their interaction, Eika was treated as an intelligent and mature woman on the basis of her being an ex-career employee in one of Japan's largest companies. In other words, Jackie appreciated qualities in Eika that had been ignored by most non-Japanese people since her arrival in Sydney.

In addition, the linguistic identities of Bill and Jackie had a great impact on Eika's agency in interacting with them. Throughout her stay, Bill's native-speaker status remained at the forefront of Eika's experience of him. In our conversation, Eika habitually mentioned her deep embarrassment about her inability to understand his Australian English. In contrast, Jackie's identity as a non-native speaker helped Eika become less conscious of her own non-native speaker identity. Jackie spoke Chinese as her first language and English as her second. According to Jackie, her Chinese accent occasionally caused minor communication breakdowns with her monolingual Australian co-workers (f23june04jackie), but she attributed this to their linguistic deficiencies rather than her own.

Agency 95

Jackie: they are really sad. they say that they can't understand me because of my accent. what are they talking about? everyone has an accent and the Australian accent is so awful! (f23june04jackie)

Jackie and her Chinese friends frequently engaged in counter discourses such as this against monolingual native speakers of English, and Eika was introduced to this alternative way of understanding (Australian) native speakers. As Foucault (cited in Burr, 2003) argued, this process was opening up possibilities for change in Eika:

> ... change is possible through opening up marginalized and repressed discourses, making them available as alternatives from which we may fashion alternative identities. (Burr, 2003: 122)

Gender identity in conjunction with age also played a significant part in Eika's interaction with her flatmates. Every now and then, Bill's maleness and seniority emerged as an issue in her narrative of living in his house. For instance, Eika did not feel comfortable sharing a bathroom with Bill. Also, Eika simply could not find common interests with Bill, who seemed to prefer a quiet retirement lifestyle with few guests coming to visit the house. It was the first time she had lived with a non-family member and she had little idea about how to negotiate her position in terms of gender and age. On the contrary, Eika and Jackie were at a similar life stage as unmarried career women and, as Eika expected, it enabled them to discuss a much wider range of issues such as work, singlehood, marriage, motherhood and, particularly, romance. The large bathroom was their common space where they shared cosmetics, clothes and anecdotes about their everyday lives.

For Chizuko, too, home increasingly became much more than just an opportunity to improve her English. As soon as she decided to go on *ryugaku*, she organised enrolment in an English language course and living with an Australian homestay family. When the contract with the host family ended, Chizuko moved into an apartment with a Japanese and a Chinese student who had been staying with the same host family, and lived with them for nearly two years. Because the Chinese student was learning Japanese in addition to English, their home language was both English and Japanese. Although the increasing use of Japanese concerned her, she enjoyed the company of the two flatmates and continued living with them until they had to leave Australia.

When I began my fieldwork with Chizuko, she had already left both the Australian family and the two Asian share mates, and was living with a Japanese family in an area known for its large Japanese population. At first, it was puzzling to me. Despite her constant complaints about the lack of opportunity to speak English at home, she showed little sign of discontent with the Japanese-speaking home environment. On the contrary, she seemed quite happy, and reluctant even to entertain the thought of leaving.

チズコ：　　やっぱりさ〜、もう本当に楽しいし楽だからあそこ出るのいやなんだよね〜。まあ、オージーと住めば、もっと英語喋る機会が増えると思うけど、子供たちと別れるのがつらいよね。

Chizuko:　well, I don't want to move out of there because it's so much fun and easy to live with them. I know that if I live with Aussies, there will be more opportunity to speak English, but it'll be so hard to say goodbye to the kids. (f6march04chizuko)

When she moved in, the Japanese family consisted of a husband, a wife and their seven-year-old and 20-month-old daughters. Chizuko's first point of contact with the family was with the husband; they were students together at a natural therapy school. Although her move into their flat was meant to be temporary, she gradually made it her home and was invariably included in family outings. In this family, she was positioned as a respected classmate by the husband, while the wife saw her as her closest friend and de facto mother of her children. The children came to consider Chizuko as their 'second mother' and the younger child often went to Chizuko to be comforted when she woke up in the middle of the night.

Obviously Chizuko's choice to live with the Japanese family contradicted her tremendous *akogare* for becoming part of Australian society and mastering English, as mentioned in Chapter 4. She believed that if she lived with English speakers 'there will be more opportunity to speak English', and yet she chose to live with the Japanese family. This contradiction can be explained by the argument by Pavlenko and Piller (2001) that language learners are capable of choosing how and how much they want to use and learn their L2. Her contradictory choice thus must be seen as a result of a tension between a beneficial learning context and other desires (see below) that were equally as important as, if not more important than, her desire to practise her second language.

For instance, Chizuko often told me about her strong wish to marry and start a family. However, she had not been able to fulfil this life goal. Although she had had a few romantic experiences, she felt unable to find a long-term partner with whom she could think of marriage. Also she was becoming increasingly concerned about her ability to give birth because of her age (she was 41 years old when she joined the study). By living with the Japanese family, she could, however indirectly, fulfil what she wanted to achieve in her life as a woman. At home, she was the 'second mother' to the children and had flatmates who considered her as part of the family. Thus her adopted

Japanese family was not something she would easily relinquish for the sake of gaining access to linguistic resources.

In my observation, Chizuko was not troubled by the fact that she had not achieved her ideal level of fluency in English. She had sufficient proficiency in English to enable her to carry out almost all her daily tasks and casual conversations at social gatherings. Particularly towards the end of my study, what appeared to be most important to Chizuko was how to obtain permanent residency and maintain the lifestyle that she cherished in Sydney (this issue will be revisited in Chapter 9); this lifestyle had come to be as important to her as her overall *akogare* for English, which formed one of the salient drives behind her decision to move to Australia.

Yuka's choice of home environment provides a similar example of multiple and changing desires. Having lived with several different Australian host families during her first five years in Sydney, she began living by herself in early 2002. This choice was motivated by her desire to gain emotional and material independence from her host families and to learn to become responsible for her own life. Although she stayed in touch with her last host family throughout her *ryugaku* years, she felt that they tended to treat her as a child and this positioning began to cause friction. This was particularly so with the host mother, who often objected to Yuka's choices in terms of education and romance and tried to persuade her to change her mind. This left Yuka feeling increasingly incapable of negotiating her values with the host mother.

When she began to study for a degree, Yuka moved into a one-bedroom apartment near the university and enjoyed the freedom of living by herself. Although she occasionally complained about being lonely, she did not want to give up her freedom and independence, which can be understood as another example of competing interests. As mentioned earlier, Yuka initially came to Australia to study English as a means of dealing with her problem of being *hikikomori* (socially withdrawn). She made a great deal of effort to learn English and to develop social skills in order to associate with other people. She acquired the NSW Higher School Certificate through TAFE before undertaking her university degree course. During my visits to her flat, I observed that she usually cooked for herself and kept the place in order. She often told me how she had changed from being a *hikikomori* teenager to being an independent woman in her twenties and, in my observation, this sense of transformation contributed to her self-esteem as a mature individual.

Furthermore, for Yuka, home was her 'base' where 'I can relax and recharge my energy so that I can get back out there and fight again' (f24june04yuka). Her choice of the term 'fight' suggests her constant struggles outside the home. During the study, Yuka regularly expressed her frustration with Australians' arrogance and their ill-treatment of Asians in university classrooms and public spaces. She had to resist being positioned as a deficient Asian speaker of English by speaking up constantly and even unnecessarily to show that she was competent in English. In fact, she went to see a university counsellor from time to time to discuss her emotional difficulties with interpersonal issues. With her long-term sense of insecurity (related to the *hikikomori* years) and emotionally exhausting daily social practice of resistance, she needed a quiet personal space where she could retreat and re-energise herself. Norton (2000) reports that a Polish immigrant woman, Eva, saw her home as a 'place of refuge' and constructed her private space to be Polish, 'where she was respected and well liked and where she could lead a relatively independent lifestyle' (Norton, 2000: 61).

5.3 Work as an ELL Opportunity

So far I have focused on my participants' choices of home environment during their *ryugaku*. This section discusses the discourse of work as an ELL opportunity. Firstly I present an analysis of the media discourse of work and *ryugaku* and secondly I present examples of my participants' agency in ELL and social participation through work.

5.3.1 Media discourses of work during *ryugaku*

Tsuda (2000) points out that many Japanese women have *akogare* for being able to work using English:

> 英語はまた「自立」の気分を与えてくれる言語でもある。日本人女性はよく「英語の使える仕事がしたい」というが、このことばからも明らかなように、英語と仕事は女性たちの頭のなかでは一つになっており、その行く先というのは「女性の自立」という到着点である。そして英語は「男女平等」という先進的な思想と結びつく言語として日本では受け止められている。
> English is a language that induces a sense of 'independence'. Japanese women often say, 'I want to work using English' and it is apparent from such comments that English and work are one in women's minds and therefore that English can be a path leading to women's independence. English is seen as a language that is linked with the modern ideology of 'gender equality' in Japan. (Tsuda, 2000: 91)

Indeed, a wide range of media, English language schools and *ryugaku* agents in Japan function as mechanisms to produce and sell the discourse of work and English. *Ryugaku* and women's magazines typically carry articles glorifying success stories of Japanese women working in an English-medium workplace.

Working in the West is also constructed as an opportunity to learn 'authentic' English. Such ideas have become a packaged product that is sold to Japanese women as a legitimate form of *ryugaku*. For instance, Koor Intercultural Programs and Education (2004), one of the *ryugaku* agents in Sydney, claim on their website, 'オーストラリア人と一緒に英語を使う環境の中で働く事は、生きた英語を学ぶ最適のチャンス (to work in an environment where you use English to work with Australians is the best chance to learn authentic English)'. In Australia, international students are allowed to work up to 20 hours a week, while working holidaymakers are entitled to work on a full-time basis for one employer for six months at a time (Department of Immigration and Citizenship, 2010).

I noticed, however, that many Japanese students and working holidaymakers in Sydney are employed in Japanese service industries such as restaurants, take-away shops, duty-free shops, *ryugaku* agencies, travel companies and massage clinics. Although they are motivated to find a job with local people in order to improve their English, getting such work requires a functional level of English. It is therefore easier to find work in a Japanese-speaking milieu. However, the difficulties of finding work in the English-speaking workplace have raised problematic issues in recent years as opportunities for exploitation have been created.

For instance, some *ryugaku* agents have taken advantage of those who had *akogare* but did not have the resources to find a job in an English-speaking environment. A typical case was reported in *The New Zealand Herald* (2004), which reported how, desperate to gain work experience with native speakers, Kayoko Sakamoto, 25, paid $2400 to a Japanese agent to find her a job in a hotel in Christchurch, New Zealand. The job consisted of serving breakfast and lunch and cleaning for eight hours a day without pay. Sakamoto thought that it was 'normal' that she was not paid:

> I didn't think about money, I wanted experience of working with New Zealanders and using English. I thought it was better than going to a language school.

When I discussed Sakamoto's case with Tokiko, one of my secondary participants (in the past she had worked as a work experience placement officer at a *ryugaku* agent in Sydney), she said that it was not an isolated incident.

トキコ： そんなケースいっぱいあるよ。お金もらわなくてもいいからとにかくオージーと仕事したいって言う人いっぱいいるもん。

Tokiko: there are many cases like that. so many Japanese are dying to work with Aussies, even for no money. (t20sep04tokiko)

For my participants, too, there was a sense of prestige attached to the concept of working with Australians. It was talked about as a window of opportunity to improve their English and to gain access to wider Australian social networks. Nevertheless, their interest in and opportunities for finding work using English varied considerably. Although the majority of my participants hesitated, or for a time chose not to work with native-speaker Australians, Yoko made a considerable investment in the L2 work discourse and demonstrated her determination to be employed in English-medium workplaces despite, as you will see below, enormously discouraging circumstances.

5.3.2 Yoko's work history in Sydney

Yoko was employed for most of her two-and-half-year stay in Sydney. She worked for three months at a Japanese restaurant, three months in a boutique hotel and 20 months at a hotel in Chinatown. Her determination to work seemed to be based on two factors. Firstly, she was freshly divorced and had limited finances to support her stay in Sydney. Secondly, she believed that work in Sydney would increase her opportunity to meet local people and improve her English.

Initially, she worked as a waitress in a Japanese restaurant patronised by Australian, rather than Japanese, customers. Her first opportunity to work in an entirely English-medium environment came about when she was enrolled on a TAFE hospitality certificate course. The course required her to gain 150 hours of work experience in the customer service industry. Following that, a classmate who was already working in a boutique hotel secured her a job as housekeeper. One week later, she was promoted to the position of receptionist. This work experience gave her an opportunity to remap her career and future plans, because she had, from that point, decided to become an international hotel receptionist. As such, she subsequently sought a job as receptionist at a three-and-a-half-star hotel in Chinatown, where she worked with a team of Australians.

Yoko's Japanese friends often complimented her on her work experience and expressed admiration of her efforts to improve not only her English but also her career prospects as an international receptionist. Working with and for Australians was a major challenge for Yoko and her job proved so stressful that she often felt physically ill on the way to work. She frequently mentioned her constant sense of exhaustion and even occasional bouts of diarrhoea.

ヨウコ： 　もう本当に朝、仕事行く時にジョージストリート歩いていると、お腹が痛くなってきちゃうんですよ。「ああ、行くのやめようかな」って、「

	やだな、また英語であの人達と仕事するの」って。でも、結局、「こんな事で、負けちゃだめだわ！」って行くんですよね。
Yoko:	well, when I'm walking down on George Street on the way to work in the morning, I get a stomach cramp. I'm like, 'oh, maybe I shouldn't go to work', 'I don't want to work with them in English'. but, I'm like, 'I can't let it beat me!' and I go to work eventually. (f9dec03yoko)

Yoko's agency drove her to take up and keep the challenging receptionist job, and it manifested in a combination of strategies. The following subsection explores these strategies, including the power of belief, asking for help, constant reminders, recognising progress, dealing with mistakes and marginalisation, and having attractive future plans.

5.3.2.1 The power of belief

Yoko had a firm belief in the possibility of 'perfecting English'. In her narratives, there was a close link between working with Australians and her mastery of English, which often generated actions producing both immediate and effective results. Her belief was so powerful that very little prevented her from seizing opportunities. Her first attempt at job hunting was typical. When, shortly after her arrival in Sydney, her flatmate told her that a nearby café was looking for a waitress, she immediately made her way there and applied for the job.

ヨウコ：	えーっと、もしここで仕事が出来たら、英語が上手くなるって信じてたんで。その時は、そういう英語だけの環境で働いたら、3ヶ月ぐらいでペラペラになるって真剣に思ってたんで＠＠
Yoko:	well, I really believed that I would be able to speak English if I could work there. at that time, I thought that three months would be enough to become totally fluent by working in an English speaking environment ＠＠ (t14june04yoko)

However, the owner of the café rejected her job application and the reason was her limited English. When I asked Yoko if she was worried with her English level at that time, she said that this issue never occurred to her.

ヨウコ：	考えませんでしたね。とにかく、英語で仕事したら英語が上手くなるからって考えてたんで。
Yoko:	I didn't think about it. all I was thinking was that my English would be better if I worked using English. (t14june04yoko)

One possible interpretation of her lack of concern was that, as a recent arrival, she was relatively free of the discourse that 'good English' was needed to find a job. However, her perseverance in seeking and performing English-medium jobs, despite her increasing awareness of the importance of linguistic skills in the workplace, suggests an unchanging strength in her belief. For example, when she was offered a position as a receptionist at the boutique hotel, she immediately accepted. When the director of the hotel expressed his concern with her English at the interview, she told him that she was perfectly capable of handling the job and had enough English to perform her job competently. She told me later that she had dissimulated in this fashion in order to secure a job working with and for local people. However, Yoko quickly grew concerned about her English competence when she began working as a receptionist and occasionally complained about physical symptoms caused by the stress of working with local people and international English-speaking customers. Even so, she continued to believe that work would improve her English. Although she often expressed anxiety, she tended to conclude her stories by saying that she would continue to do her best.

5.3.2.2 Asking for help

Yoko's patterns of asking for help at work illuminate the complex nature of carrying out such tasks in an social and occupational context. For instance, at her first workplace, the Japanese restaurant, she not only keenly observed how more experienced Japanese waitresses served customers in English, but also constantly asked them for useful English expressions, phrases and questions such as 'May I help you?', 'Are you ready to order?' and 'Would you like anything else?'. She said that she had nothing to lose by asking, since she considered herself to be at the bottom of the hierarchy of English proficiency among her Japanese colleagues and, as such, did not have to negotiate her position in terms of her linguistic identity. At the hotel in Chinatown, however, the act of asking for help from Australian colleagues became problematic. She detested asking fellow receptionists, particularly Australians, for help with her English because she was too embarrassed to admit that she did not understand seemingly simple exchanges with them or with the hotel guests.

It may appear that the differences in her agency in these two different workplaces were a matter of racial and linguistic identity: it would have been naturally easier to ask the Japanese colleagues in Japanese. However, the comment below indicates that the picture was more complex.

ヨウコ： いつもなんかわからないと、ベルボーイに聞くんですよ。「ちょっとこっちきて〜 」みたいな、で、これってどういう意味って。で、たまに

ふざけて、「いくらくれるの?」みたいに言ってくるから、「ちょっと、早くしてよ、あたし仕事しないといけないんだから」って言うんですよ。

Yoko: whenever I don't understand something, I ask the bellboys. 'come here for a second' and I ask them what it means. sometimes they joke around, asking me how much I would pay them. I tell them off saying, 'come on, hurry up. I have to get back to work!'

キミエ: へ〜、ベルボーイだったら恥ずかしくないんだ?
Kimie: hmm, you are not embarrassed to ask the bellboys?

ヨウコ: 皆若くってバカばっかりですから、向こうにバカだと思われても別に気にしません。
Yoko: they are all young and stupid, so I don't care if they think that I am stupid. (f19jan04yoko)

At the hotel in Chinatown, it was important for Yoko to construct and maintain a professional receptionist identity in the eyes of her Australian receptionist colleagues. Asking for help with English would have stigmatised her as linguistically deficient and therefore professionally unreliable. However, even though these bellboys were White Australian native speakers of English, Yoko positioned them as her subordinates, based on her higher work status and greater age. This positioning allowed her to make use of these bellhops as linguistic and social resources.

5.3.2.3 Constant self-reminders

Another characteristic of Yoko's agency in the English-medium workplace was her constant self-reminding of her *akogare* for English. It was evident that such narrative practices were often triggered by her exposure to the objects of her *akogare*: White Australian native speakers, Hollywood stars (especially Brad Pitt) and her new career prospects as a bilingual receptionist. During her stay in Sydney, she frequently went to see Hollywood movies – particularly Brad Pitt movies – usually several times, whenever she was feeling depressed about her job and her slow progress in English. Movies, in her view, reminded her of the purpose of her *ryugaku*.

ヨウコ: 映画みてて、「ああ、あたし、こういう世界に憧れてオーストラリアに来たんだった!」って思い出したんですよね。頑張ろうって思いました。
Yoko: while watching the movie, I remembered, 'I came to Australia because of my *akogare* for the world like this!' I thought that I must keep trying. (f27may04yoko)

Furthermore, Yoko's emotional investment in Brad Pitt movies and achieving success in ELL must be understood in relation to her divorce. As mentioned in Chapter 3, Hollywood movies provided moments of escape after the discovery of her husband's extramarital affairs. She used knowledge of English and Hollywood movies/stars as social capital to rebuild her self-esteem in Japan. She had a small photo-sticker of her ex-husband and his girlfriend at the back of her diary and, whenever she wanted to give up on the receptionist job, she forced herself to look at it. In other words, part of her perseverance in the job and ELL came from her desire to take revenge by transforming herself into a successful international receptionist, fluent in the international language of English.

5.3.2.4 Recognition of improvements

Drawing on the work of Leech (1983), Piller (2002: 111) argues that, due to the modesty maxim at work, 'talking about one's L2 success poses an obvious problem'. This was often the case with Yoko (and also the other participants), who tended to understate their progress in English and remained self-critical. As time went by, however, she began making positive self-evaluations and praising her achievements and this seemed to have a positive impact. Typically, although she would first stress that her overall proficiency was still unsatisfactory, this would be followed by expressions of surprise or pleasure as she noticed improvements in specific areas of her English.

ヨウコ：　イヤ〜全然まだ喋れないんですけど、なんか最近仕事場の人が何言ってるか少しだけですけど分るようになって来ました。

Yoko:　well, of course I still can't speak well at all, but recently, I feel more able to understand what my colleagues are saying. (f18jan-04yoko)

Yoko's willingness to persevere in her job also resulted from her constant acknowledgment that interaction with her Australian colleagues contributed greatly to improving her English. She often said to me and her Japanese friends, who admired her courage in working in a local hotel with Australians that, despite her struggle to understand her fast-speaking Australian colleagues and customers, it was the act of working with native speakers that contributed most to her success in English.

5.3.2.5 Dealing with marginalisation

One of the most striking forms of agency that Yoko displayed was her ability to turn her experience of marginalisation at work into strength. She was aware that some of her colleagues treated her as a deficient speaker of English and for that reason often did not pass on new information to her.

ヨウコ： 皆私が英語できないの知ってるから、「ああ、ヨウコには、言わなくってもいいよ。どうせわからないからさ」みたいな事言ってるの何回か聞いたんですよね。恥ずかしかったし、すっごく頭きましたけど、でも、彼らの言ってる事間違ってないんで、言われてもしょうがないって。だから、早く英語うまくならなきゃっていつも思います。

Yoko: everyone knows that I can't speak English well, so I've heard them say 'don't bother telling Yoko. She won't understand' a few times. I was embarrassed and angry, but I thought that it can't be helped as they aren't wrong about me. so I always think that I have to get better at English quickly. (f19march04yoko)

Her comment, 'they aren't wrong about me', indicates that she accepted their positioning of her as a limited ESL speaker. However, she did not allow this to negatively affect her socialisation with her colleagues and she was able to channel her anger and humiliation into constructive agency. For instance, whenever she was invited for a social chat with her colleagues (receptionists, bellhops and managers), she would try to participate to the greatest possible extent. This was by no means a sign of submission but rather of her willingness to take advantage of her colleagues as linguistic and social resources. In fact, she often produced a counter discourse whereby she positioned them as 'three-and-a-half-star workers with no future'. In contrast she talked about herself as someone who had the potential to work in a five-star hotel in the future. This kind of self-esteem seemed to have helped her maintain her dignity in a situation where she felt inferior and was possibly seen as inferior by her co-workers. She was determined that she would surprise them by transforming herself into a fluent speaker of English, finding work at a five-star international hotel one day.

5.4 The Choice to Work in the L2 Context

Yoko's choice to work during her *ryugaku* was more than just a financial necessity. Her determination to work in an English-medium workplace intersected with her faith in employment as an ELL opportunity, which constituted a discourse of English as empowering for internationally minded career women; in fact, Yoko's *ryugaku* and work experiences can be considered as a success story. Eventually, on the basis of a number of factors – her improved English, a certificate in hospitality she gained from a TAFE course and her work experience as a receptionist – she was offered an opportunity to work on Bora Bora Island, one of the French Polynesian islands. At the time of completion of my data collection, she had already relocated to the island to work in a major souvenir shop and then went on to work as a receptionist at a five-star international hotel (her new career will be further discussed in Chapter 9). Obviously, her relatively successful employment trajectories resulted from her efforts to create job opportunities, dealing with difficulties in interpersonal interactions and stress, negotiating her self-identity in the workplace. Her case demonstrates that the process of building a career using English is nothing like as glamorous or as easy as the media and popular discourses in Japan about English and work would have us believe.

In fact, although many other participants were equally keen to work, they chose not to pursue this option during their *ryugaku*. For one thing, the younger participants in their mid-twenties, Yuka and Ichi, had never worked in Japan and showed little interest in gaining career-oriented work experience in Sydney. Ichi also did not see work as creating an opportunity to participate in Australian society.

イチ： うん、白人の社会とかに入るのって憧れてたけど、仕事でっとは思ったこと一度もないね。

Ichi: yes, I've always had *akogare* for being part of White society. but I never thought of doing that through work. (t1july04ichi)

Ichi and Yuka both considered their education in ESL and later at university to be their top priority and considered work as a 'distraction'. Instead, they focused on finishing their university degrees so as not to financially burden their parents more than necessary (t1july04ichi).

In contrast, Eika was like Yoko; she embraced the idea of learning English through work. As mentioned in Chapter 3, she chose to embark on a working holiday rather than *ryugaku* so as to be able to work in Sydney. However, she came to believe from her early days in Sydney that her English was too limited to obtain a 'desirable' job (e.g. human resource management). She feared that she would not be considered a competent worker and decided not to pursue finding an office job, which was her preferred occupation.

Yuka, Ichi and Eika's decisions not to work were made possible by their financial situations: Yuka and Ichi's *ryugaku* was funded by their parents, while Eika made use of the large amount of savings she had accumulated in Japan. Conversely, those who were financing themselves or had limited financial resources had an urgent need to work. For instance, Chizuko worked in a Japanese-owned opal shop in Sydney's CBD for two years. This choice was mainly motivated by her personal assessment of her English fluency and her financial needs. The salary was much better in a

Japanese-speaking job servicing Japanese tourists than, with her limited fluency, she could earn in an English-speaking job. Tokiko, a secondary participant, also expressed her frustration about the difficulties of finding an English-speaking job with long-term prospects. She worked with a team of Australian and Japanese co-workers as a waitress on a showboat for two years. Being a Japanese speaker, she was able to win respect from her Australian colleagues, since up to two-thirds of the customers were Japanese tourists. At the time she had ample interactional opportunities to speak English with her co-workers. However, she did not consider being a waitress a desirable long-term career, as she did not see the customer service tourism industry as being suited to her professional identity. At the same time, however, Tokiko expressed doubts about her prospects of finding higher status employment in an English-only medium workplace in Australia.

トキコ：　でもさ、オフィスワークの経験とかしたかったけど、英語だけの環境っていうと、ちょっと正直言って怖いよね。完璧に英語が出来ないと、入りづらい雰囲気。あたしの性格的に、それはそれでストレスになる。

Tokiko: well, I wanted to get office work experience, but to be honest, it's scary to work in an English-only environment. it looks hard to get in unless you have perfect English. I decided not to do it because I know my personality and it would have been too stressful. (t28sep04tokiko)

It is important to note, however, that many of my participants were convinced that 'limited English' was not the only factor that would make their access to L2 work difficult or *scary*. From time to time they expressed concern about their Asian identity being a disadvantage, an issue that has been addressed by Piller (2011a, 2011b) in an Australian context. Based on findings from a number of Australian case studies on migrants from non-English speaking backgrounds, the researcher finds that limited English proficiency limits access to employment opportunities, but there is no guarantee that improvement in English necessarily leads to a career path consistent with prior work experience. Such access intersects with a number of non-linguistic factors, and race is increasingly shown as a major impediment (see also Alcorso, 2003; Butorac, 2011; Colic-Peisker, 2005, 2009; Colic-Peisker & Tilbury, 2007; Hawthorne, 2001; Piller & Takahashi, 2010b; Takahashi, 2009). However, in Australia, which strives to project itself as a post-racist supporter of equal opportunities and social inclusion, limited or accented English 'becomes a substitute for racial and ethnic discrimination' (Piller,

2011b). Many of the women in the study were aware of this, and their frequent comments, such as the one below, indicated to me their increasing resentment towards the environment where their *akogare* was denied on the basis of their linguistic and racial identity, by the very society they had so aspired to be part of:

トキコ： 結局さ〜、マルチカルチャーとかなんとか、うたってるけど、結局白人社会なんだよね。で、英語が喋れないと人間扱いされないみたいな。

Tokiko: in the end, they talk about multiculturalism, but it's just a song and dance, they are really a White supremacist society. on the top of that, they don't treat you as a human being if you can't speak English. (f24sep04tokiko)

5.5 Summary

This chapter presents a discussion of my participants' agency in improving their English in the two key social contexts: home and work. All of them considered living and working with native-speaker Australians to be conducive to ELL and entry into Australian society. Yoko and Ichi, for example, firmly believed in this discourse of home as an ELL opportunity. Both lived with English-speaking flatmates/homestay families during the majority of their stays in Australia and made a great deal of effort to practise English with them. However, as the decisions and experiences of Eika, Chizuko and Yuka suggest, home was not simply an ELL context and they created their living environments for a host of reasons that contradicted their claimed desire to improve English with local Australians. This finding provides support to the view of agency offered by Pavlenko and Piller (2001) that:

> in some cases L2 users may decide to learn the second, or any additional, language only to a certain extent, which allows them to be proficient, but without the consequences of losing the old and adopting the new ways of being in the world. (Pavlenko & Piller, 2001: 29)

My findings add another dimension to Pavlenko and Piller's (2001) idea above. Their view originates from studies of Western women who reject Japanese femininities while learning L2 Japanese (Ohara, 2001; Pichette, 2000) in that their hegemonic Western identities seemed to accord these women such agency. The three Japanese women's agency in rejecting the sacrifice of their private space for SLL, however, demonstrates that race is not the only source of agency nor power. My participants' views and needs changed over time and their emergent goals powerfully intersected with their agency in shaping their home environments. Home formed a crucial space in which Eika and Chizuko could nurture a sense of emotional security as an important member of the household. For Yuka, her flat was where she could take refuge from her daily emotional struggles and also nurture her new identity as a responsible adult, something that had been missing from her teenage years of *hikikomori*. The choices of home environment for long-term stayers, like my participants, have to be understood at the intersection of their previous as well as their emergent needs and desires which may have outweighed their desire to improve their English.

Yoko's work experience shows that working using English in Australia was by no means easy or enjoyable: she constantly suffered from stress, fatigue and even occasional diarrhoea as a result of having to constantly negotiate her identity and power relations with her Australian co-workers. However, her strength manifested in her ability to employ effective strategies when dealing with interpersonal difficulties and power struggles at work. Firstly, the power of her belief in the connection between work and ELL demonstrates the importance of having confidence in a chosen method of language learning, as this was key to her pursuit of and perseverance in an L2 job. Constant self-reminders of the original reason for ELL and recognition of the progress she was making also proved to be important strategies for maintaining her commitment to mastering English through work experience. Furthermore, although she may have feared the loss of status in the eyes of her Australian receptionist colleagues, she was able to position herself as superior to bellboys (Australian native speakers) and drew on them as a linguistic resource. Similarly, her self-positioning as someone with better career prospects than her colleagues helped maintain her self-respect and enabled her to engage in social interaction with them.

Furthermore, despite their exposure to the discourse of learning authentic English through work, few other participants felt able or wanted to pursue career-oriented work experience during their *ryugaku*. Yuka and Ichi had very little financial need to work and chose non-job oriented means of improving their English (e.g. socialising with university friends). Eika, conscious of her self-perceived limited English, felt she would not be able to find a job that matched her previous professional identity. Rather than experiencing a sense of status loss, she chose not to pursue employment as a means of improving her English. For Chizuko, ELL through work was a secondary concern and instead she chose the option of working in a Japanese-speaking environment which offered better financial rewards. In some participants' accounts, racism and the linguistic discrimination that they experienced in Sydney emerged as closely linked, if not identical, phenomena (Piller, 2011b; Piller & Takahashi, 2010a, 2010b). This led them increasingly to believe that Australian society did not welcome Asian non-English speaking workers, a view which greatly discouraged their dream of working with local Australians.

What their experiences demonstrate is that agency cannot be seen as a given or unchanging quality exercised by an individual. Rather, as Lantolf and Pavlenko (2001: 148) have argued, agency is 'a relationship that is constantly constructed and renegotiated with those around the individual and with the society at large'. In this light, it is possible to understand my participants' choices not to live or work in an English-speaking environment differently. As mentioned throughout this book, they were full of the desire to use and learn English at home or to work with local Australians, but their choices were made and continuously altered at the intersection of their financial needs, identity, non-linguistic desires and the power relations experienced in particular contexts. As such, the notion of agency, together with language desire, offers complex and nuanced understandings of their decisions to use or not use English in social contexts.

6 Going Home

> *Behind the ideal of living in two worlds is a parallel danger of being able to live fully in neither. Women may find themselves trapped in the space betwixt and between Japan and the foreign, outsiders both in Japan and abroad, belonging nowhere*
> Kelsky, 2001: 202

6.1 Introduction

In Chapters 2 and 3 I discussed the construction of language desire and the decision-making process, which led to my participants embarking on *ryugaku*. In Chapters 4 and 5, I recounted participants' experiences as they attempted to improve their English and create a desirable lifestyle in Sydney's multicultural society. This chapter traces my participants' narratives about 'going home'. For them, returning to Japan was not an obvious choice – many, if not most, did not want to go home. During their *ryugaku*, they were constantly seeking out other future options in light of their emergent identities.

In the following chapter I will firstly discuss notions of hybridity and the 'cultural supermarket' to examine my participants' narratives about going home. I will then explore the media discourse about Japanese women returning home from *ryugaku* (Section 6.3) and common concerns about returning home, including negotiation of their bilingual/international identity, social networking, and work opportunities using English in Japan (Section 6.4). In Section 6.5 I will examine the 'going home' narratives of Yoko, Chizuko and Eika in relation to their hybridity and global mobility. Finally, the cases of Ichi and Yuka's intercultural relationship and its link to their hybridity and future options will be discussed in Section 6.6.

6.2 Hybridity and the 'Cultural Supermarket'

To explore my participants' narratives of going home, I find the concepts of hybridity and the 'cultural supermarket' useful. When individuals cross borders geographically and linguistically, their taken-for-granted ideas are often destabilised and thus their identities become highly contested. Block (2002) explains that the result of such on-going destabilisation is:

> not a question of adding the new to the old. Nor is it a half-and-half proposition whereby the individual becomes half of what he/she was and half of what he/she has been exposed to. Rather, the result is hybridity. (Block, 2002: 3)

Hybridity, in Papastergiadis's (2000: 170) view, is 'constructed through a negotiation of difference', but it is 'not confined to a cataloguing of differences'.

> Its 'unity' is not found in the sum of its parts, but emerges from the process of opening what Homi Bhabha has called a 'third space', within which other elements transform one another. Hybridity is both the assemblage that occurs whenever two or more elements meet and the initiation of a process of change.

It is important to note here that, by looking into the hybridity of the women in this study, I do not mean to present my participants as monolingual monocultural individuals who have, in the course of their *ryugaku*, 'add-on' identity repertoires. But rather, I draw on the notion of hybridity to explore the complex ways they position themselves within and across multiple discursive categories, such as race, gender, age, occupation, marital status, multilingualism and cosmopolitanism, in their everyday decision-making practices. In the following sections, I will illustrate the ways in which their identities and emergent desires and hopes intersect in constructing their future options.

Mathews' (2000) notion of the 'cultural supermarket' is also useful for exploring the intersection between my participants' hybrid identities and future options. Mathews (2000) argues that identities are shaped at three levels: (1) the taken-for-granted level, (2) the *shikata ga nai* (it can't be helped) level, and (3) at what he calls the 'cultural supermarket' level. At the taken-for-granted level, the shaping of self occurs in language and social practices 'that condition us as to how we comprehend self and world' and is largely subconscious (Mathews, 2000: 12). The *shikata ga nai* level indicates that people become increasingly aware of what kinds of identities and lifestyles are open to them. These choices include societal, familial and institutional pressures and they feel obliged to choose certain options rather than others. The last level, situated as the most shallow and fully conscious level of one's cultural shaping, depends on exposure to 'the cultural supermarket'. Unlike the material supermarket, what the cultural supermarket offers is an almost unlimited range of information and potential identities through various channels such as the internet, mass media, books, foods and the huge variety of advertisements. Mathews (2000: 15) argues that because 'the cultural supermarket and the identities it offers are global', it enables individuals to construct identities and choices drawn from beyond national and physical boundaries. Therefore, the underlying assumption of the cultural supermarket is freedom of choice: that its 'customers' can pick and choose any of the 'products' displayed on the shelves. In other words, individuals are apparently free to choose what they want to be or what they call 'home'. However, as Mathews (2000) repeatedly acknowledges, and as was argued in Chapter 5, the idea of being free to choose is problematic because:

> [P]eople pick and choose themselves in accordance with their class, gender, religious belief, ethnicity and citizenship, as well as all the exigencies of their own personal molding, from a cultural supermarket that heavily advertises some choices and suppresses others; they pick and choose themselves in negotiation with and performance for others. (Mathews, 2000: 15)

Indeed, my participants' desire for continued residence in Australia and further transnational mobility was constrained by a host of issues, including visas and citizenship. The celebratory discourse of globalisation creates an illusion of a 'global village' or 'borderless world'. Although this idea works relatively well as far as capital flows are concerned, it fails to account for the powerful restrictions placed on the movements of people imposed by nation-states, which dictate who may enter their territories, where they can be and for how long (Constable, 2003; Ong, 1999). Every encounter with questioning officers at the immigration office in Sydney and the Australian Embassy in Tokyo reminded my participants of their limited mobility and rights (see also Piller, 2011a). They were indeed caught between contradictory discourses of the nation-state and freedom of choice in the global cultural supermarket. At the same time, their agency to bypass the state gatekeeping practices was also evident. As Mathews (2000) writes:

> We are not slaves to the world around us, but have a certain degree of freedom in choosing who we are. This freedom may be highly limited, but it cannot be altogether denied. (Mathews, 2000: 23)

In fact, my participants possessed and used significant legitimate resources (such as a Japanese passport and financial support) to pass through some of the barriers set by national gatekeeping practices. In their search for desirable homes, romance and employment, they persevered to pursue their *akogare* and claim various parts of the world as 'home'. The next section deals with the media discourse of Japanese women returning from *ryugaku*.

6.3 Media Images of Japanese Women Returning from *Ryugaku*

Since the 1980s there has been growing societal and academic interest in the issue of Japanese *kikokushijo*, or 'returnees'. In general, the term *kikokushijo* is used to refer to 'students who return to Japan after a prolonged sojourn abroad' (Kanno, 2000: 362), and much of the previous intercultural research focuses on returnee children in elementary, junior and senior high schools (Goodman, 1990; Kanno, 2000, 2003; Kidder, 1992; Yoshida *et al.*, 2003). As Yoshida *et al.* (1999: 495) point out, this child focus results from and continues to reproduce 'the misleading assumption that being a returnee is no longer an issue once one is beyond high school age'.

This assumption may explain why, despite the great amount of care and attention *ryugaku* guidebooks and magazines place on entry into a host society, problems surrounding returning home for adults are hardly dealt with. When they are mentioned, they appear to be trivialised. Indeed, in the media, young Japanese women returning to Japan are often represented as successful internationalists, able to capitalise on their newly acquired language skills and overseas experiences. A special feature on long overseas stays published in *Nikkei Woman* (2004), a magazine which targets career-oriented, internationalist women in Japan, provides a good example.

Out of 36 pages discussing various aspects of long overseas stays, 27 coloured and seven black-and-white pages were devoted to glorifying *ryugaku*. For instance, one sub-header from the special feature proclaims:

行ってよかった！自信がついた！海外で暮らしてモット大きな私になる：仕事を捨てて、家族とも別れて・・・大きな決断になる海外ロングステイ。実際に勇気を出して渡航して彼女達は、皆「自信」を手にして帰ってくる。海外で暮らすことで得られる充実感とは何だろう？
Glad that I went! I gained confidence! Personal growth by living overseas: Long overseas stay involves throwing away one's job and

leaving one's family ... Every woman who summoned the courage to go overseas comes home with 'confidence'. What is this sense of satisfaction that they can gain through living overseas? (*Nikkei Woman*, 2004: 18)

The supplement featured women who had returned to Japan after having carefully prepared their *ryugaku* and overcome the 'trivialised' problems in the host country. They were finally depicted as championing their overseas experiences after their triumphant homecoming. In contrast, only one of the 36 pages discussed the negative impacts of *ryugaku* experienced by women on their return to Japan. This page provided the results of a survey which detailed the losses that women reported they had incurred as the result of a long overseas stay. These include a loss of savings (64.4%) at the top of the list, followed by a stable job (30.4%), time (8.9%), a romantic partner (8.9%) and of a career built prior to departure (8.1%).

The adjacent page, however, reported positive gains recorded in the same survey. These overshadowed, if they did not altogether obliterate, the costs of *ryugaku* on the other page. Their claims of gains, including such highly desired qualities as confidence (77.8%), language skills (75.6%), toughness (65.2), international friends (64.4%) and internationalism (59.3%), powerfully romanticised the end-product of the women's overseas experiences.

Time spent in a foreign country can be a tremendous learning experience. However, what such media discourse of *ryugaku* makes invisible is the complex ways in which young women weigh up their *ryugaku* experiences and construct their future possibilities in the light of their perceived accomplishments, failures and new subjectivities. Furthermore, in the media and popular images, *ryugaku* is portrayed as a clearly defined act of going to a host country temporarily as an adult learner and then returning to Japan. Such media portrayal makes Japan the only legitimate physical space for a Japanese person; it is their one and only 'home'. Thus returning to the homeland of their childhood, biological family and lifelong friends is presumed to be only natural.

This alleged natural bond between the Japanese people and Japan emerged as problematic in my participants' narratives. In fact, for most of them, the idea of returning to Japan was no longer a given, but considered with great reluctance, or more often than not agonised over and sometimes altogether rejected. As their participation in Australia and other countries exposed them to an ever-growing range of information, identities and opportunities, their internal debate further intensified, often without their ever coming to a full sense of conviction about their final choice.

6.4 Ambivalence

'Going home' or 'leaving Australia' was an inescapable reality for all my participants, whose status was always that of a temporary resident. This status made it inevitable for them to consider the timing and the conditions of leaving Australia and returning to Japan. After nearly five years of fieldwork with my participants, I noticed that their stories of return to Japan were increasingly characterised by a sense of uncertainty, confusion, anxiety and even fear. In short, no one wanted to go home.

Nevertheless, their options for staying in Australia were limited. Unless they somehow obtained either permanent residency or a work permit, both of which were perceived as hard or impossible to secure, they were required to leave Australia at some point. Moreover, a lack of finance meant that none could continue as international students. The savings of Eika, Yoko and Chizuko were dwindling and Ichi and Yuka's parents had announced that their financial support would cease at the end of their tertiary education (which was in May 2005 for both). These material and legal realities limited their choice of residency in Sydney, making their return to Japan an inevitable option.

Towards the end of my research, an interesting coincidence took place. From mid-2004, all of my participants began talking about going home or leaving Australia more concretely than just in passing. Yuka and Ichi told me that they were planning to return to Japan in July 2005 after the completion of their university degrees, while Chizuko indicated a departure date of March 2005 after completing her diploma course in natural therapy. Yoko returned to Japan in September 2004 while Eika returned in May 2005. In each case, there was an increasing sense of anxiety as their dates of departure approached. I identified several common issues underlying their narratives about their return home, and these emerged at the intersection between their changing subjective positions in Sydney and their image of Japan. In the following sections, I will discuss three related issues: (1) the negotiation and maintenance of an English-speaking identity; (2) hybridity and social networks in Japan; and (3) finding English-medium employment.

6.4.1 Negotiation and maintenance of English-speaking identity

As I pointed out in Chapter 3, gaining English proficiency was one of the most influential factors in my participants' decisions to study in Australia. Unsurprisingly, the difficulties of maintaining their bilingual identity (and by association, international/cosmopolitan identity) in Japan was the most common issue that caused dispirit in my participants. During their long-term stay in Sydney, each had made tremendous investment in learning English. As discussed earlier, that endeavour often involved coping with subordination to a range of individuals, and a sense of humiliation resulting from being unable to assert themselves as worthy individuals linguistically. Having paid such a heavy emotional and psychological price, the loss of their ability to speak English had become unthinkable.

Placing a high value on the English proficiency that they had gained, all the participants feared that the maintenance of this linguistic identity would not be possible in Japan. For instance, two days before her departure, Yoko told me, with an expression of great urgency and concern, that her deepest fear was that she would lose her ability to speak English.

ヨウコ： 英語を忘れるのが一番こわいです。こんなに苦労してやっとここまで喋れるようになったのに、今帰ったら、すぐ忘れちゃうんじゃないかって心配です。

Yoko: what I am afraid of most is forgetting English. it took me so much effort to improve my English to this level, if I return to Japan now, I am worried that I might forget it quickly. (f22sept04yoko)

Underlying my participants' fears was their view of Japan as a monolingual society, which would afford them little access to an English-speaking, cross-cultural space (e.g. English-speaking *gaijins*). This concern seemed derived from their holiday visits to Japan during which they struggled to gain exposure to English. That caused such a sense of anxiety that Ichi even thought of cutting her holiday short.

イチ： もうなんか、英語忘れちゃうんじゃないかって心配で早く帰ってきちゃおうかと思ったぐらい。うち、田舎だから、英語使う機会全然無いからね。

Ichi: well, I even thought about coming back earlier because I was worried about forgetting English. there is no chance to use English in my hometown. (t1nov04ichi)

Similarly, for Yuka, not being unable to use English in her daily life during her holiday visit caused a sense of loss of her identity as 'Yuka Takano'.

ユカ： だって、英語を使わないと、高野ゆかじゃない。英語を話したくっていつもむずむずしてました。

Yuka: because, I'm not Yuka Takano if I can't use English. I was always itching to speak English. (t1nov04yuka)

She was so desperate that she even spoke to her dog in English (see Piller, 2002, for self-talk on pets).

Yuka, Chizuko, Ichi and Yoko (all of whom had been back to Japan on holiday) came from country areas where contact with *gaijins* (i.e. Western native speakers of English) was a rarity or practically non-existent. The image of monoculturality and the implied backwardness of their hometowns posed an enormous threat to the international, cosmopolitan identities which they had grown to cherish.

They reported that they actively tried to create opportunities to use English during their holiday visits, for instance, by writing emails in English (five of them), interacting with English speakers in online chat rooms (Ichi), watching American TV shows (five of them), visiting 'international' pubs in Tokyo (Chizuko), calling English-speaking friends overseas on the phone (Yuka) and self-talk with a pet (Yuka).

Yet despite their image of Japan as a monolingual society, it was evident that advanced technologies, telecommunications, bilingual TV programmes, an influx of *gaijin* visitors/residents and the creation of personal English-speaking opportunities did expose them to an English-speaking space within Japan. However, this exposure was considered as insufficient because their more immediate social and cultural spaces were comprised of family, friends and public life, all of which were, in their view, stiflingly monolingual and excruciatingly 'Japanese'.

6.4.2 English, hybridity and social networks in Japan

As discussed in Chapter 5, home in Sydney for some participants was a space where they enjoyed their bilingual and international identity. However, none of my participants thought that their actual families appreciated their valued identity as educated, cosmopolitan and bilingual speakers of English. Particularly the younger participants, Yuka and Ichi, who left Japan at a relatively early age (Yuka at 17, Ichi at 21) and had been back on several occasions, reported increasing tensions and discomfort as they shared their social space with their families. When they finally returned, they were both 25 years old. Having enjoyed freedom away from their parents for many years, they found parental interference enormously daunting. Yuka's struggle with her parents was painfully narrated in an email she sent me.

ユカ： 二週間しか日本にいないのにもう息が詰まってきた感じです・・・。こんな事親に言ったら悪いけど、やっぱりもう両親とは生活出来ないなぁと改めて感じました。生活習慣が違うし、私の場合離れているほうが優しく出来るし・・・。

Yuka: I started to feel suffocated after being in Japan only for two weeks … I feel bad about saying this to my parents, but I once again realised that I can't live with my parents any more. our lifestyle is different and I can be nicer when I am away from them … (e1dec03yuka)

In addition, all the participants other than Eika reported being unable to relate to their friends in Japan. Yoko's story illustrates this issue well. Having returned to Japan in September 2004, she tried to re-establish her social networks with her old friends and ex-colleagues. She was, however, enormously frustrated by the inability of her friends and, in fact, the entire community (most of whom had never left their hometown), to understand or appreciate her experiences in Sydney. Eventually she lost interest in reconnecting with them.

ヨウコ: まあ、期待した私が馬鹿だったんですけどね。どんなに、私がシドニーで英語を苦労しながらがんばって覚えたとか、どんなにホテルでの仕事がつらかったとか、オージーと一緒に住んでどういう思いをしたかとか、そういうの全然分かってもらえなくって。だから、結局会わなくってもいいかなって思ってきました。
Yoko: well, I was stupid to have expected it. they weren't able to understand how hard I tried to learn English in Sydney, how tough the job at the hotel was and what I experienced through living with Aussies at all. so in the end, I started to think I don't have to hang out with them. (t2nov04yoko)

These examples support Mathews' (2000) view that, although the global cultural supermarket offers an ever-growing variety of identities, in fact, choices are socially constrained. He writes:

> One's social world – outside one's mind and more, as resident within one's mind – acts as a censor and gatekeeper, selecting from the range of possible cultural ideas one might appropriate only those that seem plausible and acceptable within it. (Mathews, 2000: 22)

In contrast, Eika expressed little concern about reuniting with her family and friends in Japan. Even prior to her departure, her extensive social network was already highly 'international' in that most of her friends were long-time residents of Tokyo and/or had been overseas. Her main concern was the relationship between English and her professional identity in Japan, to which I will turn next.

6.4.3 English and work

Eika had two main purposes in coming to Australia: to master English and to explore what she could do in her life with her English skills. When asked again on her return in October 2004, her answer was rather unexpected. Having studied English and human resource management in Sydney, Eika decided that using English for work in Japan was out of question. She was not alone in this conviction, however. English proficiency by itself was not seen as a useful qualification for finding desirable employment among my participants. As discussed earlier, although English proficiency is sold as an advantage to women, Yuka and some secondary participants were ambivalent about being able to use their English skills in any future job. Others saw English primarily as a language for maintaining international friendships or even as a 'hobby' (Chizuko and Eika). Chizuko, too, saw very few links between her English skills and employment choices either in Sydney or in Japan.

チズコ： あたしの場合は、仕事で絶対英語使わないとっては思わないのね。そこまで英語力無いし、仕事では、好きな事をして、プライベートで英語とふれていたいと思っているんだよね。英語とは離れたくないからね

Chizuko: in my case, I don't feel that I have to use English for work. I don't have enough competence in English and I want to do what I want to do for work and I want to use English in my private time. I don't want to lose English. (i3oct04chizuko)

This ambivalence towards English as economic capital seemed to be linked with the perceived 'oversupply' of Japanese–English bilinguals in Japan (Matsubara, 1989). All of the participants believed that, unlike a few decades ago, there are now 'too many' English-speaking Japanese people, and they felt that they needed additional qualifications in order to find employment, even though many did have such qualifications. Eika, Chizuko and Yoko had obtained diplomas or certificates from private colleges (human resource management, natural therapy and hospitality, respectively), while Yuka and Ichi were about to graduate from university with arts degrees in gender studies and sociology, respectively. However, the first three regarded their qualifications as 'useless' in Japan, while the other two considered their degrees to be of very little value as career-building tools.

In addition, very few participants saw themselves as competitive enough in terms of their English skills, particularly against *kikokushijo*, young returnees.

The *kikokushijo* were considered by my participants to be 'true bilinguals' since they had grown up or spent a significant part of their youth overseas. Despite their long-term residency in Sydney and their functional competence in English, the majority of my participants, who had arrived in Australia in their twenties (Eika, Yoko, Chizuko, Ichi and most of the secondary participants), did not position themselves as being of equal worth to the *kikokushijo* in this sociolinguistic hierarchy of Japanese–English speakers. In fact there is no Japanese descriptive word for someone who has learned English overseas in adulthood and they felt at a loss to explain 'what they were' in linguistic terms. Without the *kikokushijo* identity or any other recognised status, many believed that their chances of accessing the competitive international job market were slim. This, in turn, meant that there was one less social space in Japan where they could maintain their cherished English-speaking cosmopolitan identity.

Even if they entertained the possibility of using their English for work, their choice seemed to be confined to the highly feminised job market. For instance, Yuka talked about working at a *ryugaku* agency as a coordinator, while Chizuko and Eika briefly toyed with the idea of teaching English to small children (many of my secondary informants who have since returned to Japan are also teaching English). Ichi considered the option of becoming a wedding coordinator for Japanese couples in the United States (see more details in Section 7.6). However, at the time of the conclusion of my research in 2006, none of my main participants had a job in which they were using their English skills.

My participants' narratives are in sharp contrast to the media image of returnees as empowered English-speaking women with promising international careers. Even with their qualifications and improved English skills, my participants revealed a sense of powerlessness in the face of the authoritarian nature of Japanese companies, which openly discriminated against women on the basis of age and gender. Over the years, therefore, my participants' take on the discourse of English as a tool of empowerment for women had shifted to a point where almost none of them wholeheartedly endorsed that discourse.

6.5 Hybridity and Global Mobility

The participants' aversion to returning to Japan was closely linked with feelings that they no longer fully belonged to their hometowns, their friends or even their families. They also started to reject mainstream Japanese characteristics such as monolingualism, communication styles (e.g. excessive politeness, stiff body language, lack of eye contact) and even physical appearance.

However, my participants' rejection of Japan was manifested in a complex way. In fact, Japan not only remained a constant reference point for them, but many also expressed a new nationalistic pride in Japan's efficiency, intellectual achievement and global economic and technological success. Moreover, their *akogare* for the West and the English language did not remain unchallenged. This was consistent with Kelsky's (2001) findings.

> ... many women returning home, by choice or not, come to reject blanket affiliations with the West, enunciating in some cases a renewed nationalist identification with the Japanese state and in other cases a vision of hybrid identity. (Kelsky, 2001: 22)

Indeed, the notion of hybridity holds the key to understanding my participants' ambivalence about the idea of returning to Japan. The notion can also be used to understand the multiple options they considered for their futures, in which Japan occupied a significant, but transitory, space. Hall (1993: 362) points out that individuals, however hybrid they may be, tend to 'retain strong links to and identifications with the traditions and places of their "origins"'. At the same time, as part of a diaspora, they were often in a state of 'belonging at the same time to several "homes", and thus to no one particular home'. In the case of my participants, Japan was no longer the only home. Sydney, too, had become a home. For instance, Chizuko, Yuka, Yoko and Ichi, said that when they returned from holidays in Japan to Sydney, they felt completely 'at home'.

チズコ: 本当に不思議なんだよね。一ヶ月日本にいて、シドニーに帰ってきた時、「あ、家に帰ってきただ」って思っちゃったんだよね。ここが家になってきているんだなって思った。うん。

Chizuko: it was amazing. when I came back to Sydney after one month in Japan, I felt, 'wow, I've returned home'. I thought that it's become my home here. Yeah. (i3oct04chizuko)

As the word 'amazing' suggests, the acknowledgement of Sydney as an additional home often evoked mixed feelings. Underlying this pleasant amazement was the feeling that they were no longer purely Japanese, but had become Japanese who felt at home in what they initially considered as a foreign country. In spite of the hardships they experienced in Australia, a new sense of 'Japaneseness' and belonging had emerged.

Furthermore, based on their short stays (Yuka and Eika) or even without their physically being in a place (Yoko, Ichi, Yuka and Eika), many participants had also begun to feel that other parts of the world could be potential homes. As is described in the following section, their imagination of future possibilities as to where they wanted to live, work or study, and with whom they wanted to share their lives seemed boundless and borderless.

In the next sections, I will explore the narratives of each of the main participants about their future movements in terms of the ways in which their options were imagined, constructed and debated in negotiation with their hybrid identity. I will start with Yoko.

6.5.1 Yoko: Bora Bora Island and beyond

After two-and-a-half years of living in Sydney as an international student and working as a hotel receptionist, Yoko decided to move to Bora Bora Island to work. This was surprising news to me and her friends for two reasons. Firstly, in my view, Yoko had the strongest *akogare* for the West among my participants. During my fieldwork, she constantly talked about her plans to move to the United States or the United Kingdom in her quest to find a White boyfriend/husband. Secondly, no one, not even Yoko, knew where the island was: it did not exist in our mental map as a possible residential, or even tourist, destination at that time. It turned out that the island was not even an English-speaking society but was one of the French Polynesian islands (its main island being Tahiti). None of this fitted Yoko's identity project described above.

She started to consider the idea of leaving Australia around mid-2004. This had been motivated by her painful break-up with her Chinese-Australian boyfriend, her increasing frustration with her financial situation (at the time, she had roughly AU$1000 in the bank in Australia), the stress of her workplace and the unlikelihood of gaining permanent residency in Australia, without which she would have to continue to pay for school fees in order to renew a student visa. However, as discussed in Section 5.4, she did not want to return to Japan. Thus, she 'jumped at' a job offer as a sales assistant by the owner of an opal shop on Bora Bora.

ヨウコ： ジョンともうまくいってなかったし、そろそろ帰ろうかなって思ってたんですよ。でも、本当に日本に住みたくなかったんで、飛び付いちゃったんですよね@@短期間で決めちゃったんですけど、あんまり後悔はしてません。

Yoko: my relationship with John wasn't going anywhere and I was thinking about going home. but I really didn't want to live back in Japan, so I jumped at it. I made the decision in a short time, but I have little regret. (t2nov04yoko)

Yoko had never heard of the island before. It was far from the homes of the White people and Hollywood stars she yearned for, and the move would entail a new occupational identity as a sales assistant which excited her very little. Yet the option of moving to the island was immensely more attractive than the idea of remaining in Sydney without any possibility of reconciliation with her boyfriend, or moving back to her small hometown where the choice of identities and employment was quite limited. In her mind, her hometown would once again turn her into a miserable 30-something divorcee and rob her of the sense of freedom to maintain her treasured and hard-earned bilingual and cosmopolitan identity.

Her move to Bora Bora also presented an opportunity to reinvent herself as multilingual rather than merely bilingual, because the official language was French. When she was back in Japan waiting for a work permit to be granted by the French Embassy, she started to study French, imagining herself as fluent in French. Although she had never been to Bora Bora or the other French Polynesian islands, in her narrative it was already her new home. However, as her email to me below suggests, her adventure was still fused in her consciousness with the world of Hollywood:

> i still can't believe i left Sydney ... i went to french embassy in tokyo yesterday [...] im just thinking about blue sky and ocean in Tahiti ... im running White beach with brad pitt ... (e30sep04yoko)

In her bedroom in her parents' house, she put up a poster of Bora Bora Island which, she said, provided an emotional oasis and the hope that her life would be more satisfactory and enjoyable once she moved to the island.

At the same time, Yoko did not see Bora Bora as her final destination. In fact, her utmost *akogare* still seemed to lie in Western English-speaking countries. She entertained the idea of moving to the United States, Canada or England after her contract on the island was over. The reality, however, was that, in order to move to any of these countries, she had to negotiate her visa status and right to work. With the United States becoming more strict about the entry of foreigners, she considered the United Kingdom, where international students are allowed to work in the same manner as in Australia, as the most feasible option.

Having been back in Japan since September 2004, the emails she sent me from her hometown conveyed both the emotional struggles she experienced as she tried to survive in Japan, and growing excitement about moving to Bora Bora. She had been trying to find a regular language exchange partner in her hometown with very little success. In October 2004, after only two weeks, she resigned her temporary job as an office worker as a result of personal conflicts with her 'unnecessarily' critical supervisor. She then moved on to work as a kiosk shop assistant at a golf course. She cleaned windows at her new workplace and this reality of her work conditions in Japan saddened me. My immediate response was that she must have felt defeated in this simple job in light of her overseas experiences. However, the ending of the email instantly reminded me of her strength:

ヨウコ： お元気ですか？私は今仕事中。窓ふきしてました。まあ深くは考えないことにして！がんばります！
Yoko: How are you? I am in the middle of my job. I was cleaning windows. I try not to think about it too much! I'll do my best! (e23nov04yoko)

In fact she sent me this email from her newly acquired mobile phone which enabled her to stay in touch with her friends overseas. However virtual that connection was, it gave her the strength to stay hopeful and look forward to her next journey to the exotic island, where her dream of working in a five-star international hotel would indeed come true.

6.5.2 Chizuko: Returning home to Sydney

Like Yoko, Chizuko expressed a firm rejection of Japan as a permanent home. For her, life in Japan was filled with stifling social rules and she felt suffocated every time she went back there for a holiday. However, after the completion of her two-year diploma course in March 2005, she had no choice but to return to Japan. While other participants were planning their moves to other countries (e.g. Yoko to Bora Bora, Ichi to the United States and Yuka to China), Chizuko was planning to return to Sydney on a permanent basis. In June 2005 she enrolled on another two-year course at a private college in Sydney and resumed living with her Japanese family friends and working in the opal shop.

As discussed earlier, she came from a rural area where a café was still a novelty. In that part of Japan she had limited access to any linguistic resources. During her holiday visits, television was the only cultural resource to help maintain her cherished English-speaking international identity.

チズコ： 二ヶ月で英語忘れるのが心配だったから、NHKの英語の番組ばっかり観てたね。すっごい安心したもん英語の音に。
Chizuko: I was worried that I might forget English in two months, so I only watched English programmes on NHK. I felt so relieved at the sound of English. (f3oct04chizuko)

In Japan she also had limited access to what she always idolised – *gaijins*.

チズコ：	日本に帰ったら、日本人ばっかりの世界じゃない。それがやなのよね。英語が喋れるか喋れないかってだけじゃなくって、外人見ると気持ちが高まるのよ。
Chizuko:	when I go back to Japan, it's a Japanese-only world. it depresses me. it's not only a matter of whether or not I get to speak English, but when I see *gaijins*, I feel uplifted. (f3oct2004chizuko)

In fact, when she was back in Japan for a two-month holiday in 2003, she spent little time in her hometown and mostly stayed in Tokyo, actively seeking out opportunities to meet foreigners. She regular visited an area called Roppongi, in order to socialise with Westerners, preferably Australians. She was disappointed that most of the *gaijins* she met were Middle-Eastern men who were fluent in Japanese but had little English proficiency. They held little attraction for her.

This lack of access to Westerners in Japan posed a serious concern for her, not only in terms of her linguistic identity, but also in terms of her prospects for romance. She had always been clear about her preferred racial type for a romantic partner, that is, a White Westerner. She repeatedly told me over the years that:

チズコ：	外人以外の人とデートするのって考えられない。ずっと結婚したいと思ってたし、年々強まるよね。私の夢は外人と結婚する事だからさ。
Chizuko:	I can't think of dating a non-*gaijin* man. I've always wanted to get married and it is getting stronger year by year. my dream has been to marry a *gaijin*. (f3oct04chizuko)

This racial preference for Whiteness was intimately linked with her investment in the English language and her English-speaking identity. Although she did not see herself as a fluent speaker of English, she believed that she could be her 'ideal-self' when conversing with a Western man.

チズコ：	何で外人がいいかっていうと、英語だと理想の自分になれるから。英語の表現ってとってもストレートじゃない？少ないボキャブラリーでやらなきゃいけないんだけどね。でもだからストレートに正直に自分が表現できるみたいな。日本語だと回りくどいのよね。
Chizuko:	The reason why I prefer *gaijin* men is because in English, I can be my ideal-self. English expressions are more straightforward,

aren't they? I have to manage within my limited vocabulary. but that's why I can be straight and honest in expressing myself. in Japanese, I have to beat around the bush. (f3oct04chizuko)

Her desire to return to Sydney thus constitutes her wish both to maintain her linguistic identity and to locate herself in a desirable romantic market. Her case demonstrates a striking example of the intimate relationship between language and romance.

Chizuko said that if an immediate return to Sydney proved impossible for financial reasons (being an international student can be very expensive), she would plan to move to Tokyo or, more specifically, into a so-called *gaijin* house. *Gaijin* houses are residential share accommodation for long-term foreign visitors who find it hard to rent accommodation because it involves complex logistics and a considerable amount of 'key money' (three months' rent plus gift money to the owner of the accommodation). At *gaijin* houses, tenants pay only about AU$500–600 per month for their rooms, paid either in weekly or monthly instalments, and thus avoid the difficulties of having to deal with real estate agents or owners of accommodation who often do not trust foreign tenants. Nowadays, *gaijin* houses have become part of the ELT industry and the owners of such businesses advertise their houses as 'domestic *ryugaku*', because they provide an opportunity for Japanese people to live with Western native speakers of English. For Chizuko, a *gaijin* house was the most attractive residential choice financially and emotionally within her temporary homeland, Japan. In her narratives, she often talked about herself as a temporary resident of Tokyo and as someone who would eventually somehow go home to Sydney. Chizuko saw herself as a *gaijin*, a traveller from the West; her self-perception as such empowered Chizuko in that she as a *gaijin* was not obliged to conform to rigid Japanese social norms.

Sydney offered more than the worlds of Westerners and English to Chizuko: there was also a strong sense of belonging to her Japanese family in Sydney. As discussed in Chapter 5, she had become a second mother to the children and the closest friend of the mother of the family. At the time of finalising my research in 2006, she was once again happily living with the family, asserting that she was more determined than ever to 'make it happen' and obtain permanent residency in Australia.

6.5.3 Eika: A long journey in search of a new life choice

For Yoko, Chizuko, Yuka and Ichi, return to Japan was a highly *shikata ga nai* (inevitable) choice, while for Eika going back to Japan was a positive choice. She told me that she wanted to go home to reflect on, and finally choose, a life option out of all the possibilities that had become available through her exposure to several countries. Before and during her stay in Sydney, she had visited Malaysia, Singapore, Thailand, Australia, New Zealand, Taiwan, Hong Kong, China and the United States.

After finishing her TAFE course in June 2004, she had no concrete plans to live in either Sydney or Japan and she decided to switch from a student to a tourist visa. Having travelled to New Zealand to renew her tourist visa in August 2004, she spent another three months in Sydney and then went on a round trip to Taiwan, Hong Kong, China and the United States, returning to Australia in January 2005. She planned to travel on the Australian east coast for another three months or until, as she jokingly said to me, her initially enormous, but now significantly reduced, savings from Japan ran out. After that, she said she 'might' think about going back to Japan to decide whether she would stay and work there for good or leave for another country. Her future beyond her eventual return to Japan, 'perhaps' some time in 2005, was an open-ended story still to be negotiated.

However, every now and then, despite her narratives of return to Japan as a 'joyful' plan, I noticed an increasing sense of reluctance. In fact she was investigating other schools that she could attend after the completion of her TAFE course and she changed and extended her visas several times (from a working holiday to a student and then to a tourist visa) and increasingly expressed her interest in working in other parts of Australia. One way to interpret her ambivalence is that her feelings were in many ways symbolic of her complex relationship with English. Despite her initial self-positioning as a competent speaker of English, her view changed dramatically during her stay in Sydney. By mid-2004, she became critical of Australia's claimed multiculturalism and the image of 'friendly Aussies', and sceptical of being able to achieve a bilingual occupational identity.

エイカ： オーストラリアに来て分かった事は、英語使って仕事するなんて、とんでもないってこと。そんな英語力無いもん。
Eika: what I understood after coming to Australia is that there is no way I can use English for work! I don't have such competence in English. (t1nov04eika)

This sense of 'defeat' became central to her self-narrative, which complicated her relationship with Japan. For instance, she clearly began investing more in her national identity, as is evident in what became a constant comment, 'I am first and foremost Japanese', which she never mentioned at the beginning of her stay in Sydney. This increased investment in Japanese identity, in turn, was problematic as it inevitably confined her prospects to the Japanese job market of which she became increasingly critical. At the beginning of her stay in Sydney, she remained fond of her previous workplace in Japan and was confident that she could easily return to work there after taking a working holiday in Australia. But this idea was increasingly challenged as she learned about work conditions in Australia through her TAFE course and from her Chinese-Australian flatmate. She began re-evaluating gendered Japanese workplace practices in light of the Australian discourse about women's employment. Thus, towards the end of her TAFE course, employment in Japan had become significantly less attractive for Eika (t28oct04eika).

Her narratives of going home entailed a great deal of emotional struggle as she reflected on her needs, wants, identities and future options. Just before she left Australia, she said with a great sense of uncertainty:

エイカ： まあ、一度日本に帰ってどう感じるかだよね。ひょっとしたら、もう窮屈でまたすぐヨーロッパとか行っちゃうかもしれないし、ゴールドコーストといっちゃうかもしれないし。全然、また日本に慣れちゃってずっと住み着いちゃうかもしれないし、本当に一回帰ってみないとわからないって感じかな。

Eika: well, it depends on how I feel when I get back to Japan. it may so happen that I feel suffocated and decide to go to Europe or the Gold Coast as soon as I get back. or I might get used to Japanese life again and decide to live back there, so I can't be sure unless I go back there once. but I want to go home once and reflect on what I've done and what my options are now. (f17apr05eika)

Eika had come to Australia for the purpose of mastering English and finding a new lifestyle. During her stay in Sydney, she found a home in a multicultural and multilingual community of friends who, as recounted in Chapter 5, respected her. She also visited her friends in Taiwan, China, Hong Kong, Seattle and New York. With all these new experiences, her search for a meaningful life commitment seemed to be an on-going and exciting journey. At the time of completing my research, she had returned to Japan and was enjoying being back in the community of her close friends, many of whom have had the experience of studying overseas. Earlier, she had rejected a job offer from her previous workplace and instead she was preparing to launch a new career as a manager at a music company specialising in jazz. Music had been her passion since her teenage years and she was delighted at the prospect of working with foreign musicians, a job which would necessitate some use of English. Having launched her new career, she began to thrive with her long-term passion for music, social skills and bilingual identity.

6.6 Hybridity and Intercultural Relationships

Piller (2006) points out that intercultural intimate relationships symbolise the new phase of globalisation. In this section, I will demonstrate that the intercultural romances experienced by my participants, particularly in the cases of Yuka and Ichi, resulted from an increase in international mobility (e.g. their studies in Australia, numerous trips overseas and visits to Japan), international data flows (e.g. internet use) and cultural exchanges (e.g. language choices and maintenance). Their narratives of intercultural romance were not only a formative site of hybrid identity, but were also where their future options were jointly constructed and constantly renegotiated. On these grounds, I decided to examine the future options of Ichi and Yuka within the framework of intercultural romance and the negotiation of their identity. Their stories provide complex connections between language desire, migration, emotional attachments and sense of home.

6.6.1 Ichi and Rod: Language desire and race

Apart from her *akogare* for the West and English, one of the significant incentives behind Ichi's *ryugaku* was her hope that an overseas qualification would improve her prospects in the chauvinistic Japanese job market. This meant that she initially intended to return to Japan. However, after her second year in Australia, she expressed an increasing desire to remain overseas by finding a job either in Sydney or in another English-speaking country. Despite the many interactional difficulties she experienced during her stay in Sydney, she maintained her *akogare* for, and identification with, Australians/ native-speaker Australians. 'Even' Singapore was one of her options for future residence as it was a 'Westernised' English-speaking country.

イチ: 終わっても、絶対に日本に帰りたくないからさ…英語圏ならどこでもいいと思ってん。シンガポールでもいいってぐらい思ってたから。

Ichi: I don't want to go back to Japan after I finish uni ... I thought any English speaking countries would do. I thought even Singapore would be okay. (i16sep04ichi)

In mid-2004, new possibilities emerged. She had met Rod, a Korean-American teacher of English living in Tokyo. They met initially through an online chat room and later met up in Japan during her holidays there. Although these meetings were relatively brief, they developed and maintained their Tokyo–Sydney relationship through email, MSN messenger and international telephone calls. After May 2004, for the sake of their relationship, Ichi was increasingly committed to the idea of moving back to Japan after completing her university studies. Their plans were that she would return to Japan in July 2005 at the end of her university degree and live with Rod until the end of his teaching contract in January 2006, after which they would move together to his hometown in Arizona, USA.

Even though her return to Japan was going to be temporary (approximately six months), Ichi expressed a great deal of anxiety, particularly with regard to the maintenance of her English proficiency. Two factors alleviated this concern: their decision to use English as their couple language and the planned move to the United States.

In fact, Ichi's relationship with Rod was highly contingent on the language they used in their everyday dealings with each other. Rod spoke fluent Japanese and initially wanted to communicate with Ichi in Japanese. She unequivocally rejected that and made it clear that her temporary return to Japan depended largely on English being used as their main communication medium.

イチ： はじめはやっぱり中学頃からの夢で、英語で大学で勉強して、海外で働くっていうのをあきらめるのには抵抗があったよね。その一つの理由に、がんばって勉強した英語。今までの中で一番勉強して努力して手に入れた物だから、簡単にはあきらめられない。そしたら彼が、「分かった」って、日本に帰っても英語を使ってくれるっていうんで。まあ帰ってもいいかなって。それじゃなきゃ、シドニーかどっかで半年間待ってようかとおもってんよ。

Ichi: I was a bit hesitant of giving up on my dream from junior high school of studying at uni in English and working overseas. one of the reasons was English which I tried so hard to learn. it was something that I worked hardest to obtain and so I couldn't give up easily. then he said, 'I understand' and he told me that we would continue to use English after my return to Japan. so I thought maybe it's okay to go back. otherwise I thought about waiting for six months in Sydney or somewhere else. (f16sep04ichi)

In this negotiation of language choice, Ichi was able to put herself in a more powerful position and this was accepted by Rod because he was more committed to her romantically and emotionally than Ichi was to him. Her ability to impose her choice of English was based on their joint knowledge that even if he was an American citizen, she had 'compromised' her *akogare* for White men. She told me:

イチ： もしロッドがアメリカ人じゃなくって、普通のただの韓国人だったら、あたし付き合っているかどうか分からないもん。ひどいかもしれないけど、やっぱり白人がいいなって今でも思う、うん。彼もそれ知ってるからさ～@@

Ichi: I am not sure if I would have gone out with him if he was not American and just a regular Korean person. it sounds awful, but I still prefer Whites, yeah. and he knows it, too @@ (f16sep04ichi)

In her narrative about Rod, she gave priority to English, which meant that her *akogare* for Whiteness had to take a back seat. However, both she and Rod knew that it did not mean the end of the allure of Whiteness for her. It did not mean that she had developed *akogare* for Asian-ness, either. In fact, she continued to have 'friendly' friendships with White male friends in Sydney, a great source of anxiety for Rod.

イチ： 彼、自分が、あたしのタイプじゃ全然ないって知っているから～@@、こっちの白人の男の子の友達の事、すっごいヤキモチ焼く、うん。

Ichi: he knows that he is not my type at all @@, so he is so jealous of my White guy friends here, yeah. (f1dec04ichi)

Thus, Rod's inescapable racial identity seemed to position him in such a way that he needed to offer something as a 'compensation' to Ichi – access to his English native-speaker and Western persona as embodied in his American citizenship.

The couple's international move from Japan to the United States further alleviated Ichi's anxiety about her six-month return to Japan. Japan became a mere transit point and as such allowed her to adopt an identity as a temporary visitor or even a tourist rather than as a permanent resident. This way, she did not have to try to fit back into Japanese society, similarly to the case of Chizuko. Although she laughed about the fact that she could not locate Arizona on a map (f12nov04ichi), she already saw it as her next home. She registered herself on an American job search website, hoping to develop a career as a wedding coordinator by capitalising on her bilingual and bicultural skills. In our conversation, her heart was already in Arizona with her imagined community, comprising Rod's family and her future American friends and colleagues.

イチ： もう、気分はアメリカだよね〜！@@　彼の家族もあたし達が来るの楽しみにしてるみたいだし、とにかく早く行きたいなって。
Ichi: I feel like I am already in America!@@ his family is looking forward to having us and I just want to get there as soon as possible. (f11nov04ichi)

Although her heart was already there, her actual relocation, of course, required a visa. Unlike Australia, the United States did not provide a partner visa unless couples were married. To overcome this issue, Rod suggested in November 2004 that they get married. She did not consider his proposal an attractive option. In fact she rejected it outright. She said:

イチ： まだ結婚したくないって言ってさ〜。真剣に付き合ったのって、これが初めてだから、まだボーイフレンド、ガールフレンドのステータスを楽しみたいって。実際、自分のお金も無いし、結婚式とか、親に頼りたくないしね。ビザは取るの難しいけど、でも、そのためだけには結婚したくないから。
Ichi: I told him that I didn't want to get married yet. This is my first serious relationship and I want to enjoy boyfriend-girlfriend status for a while. in reality, I don't have money and I don't want to rely on my parents for the wedding. I know that it's hard to get a visa, but I don't want to get married just for that. (f1dec04ichi)

She knew that marriage to an American citizen would greatly improve her mobility and access to an English-speaking society, which would further construct her as a transnational cosmopolitan. However, what was more important to her was to gain financial independence from her parents and enjoy her first serious romantic relationship. Clearly, she did not want to be legally bound to a man towards whom she lacked a feeling of total commitment, either. English and international mobility were obviously important, but not at all costs.

6.6.2 Yuka, Ali and the multilingual community

Yuka's story about her teenage years begs the question of whether she ever felt 'at home' in Japan. As mentioned earlier, Yuka became a *hikikomori* in her junior high school years and came to Australia at the age of 17 to start a new life. Her narratives of her early years in Sydney were without the slightest hint of homesickness for Japan. Instead, she talked extensively about her empowering experience of learning English and making international friends. Over the years, however, she increasingly became critical of Australians and

Australia's multiculturalism, which she saw as a failing ideology. For her, Australia emerged as a White supremacist country with a monolingual mindset. Yuka began spending more time with Asian students from her university, particularly those of a Chinese background, and such friendship was part of her resistance against exclusionist White Australians. Indeed, it was these connections with Chinese friends and also romance with a Chinese man, which opened new future options for her.

Encouraged by her Chinese friends, she began learning Chinese at university at the beginning of 2002. During the 2003 Christmas holiday, she visited her Chinese university friends, Kristy and her boyfriend Luca, in Guangzhou, China and was introduced to their friend, Ali. After returning to Australia, Yuka kept in touch with Ali via the internet and gradually developed a romantic interest in him. In September 2004, the frequency of their communication increased, particularly through MSN messenger. As her feelings grew, she became more determined to move to China and seek job opportunities on completion of her university studies in July 2005.

Her interaction with Ali, mostly online, took place within a 'cyber community' of multilingual friends in which her hybridity was greatly appreciated. She would spend hours and sometimes even the whole day chatting with Ali, Kristy and Luca on MSN messenger. She predominantly conversed in Chinese with Ali, who spoke very little English, while she mainly used English while code-switching with Kristy and Luca, who were multilingual in Chinese, Japanese and English. It was still difficult for her to chat entirely in Chinese and she often had to use a Chinese–English dictionary. Nevertheless, every opportunity to interact with Ali in Chinese gave her a great deal of enjoyment and excitement, leading her to invest more in her romance with him, her multilingual skills and her future in China. In this community, she was a woman with social capital comprised of being Japanese with the ability to speak English and Chinese (f13nov04yuka).

However, Ali, known among his friends as a playboy, did not make an 'official' commitment to her. She found his hesitation very frustrating because she was ready to commit herself to him. Due to her limited romantic and sexual experience, she often felt at a loss as to how she could advance their relationship. At the same time, she enjoyed being playful when their Chinese phone and online conversations turned romantically and sexually flirtatious. Ali even demanded 'kisses' on the phone or jokingly suggested online sex by using a web camera on MSN messenger. Yuka told me that from time to time she felt like a different woman; she felt more passionate and honest in Chinese than she could ever be in Japanese or English, although they were her 'better languages'.

ユカ： ましな方の言葉［日本語・英語］ではどうやっていちゃつけばいいのか知らないですし、イケてないチャイニーズでやろうとしてるわけですよ。信じられないです。でもどうやってさりげなく出来るかわからないんで、ダイレクトに彼に気持ちを伝えるしかないんですよね@@@。バカみたいって感じます@@@でも日本語と英語ではぜったいこんな感じじゃない。「I miss you」とかって英語で言わなくちゃいけないのってすっごい気持ち悪い。いや！日本語ではどうやって言うのかもわかりませんよ@@

Yuka: I don't even know how to flirt in my better languages [Japanese and English] and am trying to do it in my pathetic Chinese! I can't believe it. but because I don't know how to be subtle, I have no choice but to be direct in telling him how I feel @@@ I often feel stupid myself @@@ but I am never like this in Japanese or English. it feels disgusting to have to say 'I miss you' and stuff in English. ugrh! I have no idea of how to say that in Japanese @@ (foct04yuka)

Furthermore, her romantic preferences became increasingly linked with her language desire for Chinese. Her general preference now was for a man 'who speaks Chinese' and Whiteness had lost its romantic allure for her. Regardless of race, she often expressed a strong aversion to what she jokingly called 'monos' or monolingual men. She said she had always been attracted to men with 'differences' and that excluded Japanese men (f21oct04yuka). While telling me how most of her friends in Sydney were at least bilingual, she started to check her mobile phone and concluded that all the saved numbers were those of bilingual/multilingual friends.

Although Ali was narrated to be the main reason for her move to Guangzhou in 2005, their romantic prospects were not the only force prompting her move. Yuka told me:

ユカ： 中国に行こうと思ったのはアリの事が絶対あります。でも他の理由もあるんですよ。中国語を伸ばしたり、英語を保持するためには、中国で働くのが一番なんじゃないかって。日本語と中国語と英語を話せる日本人ってそんなにいないかと、だから仕事探しで結構いけるんじゃないかなって。

Yuka: Ali is definitely why I thought about moving to China. but there are other reasons as well. thinking of the best way to improve my Chinese and maintain English, I think it's best to work in China. there are not many Japanese who can speak, well, Japanese, Chinese and English, so I am sure I can be competitive in the job market. (f13nov04yuka)

Her move to China was thus aimed at maximising her social and cultural capital in the job market rather than simply the pursuit of romance with Ali. Her self-esteem arose from her identity not just as an ordinary bilingual, but a rare multilingual with proficiency in three highly valued languages in the world – Japanese, English and Chinese. Having learnt that her father's friend could help her get a highly paid job in China, she was happy to live anywhere in China and not simply in Guangzhou.

ユカ： いい仕事が中国で見つかりさえすれば好きな時にアリに会いに行けるかなって。ゴンジョウで仕事が見つかればいいですけど、工場でネジとかラジオの部品ベルトコンベアーで組み立てみたいなのを地元のチャイニーズとやるのとかっていやです！@@そんなのの為に大学で何年も勉強したわけじゃないんで。

Yuka: as long as I can get a good job in China, I can go and visit Ali whenever I want. it would be good if I could get a job in Guangzhou, but I don't want a job like making screws or putting radio parts together on an assembly line in a factory with local Chinese people! @@ I didn't spend so many years studying at uni to live like that. (f13nov04yuka)

Although her pursuit of romance was important, she was not willing to experience downward social mobility for it. Her years of investment in education, where she often felt inadequate and marginalised by mainstream Australian students, could not be wasted on 'an assembly line'. Having championed mulitilinguality and gained elite consciousness, Yuka took her future career very seriously – no compromise, not even for romance.

Furthermore, although China had the most prominent presence in her heart, there was also the sense of 'exciting' uncertainty in relation to future romantic possibilities and further international mobility. When I asked Yuka if she was going to return temporarily to Japan at the end of her university studies, she was uncertain.

ユカ： 帰るかもしれないし、帰らないかも知れないし@@@家族もいるし友達もいるし。それとオーストラリアにもたまに帰って来たいです。でも正直言えば、将来自分がどこにいくかってわからない((大きな笑み))。でもあの突然どっかの国で誰かと出会っちゃって、「きみえさん、私彼とヨーロッパに行きます！」とかになっちゃったりして。中国に行くのは楽しみですけど、何をしてるかとか、その後どうするかとかまだわかりません。

Yuka: I might go back, but may not either @@@ I have my family there and a few friends ... and I would like to come back to Australia to visit sometimes. but to be perfectly honest, I don't know where I am going to be in the future ((big smile)). but, like, suddenly I might meet someone in some country and say, 'Kimie-san, I am going to Europe with him!' I am excited about moving to China, but I am not sure what I will be doing or where I am going to be after that. (f21oct04yuka)

Although her lack of certainty was apparent in this comment, it entailed little sense of insecurity. Rather, she was a woman who saw Japan, Sydney and China as her homes, and possibly even the rest of the world. What a transformation it has been.

6.7 Summary

This chapter has examined the Japanese women's narratives of going home and the ways in which their hybridity has intersected with their future options. Their growing resistance to the idea of returning to Japan was closely linked to their views of life in Japan and their desires for language maintenance and career opportunities. In their hometowns, Ichi, Chizuko, Yoko and Yuka considered it impossible to cultivate their experiences in Sydney and maintain their cosmopolitan, English-speaking identities. At the same time, they had growing doubts about English as a career-building tool in Japan, fearing that their linguistic investment could be wasted.

I also explored the ways in which my participants constructed future options in negotiation with their hybridity. For Yoko, Chizuko and Eika, Sydney as well as other parts of the world had become 'homes' of great personal significance. Through Ichi and Yuka's stories of intercultural relationships, it was evident that their choices of home and romance profoundly intersected with their language desire (Ichi for English and Yuka for Chinese and multilingualism) and their increasingly complex hybridity. This transnational movement of my participants sharply contradicts the discourse of *ryugaku*, which embeds in a 'return ticket' between the host country and Japan. In the following final chapter, I will attempt to theorise the link between language desire, multiple identities and transnational mobility.

7 Conclusion

7.1 Introduction

In this book, I have explored the notion of the language desire of young Japanese women and their experiences in Japan and Australia. In this concluding chapter I will firstly draw together the main findings presented in Chapters 2–6 and, based on these findings, I will offer a conceptualisation of language desire within the poststructuralist framework of identity, language and desire. Finally, I will discuss some implications of these findings for the fields of SLA and ELL in Japan as well as for the Japanese nation-state.

7.2 Japanese Women on the Move Revisited

This section provides insights into the set of inquiries that I set out to explore in this research (Chapter 1).

7.2.1 Construction of language desire in Japan

First of all, on the basis of my initial analysis of Japanese women's *akogare* for English, I came to the view that it was crucial to explore how *akogare* was constructed in the Japanese context. As discussed in Chapter 2, all my primary participants reported having developed their *akogare* for the idea of the West during their teens as a result of listening to foreign (mostly American) music, watching Hollywood movies and/or their adulation for Western male celebrities. Such gendered *akogare* was talked about as a key driver behind their positive attitudes towards learning English and, in many cases, led to the immediate and/or increased use of the language in their lives. Direct exposure to Western men and boys in their teenage years also fostered their *akogare* for English in the cases of Chizuko, Ichi and Yuka. What these findings suggest is that their *akogare* for English became conflated with their desire for the West and Western men at an early stage in their lives. Furthermore, we have seen that the media had a strong impact on the early construction of their language desire. The Japanese media constantly presents the English language as a means for appropriating what is 'desirable', that is, Hollywood stars and singers, most of whom are White Western men.

This romanticised link between English and Western men was evidenced in my analyses of women's magazines, ELL promotional materials and *renai* English materials (see Chapter 2). In the media space, White Western men were often represented as desirable teachers of English who were attractive and gentlemanly. *Eikaiwa* schools in Japan often used gendered advertising to attract customers, suggesting White Western men as an effective means for ELL. Furthermore, we have seen how the media discourse of *renai* English promotes and draws extensively on this romanticised link. For instance, English was notably represented as a means of developing/maintaining romance with Western men. Examples of romantic English phrases from movies were used as legitimate sources of ELL and, in this way, the allegedly Western style of heterosexual romance was presented as desirable and ideal. As we have seen in Chapter 2, the *renai* English discourse endorses particular subject positions of sexy, provocative but also demure femininity for young Japanese women, together with good-looking, chivalrous and powerful masculinity for Western men. As such, the media constructs English and romance with Western men as objects of consumption. I will return to this aspect of language desire in Section 7.3.

7.2.2 The meaning of *ryugaku* in Australia

The second area of inquiry in this book was concerned with what it meant for the Japanese women to undertake *ryugaku* to Australia. Firstly, to situate my participants' decision to come to Australia in a wider social context, I looked at the media representation of *ryugaku*. It emerged that inner circle countries (Kachru, 1992), that is the United States, United Kingdom, Canada, Australia and New Zealand, were presented as ideal language *ryugaku* destinations while there was little mention of outer circle countries. Furthermore, the Japanese media commonly painted *ryugaku* as a glamorous means of identity transformation and of finding/starting a new lifestyle.

Consistent with the media discourse of *ryugaku*, my participants all narrated their decisions on *ryugaku* as a means of changing their lives through ELL, further education and/or work experience in Sydney. As discussed in Chapter 3, their idea of *ryugaku* seemed significantly motivated by their desires to reinvent their problematic identities in their hometowns (Yuka,

Chizuko and Yoko), to realise their teenage *akogare* of mastering English (all participants), and to enhance their future careers after their return to Japan (Ichi and Eika). As the cases of Yoko and Chizuko revealed, some participants resurrected their teenage fascination and acted upon *ryugaku* as a means of transforming the unfavourable life circumstances that they faced in their late twenties and thirties in Japan.

Although mastery of English was central to their *ryugaku* narrative, factors involved in their choice of Australia seemed to be also closely concerned with lifestyle choices rather than just with the conditions for learning English. Australia was favoured because of its relatively low cost of living/studying, its relative safety, good climate and work conditions. It was also found that, apart from the younger women (Yuka and Ichi), my participants' age played a crucial role in their decision-making processes in that they saw *ryugaku* as their last opportunity to realise their aspirations in relation to language learning and the possibility of lifestyle change.

Moreover, their prior images of Australia as a White Western nation and of Australians as friendly people were influential in their decisions to choose Australia. For all my participants, their life in Australia was often imagined as involving extensive socialisation with (White) Australians through whom they expected to improve their English and knowledge of the West. In sum, for my participants, coming to Australia was a financial, emotional and educational investment in the identity transformation that they believed would result from ELL and their experiences in Australia. Their personally and socially constructed meaning of *ryugaku* had a strong bearing on their social, linguistic and romantic practices in Sydney, which was the focus of the third area of inquiry as discussed next.

7.2.3 Language desire, identity and ELL in Sydney

Having analysed their initial desire and decision to study in Australia, I moved on to explore how young Japanese women's language desire and their identities might intersect with the processes, practices and outcomes of learning English in Sydney, and how these, in turn, impact upon their identities. To provide insights into this inquiry, I looked into the notion of desirable interlocutors (Chapter 4) and agency (Chapter 5).

The majority of my participants considered access to White Australian society as crucial to ELL and their overall *ryugaku* project. However, they believed that their temporary resident status, Asian identity and limited English made this access excruciatingly difficult. Against this background, the discourse of native-speaker men as special learning aids emerged as one area on which they could capitalise. Having a native-speaker boyfriend was considered to be conducive to their ELL due to the amount and quality of time spent in L2 interaction in romantic and sexual contexts. In those situations, my participants felt more able and at ease using English. Native-speaker boyfriends also provided a discursive and emotional path into the Western world through, for example, the use of terms of endearment such as 'darling' and 'sweetie', which fulfilled their desire for romantic attachment and intimacy.

However, further analysis revealed that their concept of desirable male interlocutors was much more complex than just a matter of linguistic (i.e. native speaker of English) or racial identity (White). Rather than welcoming all types of male native speakers, all my participants were highly discerning as to who they 'allowed' to speak to them. Their idea of 'desirable interlocutors' intersected with factors such as race, native-speaker identity, bilingualism in Japanese and English and physical appearance in complex ways. They actively avoided men who they considered to be 'losers' even if they were native-speaker Australians. These findings suggest that, although improvement in English was important for my participants, social interaction in Sydney was not solely about ELL. Socialisation with male speakers of English was often a site of identity negotiation where my participants were aware of their worthiness as a single woman in demand.

In addition to this gendered notion of ELL and language desire in Chapter 4, I also highlighted a wider range of my participants' agency in the social spaces of home and work in Chapter 5. In the media discourse, living with Australian native speakers of English was portrayed as an ideal situation, in which Japanese students of English were guests in need of care by their host family/share mates who, in turn, were caring individuals capable of looking after their young Japanese house guests/share mates.

My participants all considered living with Australian English native speakers as conducive to ELL and learning Australian culture. But their actual choice of home was complex, intersecting with a host of both existing and emerging needs and desires. As the cases of Eika, Chizuko and Yuka showed, home was considered as not just an ELL opportunity, but also a secure environment where they did not have to struggle with cultural differences in some cases, or a place in which they felt accepted by others. Compared to her Australian native English speaker flatmate, Eika's non-native speaker flatmate contributed not only to her increased L2 interactions, but also to a sense of being a worthy individual and of belonging to a multilingual community. Chizuko was able to find her place as a worthy family member in a Japanese-speaking home environment. In the case of Yuka, having reached a relatively high level of English proficiency, it became important that she had a living space to herself and could learn to be responsible for herself. This in turn contributed to her sense of identity transformation from the status of a *hikikomori* to that of an independent, educated woman in her twenties. What these findings suggest is that, for long-term stayers like my participants, the desire to improve their English was sometimes overridden by the emerging importance of creating a home environment where their worth as individuals could be acknowledged (Chizuko and Eika) or where they were able to nourish their new identity (Yuka).

Similarly to the media discourse of *ryugaku* and the home environment, working with native speakers of English was often framed in the media discourse as an opportunity to learn and use 'authentic' English. Such discourse was found to create opportunities for the exploitation of those desperate to find work with local people for the sake of improving their English. In fact, many Japanese students and working holidaymakers I met found working with local people to be daunting, if not impossible, due to their perceived limited command of English and local knowledge. Many opted to find jobs in Japanese-speaking workplaces such as souvenir shops and restaurants or as tour guides for Japanese visitors where, of course, they heard and spoke very little English.

My participants' abilities to find a job in English-speaking workplaces varied considerably. The case of Yoko's work experience in Sydney highlighted the fact that finding and maintaining employment in the L2-medium workplace required a great deal of effort and perseverance. In fact, even though my other participants admired Yoko and generally believed that work with and for Australians would contribute to improvement in their English and would create opportunities to make friends with locals, many chose not to pursue this option for various reasons. For some, there was no financial need to work (Ichi, Yuka and Eika), while for Chizuko there were more financial incentives in Japanese-speaking workplaces. Eika gave up on her job search because she felt she could not find a job that matched her previous professional identity with her level of English. All this suggests that agency is not a pre-given quality, but co-constructed at the intersection of desires and needs in negotiation with people around us.

7.2.4 Consequences of *ryugaku*

The final area of inquiry was concerned with the consequences of *ryugaku*. As discussed in Chapter 3, the Japanese media tended to focus mainly on the positive outcomes of *ryugaku* for women who return to their home country. They were mostly presented as being more mature, more professionally-qualified and more linguistically advanced than they were before their *ryugaku*.

Ryugaku was also represented as a 'return ticket' scenario which involved going overseas and then coming back to Japan. However, analysis of my participants' narratives about 'going home' revealed a different picture that challenged the mainstream assumption.

In the beginning of their *ryugaku*, all my participants considered it natural for them to return to Japan. However, that taken-for-granted option increasingly became problematic towards the end of their stay in Sydney. As reported in Chapter 6, all my participants expressed increasing ambivalence towards the idea of returning to Japan and I identified several underlying factors common to them. For instance, they feared that they would not be able to maintain their English proficiency in Japan; they were concerned that they would not be able to affirm their new subjectivities with their families and/or friends, and they were pessimistic about their chances of finding a job in Japan that would allow them to capitalise on their English-speaking skills and international identity. As a result of these concerns, all of my main participants began exploring a wider range of future options, including a move to another foreign country (Yoko, Ichi, Eika and Yuka), extending their stay in Sydney (Eika, Chizuko and Yoko), or gaining permanent residency in Sydney (Chizuko). Furthermore, international romance was found to be linked with their (new) language desire, resulting from and leading to more identity and residential options (Yuka and Ichi). In sum, although their material conditions, such as their temporary residence status or limited funds, imposed restrictions on their ability to stay in Sydney or to move to other parts of the world, they also had the resources, such as their English proficiency, multilingualism, Japanese passports, work experience and parental support, that allowed them to negotiate future mobility. These findings suggest that one of the most significant consequences of their long-term *ryugaku* was their access to a wider range of identity positions that, in turn, profoundly intersected with the imagination and construction of their future options of residence, occupation and romance.

7.3 Language Desire Revisited

In this section, I will offer a conceptualisation of language desire, the main theme and theoretical framework of the research. Based on the findings revisited above, language desire can be conceptualised at two levels (see Figure 7.1): (1) construction (historical contexts, discourses of women's life course and the media); and (2) possible effects (approaches to SLL, migratory desire and gendered life choices).

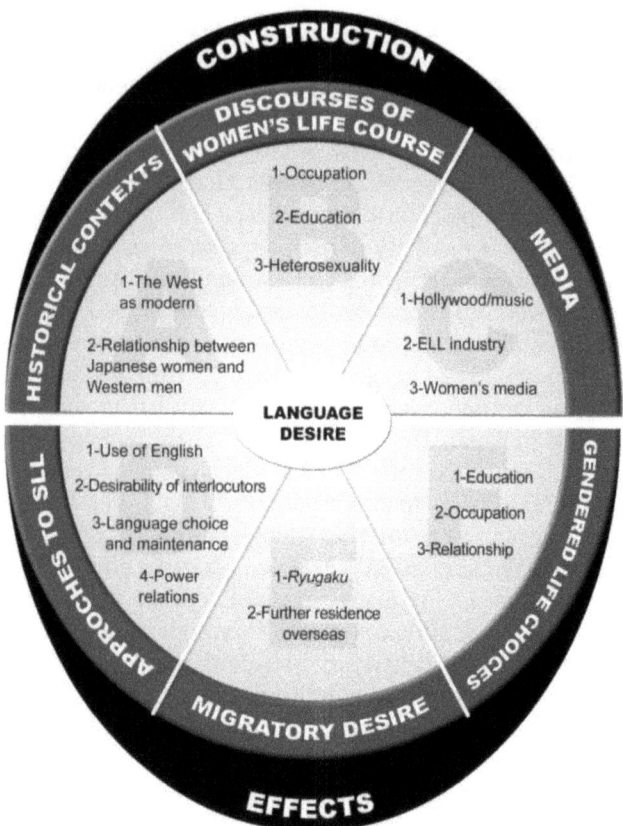

Figure 7.1 Model of language desire in the case of young Japanese women

7.3.1 Construction of language desire for English

Language desire among young Japanese women can be considered as a construction linking three discursive spaces: ELL, Western masculinity and identity transformation. Firstly, it is important to understand that language desire is not a private, individual construction in the minds of female language learners (Cameron & Kulick, 2003). As is demonstrated throughout this book, it is constructed at the intersection between the macro-discourses of the West and foreign men and ideologies of Japanese women's life-courses in terms of education, occupation and heterosexuality.

As modelled in Figure 7.1, the construction of language desire has to be understood with reference to historical discourses of the West as modern

(A-1) and Western men (A-2). Particularly since the end of WWII, there has been much fascination and also scepticism towards interracial romance in conjunction with the intensification of the nationalistic discourse of internationalisation since the 1980s. Furthermore, language desire is closely embedded in the gendered discourse of English-related occupations (B-1) and English language education (B-2) as a women's domain in Japan. Such discourse is generally age/stage specific. Many Japanese women are pressured to make the 'right' life choice in terms of the timing of study, work and marriage, hence affecting their decision about whether or not to pursue their dream of learning English and/or going overseas (Chapter 3). In addition, language desire is exclusively based on the ideal of heterosexuality (B-3). In the popular literature (e.g. Ashima, 2002; Ieda, 1991; Igata, 2001; Oguri, 2002, 2004; Ozawa & Shirakawa, 2004), including the genre of *renai* English (Ootomo, 2004; Ozeki, 2002, 2003a, 2003b; Toda, 1999), the discussion of intercultural romance almost always assumes and thus reproduces the ideal of heterosexuality (Piller, 2011a). Subject positions available in such media spaces endorse sexy, provocative but also demure femininity for Japanese women on the one hand, and good-looking, chivalrous but also powerful masculinity for their intercultural partners on the other. My participants' exposure to such macrodiscourses was crucial in developing their language desire. Thus, one's language desire emerges with exposure to the historical, social and cultural contexts in which language learners have been situated.

In this light the role of the media (C) is obviously crucial to the construction of language desire. As discussed in Chapter 2, for commercial purposes the Japanese media draw on and, in effect, promote connections between ELL and romance with Hollywood stars/singers (C-1) and Western men. The ELL industry functions with the media to construct ELL and Western masculinity as not only mutually constitutive but also objects of consumption for the purpose of identity transformation. As such, young Japanese women develop their language desire for English not simply as students, but also as consumers of ELL, *ryugaku* and Western masculinity as commodities. Given young Japanese women's power of consumption of goods and services, such as English lessons, textbooks, Hollywood movies and overseas trips/*ryugaku*, the ELL industry and the media are largely dependent on their ability to sell the dream of English proficiency, the West and Western men and identity formation as a package to Japanese women.

Although my participants were seemingly susceptible to the allure of this dream, they proved to be also highly discerning consumers. That they actively evaluated and selected information produced by the media was evidenced in their decision-making processes in choosing Australia as a *ryugaku* destination (Chapter 3). Moreover, they become ever more critical consumers/observers of the media as a result of their contact with the reality of life in Sydney (Chapter 4). Some of my participants, Yuka and Eika in particular, showed antipathy towards the notion of *akogare* and media representations of Japanese women in love with English and the West. Thus, although the media may provide a platform for the construction of language desire, it should not be viewed as a determining agent.

In fact, although language desire, which emerged at an early stage in some Japanese women's lives, had a lasting effect, its form or effect was not permanently fixed. As noted above, my participants' desire often shifted as a result of their experiences of interacting with various people in Sydney. That often led to changes in their desire as to whom they chose to socialise with, hence impacting on their processes of SLL and its use in Sydney. For instance, Yuka and Eika expressed a reduced desire to associate with White Australians as a result of being negatively positioned as deficient English speakers or submissive Japanese women, neither of which identities fitted their own subjectivities. Over time, they both found pleasure in becoming respected members of their respective multilingual communities in which there were few White native speakers of English. Both were losing interest in gaining approval from White Australians as they increasingly found emotional security in the sense of belonging to, and appreciation by, their community of multicultural/multilingual friends. This suggests that language desire needs to be understood as something that is continually shaped and reshaped in relation to experiences of negotiation of identity in the communities in which language users are located.

7.3.2 Possible effects of language desire

Possible effects of language desire in the case of young Japanese women include the processes of SLL, migratory desire and gendered life choices. I will discuss each in turn below.

7.3.2.1 Processes of SLL

Based on my findings, language desire seems to link with four aspects of SLL processes: the nature of use of English (D-1); desirability of interlocutors (D-2); language choice and maintenance (D-3); and power relations (D4).

Firstly, my participants' language desire seemed to encourage the use of English for communication purposes (D-1). In Japan, it is probably fair to say that, even though the communicative approach has been a 'buzzword' for some time now, school-level students who seek out an opportunity to actually use English are still in a minority. However, my participants who developed language desire early on tended to use English as a means of communicating their desire and performing their heterosexual and international identities (see Chapter 2). For instance, despite their limited proficiency in English, Eika and Chizuko attempted to write fan letters to their Hollywood hero in their secondary school years. Ichi and her classmates asked their classroom teacher to organise a special English conversation class with a native speaker of English for whom Ichi developed romantic feelings. Furthermore, in their early adulthood in Japan, many actively sought to practise English by socialising with foreigners (Yoko, Chizuko and Eika) and enrolling in English conversation schools (Eika, Yoko and Ichi). What these findings suggest is that language desire often acted as a catalyst that encouraged them to find more opportunities to practise and to use English beyond the social contexts available through formal language learning. Furthermore, their actual experience of (romantic) intercultural communication seemed to further intensify their existing *akogare*. Thus, it can be claimed that there is a reciprocal relationship between language desire and actual use of English.

Secondly, in the gendered interactional context in Sydney, language desire functioned to mediate the ways in which my participants evaluated the desirability of their interlocutors (D-2), hence affecting their choice of engagement and dis-engagement in interactions. In the case of Ichi, whose *akogare* for Western society and White men was strong and long-lasting, the racial and linguistic identity of interlocutors were important markers of their desirability. Throughout her stay, Ichi continually placed importance on seeking interactional opportunities with White Western men as friends and romantic partners, while at the same time she reported avoiding socialisation with Asian non-native speakers. Similarly, despite her ambivalent feelings about her White Western male friend mentioned earlier, Yoko considered him desirable as a friend on the basis of his racial and linguistic identity and continued to socialise with him.

As time went by, however, many participants came to see White men, represented in the media and other discourse as romantic, courteous and chivalrous, as not necessarily all that they had imagined. Thus, they responded to the racial attributes of male interlocutors in various ways: some continued to pursue the ideal White man, others gave up on the stereotype, and yet others settled for the best available. As discussed in Chapter 4, the racial identity of male interlocutors did not determine their value and hence did not always lead my participants to engage in interaction. For instance, despite their constantly claimed passion for White men, both Yoko and Ichi developed serious relationships with partners of an Asian background during their stay in Sydney. What became more important for Yoko, who was increasingly frustrated by her slow rate of improvement in English, was to have a native-speaker partner who cared about her as a woman and satisfied her linguistic needs. In fact, this romantic choice was made after she rejected the romantic approaches of a 41-year-old White Australian man and later the approaches of another Western man as she did not consider either of them as potential partners. Similarly, Ichi decided to have an online relationship with a Korean-American man living in Japan because he won her over with his strong commitment to their relationship. Although he was not physically or racially attractive (she often complained about his short stature and his Asian looks), he was still an American native speaker of English and it made her feel good to be 'wanted'. Obviously this sense of being desired seemed to outweigh her *akogare* for White masculinity. Furthermore, although Chizuko, whose fantasy was to marry a White man, had been genuinely wanted by a White Australian man, his lack of sexual attraction meant she did not consider him as a desirable romantic partner or even as a friend.

What their contradictory choices may suggest is that the language desire of my participants was not static, but was fluid over time and across different contexts. *Akogare* was negotiated and occasionally compromised, as a range of other priorities moved to the foreground of their lives. Thus, the effects of language desire on their process of SLL profoundly intersect with existing as well as new social, linguistic and romantic desires.

Thirdly, language desire has a profound impact on language choice and maintenance (D3). In my study, the issue of language choice was particularly pronounced in the contexts in which my participants interacted with speakers of English who also spoke Japanese. Eika's dilemma over her bilingual Australian boyfriend with regard to language choice provided an interesting example (see Chapter 4). She clearly expressed her desire to use English as she relied on her boyfriend as a language-learning aid. However, despite her protests and expressions of disappointment, Eika's boyfriend increasingly used Japanese in their relationship. Towards the end of their three-month relationship, she not only seemed to have given up on the struggle over language choice, but began to enthusiastically help him improve his Japanese.

What Eika's example suggests is that language choice is a site of ongoing negotiation of desire, identity and power (D-4). Although both she and her boyfriend desired to use the other's language, she had less bargaining power on this issue due to both linguistic and non-linguistic factors. Among these was the fact that she was a recent arrival in Australia without much local knowledge and that her initial confidence in her English was rapidly diminishing. She was also self-conscious about the age difference of 10 years between this man and herself and did not feel able to perform her cherished identity as a mature woman in her first romantic relationship, in English. In contrast, her boyfriend was a Sydney local with an extensive social network and he had had several romantic experiences with older Japanese women. In their relationship, therefore, Eika had to compromise her desire for English as in this way she was able to avoid the embarrassment of sounding linguistically immature and also to establish herself as a mature adult woman and a capable helper in Japanese.

This negotiation of desire was also evident in Ichi's relationship with her bilingual American boyfriend (Chapter 6). In her case, however, she was in a position of power that allowed her to negotiate the choice of language the couple used together. His identity as the 'chaser' of Ichi's heart enabled her to exercise her power over this choice at that time of negotiation. Thus language desire that is conducive to the choice of a particular language does not always lead to the desired result, but needs to be negotiated in relation to the multiple identities that emerge in a relationship.

Furthermore, language desire profoundly intersects with language maintenance. As discussed in Chapter 6, all of my participants expressed their anxiety about not being able to maintain their English proficiency after they went back to Japan. Their wish to maintain their English proficiency, however, is not so much a linguistic matter as it is about their desire for maintaining their hard-earned bilingual/international identities in Sydney. To avoid the 'loss' of such identity during their holiday visits or after their eventual return to Japan, all of my participants used whatever resources they could find in an attempt to maintain their bilingual/international identities. However, as was the case with their language choice, desire for maintaining their English and multiple identities was often compromised by the factors in their immediate environment (e.g. family, friends and monolingualism) that were believed to offer only limited, and undesirable, identity options. They were often frustrated and anxious due to their perceived inability to maintain their English proficiency in Japan. Such negative emotions underlay their emergent desire to leave Japan altogether and migrate elsewhere, the focus of the next section.

7.3.2.2 Migratory desire

The findings presented in this book clearly suggest that language desire is closely linked with migratory desire (E-1 and E-2). My participants' language desire was a significant factor in their initial decision to go overseas (Chapter 3) as well as their emergent aspiration to stay overseas rather than return to Japan (Chapter 6). Prior to their *ryugaku* and working holiday in Australia, all of my participants had already been overseas (except Yuka). In their secondary school years, Eika (the United States) and Ichi (Australia) had been on a short-term language *ryugaku* to an English-speaking country. They reported that their teenage *ryugaku* experiences not only intensified their *akogare* for English and the West, but also formed the basis of their long-lasting dream of returning to the overseas country for tertiary education.

In their early adulthood, my participants also travelled to the United States (Chizuko, Yoko and many secondary participants) and Australia (Yoko and Eika) with the explicit purpose of gaining exposure to 'authentic English' and Western culture. Their emergent aspiration either to continue their stay in Sydney or to move to other countries was linked to their desire to maintain their English proficiency and heightened hybridity, which they considered would be impossible in Japan. In this light, language desire functioned as a basis of their agency to situate themselves in a country where they could continue to perform and maintain their cherished linguistic and gender identities.

However, such aspiration for migration is not without cost. Staying either in Sydney or moving to another country imposed serious financial burdens on themselves (Eika, Yoko and Chizuko) or their parents (Ichi and Yuka). Unlike the elite international Japanese women depicted in Kelsky's (2001) study, my participants were unemployed (Ichi, Yuka and Eika) or had to survive on the minimum wage (Chizuko and Yoko) in Sydney. And in contrast to the glamorous media image of English-speaking Japanese career women, many participants came to believe that their limited English skills would not secure highly paid English-speaking jobs in either Sydney or Japan. Yet maintaining English through living overseas had become one of their priorities. What this might suggest is that their desire for migration is not primarily economically based, but rather linked with their desire to maintain their emergent identities. Their belief that this was possible only outside Japan is central to the relationship between language desire and migratory desire. Indeed, language desire had a significant and long-lasting impact on their life choices, an issue which I explore in the next section.

7.3.2.3 Gendered life choices

Language desire intersected with several key choices that my participants made as single young women. Such choices included, but were not limited to, education (F-1), occupation (F-2), relationships (F-3) and residence (as discussed in the previous section). All the participants studied English outside a formal educational context, such as in English conversation schools, with language exchange partners and through teenage *ryugaku*. Eika and Yuka, determined to go overseas for tertiary education, majored in English in a college in Japan. Their choice of English education obviously intersected with the existing discourses that English education was indispensable for women and also the availability of large varieties of ELL education in the commercialised sector. Language desire among young women is thus both ideologically and commercially promoted within Japanese society (Kitamura, 2011).

As discussed in Chapter 5, some media represent English as a path leading to career success and economic independence (Bailey, 2002; Kelsky, 2001; Kitamura, 2011; Tsuda, 2000). In fact, all my participants fantasised about finding work using English at one stage or another. For them, an L2 job in Australia constituted a golden opportunity to improve their English, learn Australian business culture and gain entry into the wider Australian society. However, their ability to obtain employment in an English-speaking medium workplace varied considerably (Chapter 5) and often other priorities deterred them from working in English-language jobs in Sydney. Some participants were preoccupied by university studies or other educational courses (Yuka and Ichi). Japanese-speaking jobs in Sydney provided more financial rewards (Chizuko) and there was also a fear of being positioned as an incompetent worker due to their perceived limited English proficiency or local knowledge (Eika, Chizuko and many secondary participants). Thus, although language desire pointed to particular occupational choices in English-speaking local companies, such choices had to be negotiated and sometimes compromised due to financial, social, linguistic and emotional factors. As shown through the case of Yoko, the dream of working in English with local Australians was possible only through her unfading language desire and extraordinary perseverance, often at the expense of her emotional and physical wellbeing.

Furthermore, as reported in Chapters 4 and 6, their language desire intersected with their perception of desirable partners differently. As evidenced in the narratives of Ichi, Yoko, Chizuko and many secondary participants, their preference was first and foremost for White Western men (Chapter 4). At the same time, other factors also played a role in constructing their romantic choices. For instance, physical appearances significantly mediated their selection processes in this regard. Chizuko, Yoko, Eika and many secondary participants unequivocally rejected romantic approaches from physically and sexually unattractive White native-speaker males. In other words, racial and linguistic identity was only some of a wide range of qualities they considered in a male romantic partner. In order to understand engagement or disengagement in communication in the gendered context, we need to pay close attention to the context and a wide range of attributes that individuals consider as desirable in an interlocutor.

Moreover, White native-speaker men who spoke Japanese were also often rejected as romantic possibilities as they were considered, in Yoko's words, to be 'Japanese lady killers'. Native-speaker identity, particularly monolingual speakers of English, was an attractive quality in potential and actual romantic partners by all my participants, so much so that it sometimes outweighed their *akogare* for White masculinity (Yoko and Ichi). A partner's native-speaker identity worked as a decisive factor in some of my participants' romantic engagement, although the non-White identity of their partners was continuously phrased as a 'problem' (Yoko and Ichi). Few participants expressed the same romantic interest in non-native speakers (particularly Asian non-native speakers of English) and some who had romantic experiences with such men tended to consider their partners' linguistic identity as 'problematic'. In some cases, they openly admitted that it was one of the major reasons for ending these relationships.

In examining the relationship between language desire and romance, the case of Yuka and her Chinese partner provided an interesting insight (see Section 6.4.3). As with the rest of the participants, she initially had *akogare* for White men after her arrival in Sydney. The first four individuals for whom she developed romantic feelings were all White (monolingual) native-speaker men (none of these liaisons led to a long-term relationship). As her interest in the Chinese language developed at university, her preference for men also began to shift to Chinese natives or men who at least spoke Chinese and Japanese. Her romantic preference for such men obviously matched what she valued as part of her multiple identity (a fluent speaker of Japanese, English and Chinese). Furthermore, her newly emergent desire for Chinese-speaking men can be understood as her personal counter-discourse to White monolingual men or the English/Japanese bilingual men whom she grew to despise.

In sum, my participants' concern with their English and their *akogare* for White men tremendously affected their choice of romantic partners in Sydney. This is consistent with some of the findings by Bailey (2002) and Kelsky (2001). However, as exemplified above, their evaluations of potential romantic partners were complex. In some contexts, the women in this study prioritised selecting a native-speaker partner and compromised their *akogare* for Whiteness. Furthermore, although most participants were aware of the circulating discourse that positioned White native-speaker men as symbols of upper social mobility, they did not necessarily agree with this wholeheartedly. The women in my study were all relatively secure financially and thus had little economic incentive to associate with White men. This provides a different picture from that of Gal (1978), who found that young women in the Austrian-Hungarian bilingual town of Oberwart were motivated to find German-speaking partners to escape their hard life in the Hungarian-speaking villages. This difference could have been due to my participants' access to a wider range of means to achieve financial stability and upper social mobility, if desired. In addition, many were aware of their 'problematic' popularity among foreign men and reported frequent approaches from a wide range of men in Sydney. These socioeconomic factors as well as local sexual politics often put my participants in a powerful position when it came to selecting who they wanted to interact with in a social context. The effect of language desire on romantic choices was fluid, neither uniform nor static.

7.4 Implications

In this section, I will offer some implications of the findings presented above. I will begin by urging a more nuanced approach to understanding the gendered processes of language learning and then move on to make some suggestions for English language teaching in a Japanese context. Finally, I will call for a more socially inclusive approach to nation-building in Japan in the 21st century.

7.4.1 The field of SLA

At the beginning of my data collection, I was both troubled and fascinated by the differences between Japanese female students and their male counterparts in their views on and approaches to ELL (see Chapter 1). Having completed my analyses, I am convinced that SLL cannot be fully understood without putting due emphasis on gender-related factors (I have also demonstrated this point in Piller & Takahashi, 2010a; Takahashi, 2012). Two areas of study in SLA to which the concept of language desire may contribute are the notions of motivation and of power relations. Furthermore, I argue that SLA theory needs to be expanded to include the link between language desire and transnational mobility.

7.4.1.1 Motivation and power revisited

Existing SLA theories pay little attention to the role of romantic desire in understanding experiences in the process of learning L2. There has been a tendency to portray language learners as a-gendered or a-sexual beings, wanting to study and use L2 for either instrumental and/or integrative reasons, which in turn are presented as fixed entities. While Norton's (2000) study on immigrant women drew attention to the importance of gender and identity in SLL and L2 use, the link between romantic/sexual desire and SLL remained unaddressed in the field. In contrast, the notion of language desire can offer a new dimension to understanding the gendered ways in which individuals become motivated to learn L2, why they do or do not engage in L2 interactions, and with whom they choose to do so (see also Kinginger, 2006, 2008 for her series of work on romance and language learning in a French context).

First, the concept of language desire emphasises that motivation to learn L2 is not a private construction of language learners. Rather, it is socially and historically constructed and reshaped at the intersection between individuals' practices and macro-discourses. As is demonstrated in this book, the Japanese media and the ELL industry capitalise on Japanese women's *akogare* for foreign men and thus function to promote a gendered, and sometimes sexualised, incentive for Japanese women to learn English. Of course not all media have the same impact. Nevertheless, this understanding indicates that future theorising about SLL motivation needs to take into account the role of the media and the language industry in promoting gendered desire in a given country. Equally important is for SLA theory to take into account the ways in which language learners interpret, valorise or reject macro-discourses of language learning in a given context.

Second, the concept of language desire promotes a new way of understanding why language learners may or may not decide to interact in L2. My participants, in line with the findings of several other studies (e.g. Blackledge, 2001; Butorac, 2011; Kanno & Applebaum, 1995; Kinginger, 2004; McKay & Wong, 1996; Norton, 2000), often felt marginalised and could not fully participate in the L2 interactions. However, the reason was not always primarily because of their limited English, language anxiety (Horwitz & Young, 1991; Lucas, 1984; MacIntyre, 1999; Young, 1992), fear of making mistakes (Lucas, 1984), or cultural differences in communication and learning styles (Oxford, 1990; Oxford & Anderson, 1995). In fact, they often did not want to talk to their interlocutors; they simply did not find them socially, romantically and/or sexually attractive even if they were Australian native speakers or English teachers. For them, interaction in L2 was not always about SLL. Their decisions to interact or not to do so involved the negotiation of identity, gendered needs and desires (e.g. romance, marriage, sexual urges, male approval), depending very much on the life stages at which they were located.

This understanding of their agency throws new light on the relations between power and identity in SLL. This issue has, of course, been investigated by many critical SLA researchers. There is no doubt that there was a power imbalance between my participants and their interlocutors due to their backgrounds, mediating their access to linguistic resources and the nature of their interaction. Based on my data, however, I urge a need to go beyond the essentialist dichotomies of native speakers versus non-native speakers, Western versus Asian, teachers versus students, men versus women and hosts versus guests, in our future theorising of power and identity. Language learners are not just non-native speakers or Asians or women, in the same way that their interlocutors are not simply native speakers, or teachers, or men. Individuals position themselves and their interlocutors, and both are positioned by others, in relation to multiple identity categories available to them. Some categories are visible (e.g. gender, race, attractiveness) or audible (e.g. accent), while others are less visible (e.g. socioeconomic status, educational background, marital status) (Zimmerman, 1998). Each identity is given a different weight depending on a given context and time. Thus, the examination of power relations needs to be context sensitive. For my participants, who were singles in their twenties and thirties, self-assured about their physical appearance and had relatively secure economic status, male interlocutors were positioned not only in terms of their linguistic or racial identity, but also in terms of their physical, romantic and sexual attractiveness. My participants carefully assessed whether these men deserved their efforts to speak.

Furthermore, in many contexts, their exposure to the widely circulating discourse of Western men targeting Japanese women, empowered rather than disempowered my participants in a sense that the discourse implied their value in the romantic market. Indeed, in the social space in which romantic and sexual politics were at work, it was often my participants who decided whether or not an interaction took place and for how long. Such decisions were often based on their assessment of their interlocutors' worthiness as men. Other than Whiteness and native-speaker status, their assessment categories included factors such as socioeconomic status (e.g. type of occupation, assets), education, age, body size and shape (e.g. fat, thin, masculine), clothing, teeth, hairstyle, facial attributes (e.g. eye colour and nose size), skin quality, jewellery and sexiness. Each of these attributes was assessed in combination and given differential values in different contexts. For instance, many of my participants fantasised about making friends with 'good-looking young Australian men'. Yet 'good-looking' and 'young' are very relative values, as I discovered in the following social event.

One night in October 2004, I joined two of my participants, Eika and Tokiko (a secondary participant), on their night out to a pub in Sydney. This pub was widely known among my participants and locals as 'a pick-up joint'. As soon as we sat down at a table, a group of White Australian men approached us and started to talk to Eika and Tokiko. The men were in their early twenties and had moved on to this pub after their friend's wedding. Knowing my participants' taste in Western men (they both highly valued 'youth', that is, men in their early twenties), I thought the attention of these men would be welcomed, particularly as several of them could be considered 'good-looking' and 'youthful'. However, Eika and Tokiko showed little interest in the men. They were reluctant to interact with them because, as they told me in Japanese, they were too young and they were not interested in 'country boys' (f2oct04eika). Soon, both women got up from the table and left for the dance floor, saying to them, this time in English, 'Kimie speaks better English' (f2oct04eika). Eika and Tokiko saw these men as 'country boys' because they lived in Sutherland, a suburb a mere 30 km south of inner Sydney. This suburban identity (reinforced by the type of 'uncool' clothing they were wearing), along with their immaturity signalled by age and interactional manners, was shunned by the two women who were fashion conscious and came from metropolitan Tokyo. Obviously discouraged by the women's leaving, the men nevertheless tried to restore their self-esteem by saying to me, 'these Japanese girls are shy, aren't they? It's hard to understand what I'm saying in English. It's kind of noisy in here' (f2oct04eika).

The men's interpretation of my participants' disengagement as 'shyness' was probably built on a widely circulating cultural stereotype of Japanese women as shy. The same can be said of SLA researchers who, when they observe silence among Japanese learners of English, tend to jump at stereotypes, rather than seeking alternative ways of understanding 'silence' and power (see Nakane, 2007 for her illuminating study on the notion of silence among Japanese students in Australian universities). In the field of SLA and in the minds of many English language teaching practitioners as well as students themselves, there is a prevalent dichotomy between the native speaker as powerful and the non-native speaker as powerless. As the example above demonstrates, however, it is not necessarily always White native speakers who decide who can talk. At night clubs, parties, in cafes and in many other social spaces where the purpose of social interaction was particularly linked with romantic or sexual possibilities, many women in this study demonstrated their agency in deciding who could and could not talk to them, how they could talk, for how long and on what conditions. In this light it is no longer feasible to associate Asian identity, non-native speaker status, and womanhood or migrant status with static powerlessness. It is not only counter-productive but also theoretically meaningless; such essentialisation only reproduces the dated, inadequate cultural explanation for learner motivation (e.g. Japanese women don't want to speak in English because they are shy), and prevents us from asking questions differently, through which we can develop a new way of understanding the intersection of identity, desire and power in the SLL context.

7.4.1.2 Language desire and migration

In Chapter 6 I highlighted the ways in which the women's increasing desire for more transnational mobility was profoundly embedded in their language desire. However, existing theories of SLL basically do not address the link between language learning and desire for international mobility or migration. This may be due to the fact that SLA researchers tend to see language learners as bounded in their home countries. Language learners are often conceptualised to be students in their own countries, or short-time overseas sojourners in a host country, or immigrants who are already living in the host country permanently. These groups of language learners probably present very little desire for future international mobility to researchers, as plans for transnational movements are rarely part of SLA research agendas.

Similarly, the current international migration theories do not adequately address the role of gender in issues surrounding student migration (Ono & Piper, 2004). Although the increasing feminisation of migration in recent years is often considered 'a key development' (Castles, 2000: 105), the research focus seems to be concentrated either on migrant women of low socioeconomic status such as domestic servants or sex workers, or on the 'brain drain' of skilled women migrating from developing countries to the first world. Thus, it fails to explain the international migration patterns of female international students whose purpose of movement is not primarily economic advancement (Habu, 2000; Kim, 2011), but is socially, linguistically and ideologically based, as is evident in the case of my participants, who may be identified as 'post-materialists' (Inglehart, 1982).

The few studies that have exclusively investigated middle-class Japanese international students with a gender perspective pay little attention to their desire for further international migration (Andressen & Kumagai, 1996; Habu, 2000; Matsui, 1995). Most existing research on international Japanese female students concentrates on analyses of social issues in Japan, such as gender inequalities in career opportunities, pressure for marriage and childrearing and the gendered division of labour, as primary incentives for study overseas. They fail, however, to examine equally crucial factors: language desire and its constructed nature in prevalent media discourses, as part of their analysis. As such, current international migration theory offers only limited understanding of the impact of language ideologies on differential types of study abroad and the future migration patterns of young women.

It is evident that time spent overseas often leads to a strong reluctance to return to Japan and a desire for prolonged residence overseas (Habu, 2000; Kelsky, 2001; Matsui, 1995; Ono & Piper, 2004). For instance, Matsui reports that the Japanese women involved in higher education in the United States were not keen to return to Japan 'because they don't want to conform to the social norm of femininity imposed by their families, workplaces and society' (Matsui, 1995: 375) and 'they see very limited career prospects' (Matsui, 1995: 376). These studies, however, tend to conceptualise Japanese women's *ryugaku* as a 'return ticket' movement between the home (producing push factors) and the host country (producing pull factors) while the impact of the long-term overseas residence on their further movement is left unclear. Ono and Piper (2004: 116) conclude that further research is needed to investigate such questions as:

- Does their experience of study abroad lead to renewed migration?
- Do they prefer to return to the country in which they have studied?

- Are they also open to migration to other destinations?
- How are other aspects of their lives affected by the 'study abroad experience' (marriage, family, parental relations)?

By making language desire its analytical focus, this book has provided some answers to these questions.

For many Japanese women in my study, language desire functioned as a strong impetus for their decision to travel to Australia and was also an influential factor in their socialisation patterns in Sydney. Interactions with people of different backgrounds across various social contexts led to constant questioning of their identity, and to a sense of belonging to multiple global and local communities. This created even more fluidity in their sense of identity, leading to an emerging sense of being internationally minded individuals. Their perceived inability to maintain their English-speaking cosmopolitan identity and fear of having once again to conform to the traditional social, gendered and occupational expectations in Japan powerfully encouraged further international mobility, either short-term or long-term. This, in turn, was made possible by their economic background, transnational employment opportunities, cross-cultural romantic affiliations and ease of international transportation, all of which are hallmarks of globalisation.

These findings suggest that SLL theory can no longer leave out the question of migration in relation to ELL. Future research is needed to theorise the ways in which historically and commercially promoted language desire intersects with language learners' migratory intentions, and how such desires may shape their access and approaches to language learning, socialisation and employment opportunities in a given country. As my study and those of others (Habu, 2000; Kelsky, 2001; Matsui, 1995) have shown, language desire and overseas experiences are intimately linked with identity transformation and further international mobility. Many Japanese women who return to Japan do not do so because they see themselves nationally, socially, politically, culturally, linguistically and 'exclusively' belonging to Japan. It is more often than not a compromised choice made on the basis of their binding citizenship and lack of access to other migratory options. I will address this aspect further in relations to implications for Japan in the final section of this chapter.

7.4.2 ELL in Japan

Kobayashi (2002) criticised the uninformed manner in which many young Japanese women make decisions about learning English simply on the grounds that it is considered a gender-appropriate area of study. Kubota (1998) points out that not only Japanese women, but also the Japanese public

Conclusion 159

in general, are uncritical consumers of the media discourses that glamorise inner circle English (that of America and Britain, in particular) as an international language. As is reported in this book, language desire profoundly informs Japanese women's life choices in terms of education, occupation, residence and even romantic relationships. Given this, it becomes important that Japanese women are more informed about ELL (Kitamura, 2011; Piller et al., 2010).

Researchers such as Kubota (1998), Matsuda (2003) and Tsuda (1995, 2000) promoted the introduction of a critical pedagogy in Japan to raise an awareness of English domination and its problematic legacy. Kubota writes that:

> in order to effect change, the most powerful strategy in ELT seems to be to foster critical awareness with regard to English domination, construction of identities and social, linguistic, racial and ethnic inequality. (Kubota, 1998: 302)

Kubota (1998) reports on efforts being made in Japan to achieve these aims, such as a variety of proposals to introduce a number of other foreign languages or the use of English textbooks that promote a multicultural perspective. However, my literature review reveals that, although race and the political economy of English and other languages are being addressed, critiques of the role of the media and the ELT industry in constructing gendered and sexualised images of ELL remain limited. Based on my findings, I argue that, for such a strategy to be effective, the introduction of critical discourse analysis on the media construction of gender and sexual identities in relation to ELL is vital.

For instance, the general media commodification of Western masculinity needs to be challenged. There are ample examples of advertising by companies that try to sell products such as food, clothing, electronics, cosmetics and English language programmes by exploiting images not only of famous Hollywood stars (e.g. Japander.com), but also of unknown White actors (Piller & Takahashi, 2006; Tsuda, 2000). Such peddling of images for commercial gain needs to be closely examined. The pedagogy should also include an analysis of media stereotypes of relationships between Japanese women and foreign men. Research evidence, such as that of Russell (1998), is a useful reference in this regard. He reports that the Japanese media tend to construct an identity of Japanese women who develop romantic interests in black men as 'randy, rebellious teens, naïve, trend-conscious office ladies' (Russell, 1998: 152). In contrast, the media stereotype of Japanese women who seek White Western male company is that of 'career women whose preference for White men is thought to be indicative of their cosmopolitan sensibilities, their relationships motivated not so much by sexual passion as by a yearning for stable, long-term relationships with equally sophisticated, highly educated White men' (Russell, 1998: 152–153). Contrasting macro-discourses of Japanese women with White partners, such as the 'yellow cab discourse' discussed in Chapter 1, also highlight the constructed nature of Japanese women's identities. In addition, the introduction of *renai* English learning materials and advertisements in this research may help highlight the commercially produced link between language learning and cross-cultural/racial romance.

Equally importantly, the critical pedagogy that challenges the dominant *akogare* view on English and Westerners in the media should be part of English teacher training. Teachers have a significant impact on how students' image of English is constructed. For instance, a comment by one of Habu's informants (2000) illustrates how her English teacher's views on English were influential in making her decide to learn English and study abroad at great expense.

> I wanted to get a job after I finished my degree, but I couldn't find one. One of my teachers told me, 'Rather than doing an unsatisfactory job, if you improve your English, a much better job might turn up for you'. I had been thinking about whether to study abroad anyway, so I thought this might be the time to go. (Habu, 2000: 55)

However, my own findings and other research evidence suggest that English fluency can be a double bind and, therefore, English teachers should be trained to critically evaluate the discourses of English as an advantage for women. Of course, changes in the perception of English are by no means easy to achieve, particularly when so many vested interests are involved in the ELL industry. What is being proposed here is not to train teachers to discourage students from studying English altogether, but rather to equip students with the skills to assess the various discourses of English and to develop a more nuanced approach to the teaching of English (see Piller *et al.*, 2010 for a focused discussion on the overconsumption of English as a commodity in Japan and Korea).

7.4.3 Japan: Towards an inclusive society

My participants' lived experience in Australia, together with their acquired alternative perspectives and capacity to communicate cross-culturally in English, is probably one of the most desired outcomes for Japan's internationalisation project. However, many of the internationally minded Japanese women feel excluded and discriminated against in various social and occupational contexts within Japan. As is demonstrated in Chapter 6, this was also true for my participants.

One possible way of understanding this gap between intentions and outcomes is to view the encouragement given by the Japanese government, media and society to Japanese women to go overseas for cross-cultural experiences and mastering English, as conditional. There seems to be a tendency to reward those women who assimilate back into the Japanese value system and to ostracise those who do not, stigmatising them as sociocultural misfits, tainted by the Western ideologies of feminism and individualism. Some of the participants in an online video exhibition, *Japanese on the Move: Life Stories of Transmigration* (Piller & Takahashi, 2012), speak of their experiences of social exclusion on their return to Japan, which resulted in their desire to stay overseas. One participant (see http://www.languageonthemove.com/kayu-hashimoto), for instance, talks about how, during her final year at a university in Japan, she found that English-speaking foreign-educated women, including herself, had little chance of finding work with Japanese companies as they tended to see these women as 'too independent', and hence problematic job candidates.

As a matter of fact, exclusionary attitudes such as these form a new mass-mediated discourse about overseas-educated women, as is apparent from an article in *an-an* magazine (Magazine House, 2002b). The article features three male celebrities (two comedians and one artist) who are highly critical of Japanese women who are proficient in English. One of the comedians comments, 'I don't like women who have Americanised manners and speak Japanese mixed with English' (Magazine House, 2002b: 55). Equating English with the 'juggling' of a street entertainer, the artist argues that a woman's ability to speak English should be hidden and should be used subtly and only when absolutely necessary (Magazine House, 2002b: 55). Of course, this type of misogynist and anti-Westernisation discourse of Japanese women is nothing new. The *pan-pan* discourse of the 1940s, the *Yellow cab* discourse of the 1980s and the reported difficulties of returnees are reminders of Japan's resilient nationalistic project to maintain its racial and cultural purity and its intolerance of heterogeneity in language choice and (gender) identities.

Indeed one of the key sources of dissatisfaction for Japanese women who return from overseas lies in the persistent gender discrimination present in Japanese society. This was part of the reason why some of my participants (Eika, Yoko and Ichi) left Japan in the first place, and this discrimination became more and more salient for them from afar, particularly during their return visits. In response to the emergent tendency for late marriage or the rejection of marriage altogether, as well as the rising divorce rate and the decreasing birth rate, criticism against Japanese women in their late twenties and thirties has become ever more relentless (e.g. Misago, 2004). Reluctance to live in Japan and the further migratory desires expressed by many of my participants (Chapter 6) are a loud and clear rejection of these nationalist and sexist discourses about Japanese women.

Increased international mobility is encouraged by the Japanese national project of internationalisation, and is enabled by the globalisation of transportation and the wider migratory options made available by receiving countries such as Australia. As this book has shown, migrant Japanese women were exposed to alternative discourses of language, work, gender and romance through participating in multiple communities in Australia and across the world. However, they also believed that these hard-earned qualities would not be appreciated back in Japan. One of the consequences of such experiences was the strong desire to reside outside Japan.

This book goes to press in 2012 and the 2008 global financial crisis has fundamentally altered Japan's internationalisation project and individuals' choices as fewer and fewer young people today choose to study overseas. Since 2000, undergraduate enrolment of Japanese students in US universities has decreased by 52% and graduate enrolment by 27% (Harden, 2010). Australia also has seen a significant drop in the number of Japanese students (Wallace, 2011): in 2004–2005, close to the end of my fieldwork, 11,277 international student visas were granted to Japanese nationals, but by 2010–2011 that number had dropped to 5736, constituting almost a 50% decline (Department of Immigration and Citizenship, 2011).

Japanese academics, politicians and business leaders alike have chided today's Japanese youth as 'inward-looking grass-eaters', afraid of venturing overseas (Takahashi, 2010b). Rather than stigmatising this new generation as 'losers' afraid to venture abroad, it may well be that emerging accounts of experiences such as those presented in this book and which increasingly circulate in the media (e.g. Tabuchi, 2012) and through social networks, serve to discredit the promise of English and of study overseas (Kim, 2011; Tabuchi, 2012). Japanese women, in particular, are increasingly questioning the discourse of English and overseas experience as a career booster (Kitamura, 2011), as their country remains consistently ranked extremely low in terms of gender equality (Hausmann et al., 2011). Japan was ranked 98th among the 135 countries included in the WEF's Global Gender Gap Report 2011, one of the lowest among the OECD countries (Hausmann et al., 2011). Why venture out to unknown foreign countries and risk a sense of isolation and myriads of challenges, when the rewards of increased linguistic proficiency and overseas qualification are likely to be small? Similarly, why return to

Japan, when their chances of career advancement, even with high English proficiency and overseas qualifications, will be limited?

This book points to the need for Japan to transform itself to become an attractive, inclusive society, which is something more than a *shikata ga nai* ('can't be helped') choice for its young people. Without a serious commitment towards gender-inclusive nation building, the Japanese women of today and of the future, particularly those who are part of multiple linguistic, cultural and racial communities, are likely to remain as discontented citizens. The country cannot expect these dissatisfied individuals wholeheartedly to invest in the future of national welfare. Two studies point to the need for Japan to reform occupational mechanisms and for hiring practices to be more flexible in accommodating and capitalising on returning international students. Balaz and Williams (2004) report that a substantial number of Slovakian international students who went back to Slovakia from the United Kingdom viewed their return positively, reporting that their overseas experience and their new language skills in English were instrumental in improving their jobs and incomes, even after relatively short stays overseas. Such positive views were simply absent from the narratives of my participants as well as from the Japanese female students in the United States in Matsui's (1995) study. Matsui (1995: 376) argues that: '[u]nless the Japanese occupational structure becomes more flexible and open to women, particularly foreign-educated women, American education will continue to provide Japanese women with nothing more than an opportunity for psychological liberation or for becoming expatriates.'

In light of the research presented in this book, the success, or otherwise, of Japan's internationalisation project seems to lie not so much in individuals gaining proficiency in English. Rather, it requires moving away from approaches that see differences as a threat to national identity, and towards building an inclusive society that can cultivate those who can bring to it global viewpoints. Through such a transformation, Japan might begin to be seen as a more attractive choice of residence for many of its young women, including my participants, whose potential to contribute to and thrive in such a society is significant.

Appendix: Description of Secondary Participants

Name	Nationality	Gender	Age	Visa	1st contact	Recruitment
Bon	Japanese	M	22	S	Jul-01	I met Bon at the English school at the exploratory stage. I asked him basic questions about his attitude towards studying English and his social interactions in Sydney.
Haru	Japanese	F	31	DF	Mar-04	I met Haru once through the main participant, Yoko. Haru had just arrived from Japan and was in a de facto relationship with her Australian boyfriend. Questions were asked about her reasons for studying English and her experiences in using English with her Australian boyfriend.
Ikuko	Japanese	F	25	WH	Apr-04	I met Ikuko through a personal contact in Sydney. She was studying English and working as a masseuse. I saw her several times during April 2004, and questions were asked about her motivation for coming to Australia and her attitudes towards learning English.

(*continued*)

Name	Nationality	Gender	Age	Visa	1st contact	Recruitment
Jackie	Australian (Chinese)	F	37	C	Jan-04	Jackie was Eika's share mate. I often had conversations with her when I visited Eika at home in 2005.
Kaori	Japanese	F	28	S	Aug-01	I met Kaori at the English school at the exploratory stage. At that time she was studying English in order to gain entry onto a master's programme at a university and our conversations often centred on her struggles over improving her English.
Mie	Japanese	F	37	PR	Jan-03	Mie was a long-term permanent resident in Australia and a university lecturer. At the time of contact, she was in a relationship with an Australian man and was considering marriage. Our conversations often centred on her attitudes towards English and her relationships with Western men in Sydney.
Miri	Japanese	F	32	S	Aug-02	I met Miri once through a personal contact at Sydney University. Prior to *ryugaku* in Australia, she had taught English at a private English school and decided to undertake a master's degree in English teaching in order to boost her career. At the meeting, our conversation centred on her *akogare* for Hollywood stars and her experiences in learning and teaching English.
Mitsuo	Japanese	M	40	PR	Mar-04	I met Mitsuo through a personal contact on the Gold Coast. He was running a tour company for Japanese tourists and questions were asked as to his views on Japanese female workers at his company.

(continued)

Name	Nationality	Gender	Age	Visa	1st contact	Recruitment
Natsu	Japanese	M	29	WH	Jul-04	I was introduced to Natsu by Yuka. Natsu was studying English in a private college and looking for a job at that time. I met her twice with Yuka, and questions were asked about her motivation for coming to Australia and studying English.
Philip	Australian	M	34	TEJ	Mar-03	I met Philip through a personal contact in Japan. He has taught English in Japan for more than ten years and questions were asked about his views on English education and Japanese students of English in Japan.
Rina	Japanese	F	22	S	Dec-03	I met Rina once through Eika. She was studying English in Sydney for one year and was soon due back in Japan at the time of contact. Our conversation centred on the topic of *akogare* for English and her romantic relationships in Sydney.
Sato	Japanese	F	29	S	Feb-04	I met Sato through a personal contact at Sydney University. She was studying psychology and was in a rather difficult relationship with an Australian man. I had conversations with her several times and the main topics discussed included her *akogare* for Western singers, her attitudes towards learning English and her relationship problems.

(continued)

Appendix: Description of Secondary Participants 167

Name	Nationality	Gender	Age	Visa	1st contact	Recruitment
Sen	Japanese	M	25	S	Aug-02	I met Sen at the English school at the exploratory stage. I had several brief conversations with him at that time and questions were asked as to his motivation for coming to Australia and studying English in Sydney.
Suzu	Japanese	F	28	P	Mar-04	I was introduced to Suzu by Ichi. She arrived as an international student in 2000. At the time of data collection, she was studying at a university and living with her Australian partner in Sydney. I met Suzu once for approximately two hours.
Tokiko	Japanese	F	32	S	Apr-04	I met Tokiko through Eika. They were studying together at TAFE in Sydney. I was often invited to socialise with Tokiko and Eika and thus my fieldwork with Tokiko was continuous until she returned to Japan in early 2005. The main topics discussed with Tokiko centred on her attitudes towards learning English, socialisation in Sydney and future options in Japan.
Tomo	Japanese	F	23	S	Sep-02	I was introduced to Tomo by Yoko. Tomo was studying English in a private college and was working in a Japanese restaurant. I met her once and questions were asked as to her motivation to come to Australia and her experience of learning and using English in Sydney.

(*continued*)

168 Language Learning, Gender and Desire

Name	Nationality	Gender	Age	Visa	1st contact	Recruitment
Yoshi	Japanese	M	38	PR	Jul-02	I contacted Yoshi though his website. He was running a *ryugaku* agency from home. At the time of the meeting questions were asked about his views on Japanese students coming to Australia to study English.
Yu	Japanese	F	21	S	Jul-01	I met Yu at the English school at the exploratory stage. Questions were asked about her attitudes towards learning and using English in Sydney, while Yu was particularly interested in discussing her romantic issues with her Korean boyfriend.
Yukari	Japanese	F	29	WH	Apr-04	I was introduced to Yukari by Eika. Yukari was studying English in Sydney and was considering applying for permanent residency. I met Yukari several times through Eika and notes were taken on our conversations relating to the use of learning and using English in Sydney.

*Visa status: S = Student visa; DF = De Facto visa; WH = Working Holiday visa; C = Australian Citizen, and TEJ = Teaching English in Japan.

References

Ahearn, L.M. (2001) Language and agency. *Annual Review of Anthropology* 30, 109–137.
Ahearn, L.M. (2003) Writing desire in Nepali love letters. *Language and Communication*, 23, 107–122.
ALC (2002) Kuni betsu gogaku ryugaku jijyou [Conditions of gogaku ryugaku by country]. In *Gogaku ryugaku jiten [Encyclopedia of Language Study Overseas]* (p. 8). Tokyo: ALC.
Alcorso, C. (2003) Immigrant employees in hotels. *Labour and Industry* 14 (1), 17–40.
Andressen, C. and Kumagai, K. (1996) *Escape from Affluence: Japanese Students in Australia* (Vol. 79). Brisbane: Centre for the Study of Australia–Asia Relations.
Ashima, S. (2002) *Oosutoraria tairiku ikiatari battari: Tayori wa dokyoo to chokkann nomi*. Tokyo: Chienomori bunko.
Atsumi, R. (1992) A demographic and socio-economic profile of the Japanese residents in Australia. In *The Diverse Asians: A Profile of Six Asian Communities in Australia* (pp. 11–31). Brisbane: Centre for the Study of Australia–Asia Relations.
Australian Bureau of Statistics (2008) *Year Book Australia, 2008*, accessed 2 November, 2010. http://www.abs.gov.au/ausstats/abs@.nsf/7d12b0f6763c78caca257061001cc5 88/636F496B2B943F12CA2573D200109DA9?opendocument
Australian Bureau of Statistics (2010a) *3101.0 – Australian Demographic Statistics, December 2009*, accessed 18 August 2010. http://www.abs.gov.au/ausstats/abs @.nsf/mf/3101.0
Australian Bureau of Statistics (2010b) *3218.0 – Regional Population Growth, Australia, 2008–09*, accessed 18 August 2010. http://www.abs.gov.au/ausstats/abs@.nsf/ Products/3218.0~2008-09~Main+Features~New+South+Wales?OpenDocument# PARALINK4
Australian Bureau of Statistics (2010c) *National Regional Profile: Inner Sydney (Statistical Subdivision)*, accessed 07 August, 2012. http://www.abs.gov.au/AUSSTATS/abs@.nsf/ Previousproducts/10505Population/People12002-2006?opendocument&tabname=Sum mary&prodno=10505&issue=2002-2006
Australian Education International (AEI) (2000) *2000 Preliminary International Student Numbers*. Canberra: Department of Education, Training and Youth Affairs.
Bailey, K.D. (2002) Living in the eikaiwa wonderland: English language learning, socio-economic transformation and gender alterities in modern Japan. Doctoral dissertation, University of Kentucky, Lexington, KY.
Balaz, V. and Williams, A.M. (2004) 'Been there and done that': International student migration and human capital transfers from the UK to Slovakia. *Population, Space and Place* 10, 217–237.

Blackledge, A. (2001) Complex positionings: Women negotiating identity and power in a minority urban setting. In A. Pavlenko, A. Blackledge, I. Piller and M. Teutsch-Dwyer (eds) *Multilingualism, Second Language Learning, and Gender* (pp. 53–75). Berlin: Mouton de Gruyter.
Block, D. (2002) Destabilized identities and cosmopolitanism across language and cultural borders: Two case studies. *Hong Kong Journal of Applied Linguistics* 7 (2), 1–19.
Bourdieu, P. (1991) *Language and Symbolic Power*. Cambridge, UK: Polity Press.
Bucholtz, M. and Hall, K. (2004) Theorizing identity in language and sexuality research. *Language in Society* 33, 469–515.
Burr, V. (2003) *Social Constructionism*. London: Routledge.
Butorac, D. (2011) Imagined identity, remembered self: Settlement language learning and the negotiation of gendered subjectivity. PhD thesis, Macquarie University, Sydney. Online document: http://www.languageonthemove.com/wp-content/uploads/2012/03/DButorac_PhD.pdf
Cameron, D. and Kulick, D. (2003a) Introduction: Language and desire in theory and practice. *Language and Communication* 23, 93–105.
Cameron, D. and Kulick, D. (2003b) *Language and Sexuality*. Cambridge: Cambridge University.
Cameron, D. and Kulick, D. (2005) Identity crisis? *Language and Communication* 25, 107–125.
Canagarajah, A.S. (1993) Critical ethnography of a Sri Lankan classroom: Ambiguities in student opposition to reproduction through ESOL. *TESOL Quarterly* 27, 601–626.
Castles, S. (2000) *Ethnicity and Globalization*. London: SAGE.
Chang, C-L. (2011) Not learning English in Sydney. *Language on the Move*, blog. http://www.languageonthemove.com/language-learning-gender-identity/not-learning-english-in-sydney
Chang, J. (2004) Ideologies of English teaching and learning in Taiwan. Doctoral dissertation, University of Sydney.
City of Sydney (2005) *The City of Sydney 2004/2005 Annual Report*, accessed 14 January 2006. http://www.cityofsydney.nsw.gov.au/Council/FormsPoliciesPublication/AnnualReport.asp
Clyne, M. (2005) *Australia's Language Potential*. Sydney: UNSW Press.
Colic-Peisker, V. (2005) 'At least you're the right colour': Identity and social inclusion of Bosnian refugees in Australia. *Journal of Ethnic and Migration Studies* 31 (4), 615–638.
Colic-Peisker, V. (2009) *Migration, Class, and Transnational Identities: Croatians in Australia and America*. Champaign, IL: University of Illinois Press.
Colic-Peisker, V. and Tilbury, F. (2007) Integration into the Australian labour market: The experience of three 'visibly different' groups of recently arrived refugees. *International Migration* 45 (1), 59–85.
Constable, N. (2003) *Romance on a Global Stage: Pen Pals, Virtual Ethnography, and 'Mail Order' Marriages*. Berkeley: University of California Press.
Coupland, J. (1996) Dating advertisements: Discourses of the commodified self. *Discourse & Society* 7, 187–207.
Deleuze, G. and Guattari, F. (1996) *A Thousand Plateaus: Capitalism and Schizophrenia*. London: Athlone Press.
Department of Immigration and Citizenship (2010a) *Visas, Immigration and Refugees: Working Holiday*, accessed 27 October 2010. http://www.immi.gov.au/visitors/working-holiday/417/

Department of Immigration and Citizenship (2010b) Working holiday maker program, accessed 07 August 2012. http://www.immi.gov.au/facts/49whm.htm# numbers
Department of Immigration and Citizenship (2011) *Student Visa Program Trends: 2004–05 to 2010–11*. Online document: http://www.immi.gov.au/media/statistics/study/pdf/student-visa-program-trends-2010-11.pdf
Dörnyei, Z. (2005) *The Psychology of the Language Learner: Individual Differences in Second Language Acquisition*. Mahwah: Lawrence Erlbaum.
Dörnyei, Z. and Ushioda, E. (2009) Motivation, language identities and the L2 self: A theoretical overview. In Z. Dörnyei and E. Ushioda (eds) *Motivation, Language Identity and the L2 Self* (pp. 1–8). Bristol: Multilingual Matters.
Dower, J. (1999) *Embracing Defeat: Japan in the Wake of World War II*. New York: Norton.
Eckert, P. (2002) Demystifying sexuality and desire. In K. Campbell-Kibler, R.J. Podesva, S.J. Robers and A. Wong (eds) *Language and Sexuality: Contesting Meaning in Theory and Practice* (pp. 99–110). Stanford, CA: CSLI Publications.
Ellis, R. (1994) *The Study of Second Language Acquisition*. Oxford: Oxford University Press.
Evans, G. (2005) Australia's change. *Language Travel Magazine*, accessed August 2012. http://www.hothousemedia.com/ltm/ltmbackissues/feb05web/feb05marketreport.htm
Flick, U. (2002) *An Introduction to Qualitative Research*. Thousand Oaks, CA: Sage.
Foley, D. and Valenzuela, A. (2005) Critical ethnography: The politics of collaboration. In N.K. Denzin and Y.S. Lincoln (eds) *Handbook of Qualitative Research* (pp. 217–234). Thousand Oaks, CA: Sage.
Foucault, M. (1978) *The History of Sexuality. Vol. I: An Introduction* (trans. Robert Hurley). London: Penguin Books.
Foucault, M. (1980) *Power/Knowledge: Selected Interviews and Other Writings 1972–1977*. New York: Pantheon Books.
Freed, B.F. (1995) What makes us think that students who study abroad become fluent? In B.F. Freed (ed.) *Second Language Acquisition in a Study Abroad Context*. Amsterdam: John Benjamins.
Gal, S. (1978) Peasant men don't get wives: Language and sex roles in a bilingual community. *Language in Society* 7, 1–17.
Gardner, R.C. (1985) *Social Psychology and Second Language Learning: The Role of Attitudes and Motivation*. London: Arnold.
Gayn, M. (1946) *Japan Daily*, p. 234.
Gerteis, C. (2009) *Gender Struggles: Wage-Earning Women and Male-Dominated Unions in Postwar Japan*. Cambridge, MA: Harvard University Asia Center.
Goodman, R. (1990) *Japan's 'International Youth': The Emergence of a New Class of Schoolchildren*. Oxford: Oxford University Press.
Habu, T. (2000) The irony of globalization: The experience of Japanese women in British higher education. *Higher Education* 39, 43–66.
Hall, S. (1993) Culture, community, nation. *Cultural Studies* 7 (2), 349–363.
Harden, B. (2010) Once drawn to U.S. universities, more Japanese staying home. *The Washington Post*. http://www.washingtonpost.com/wp-dyn/content/article/2010/04/10/AR2010041002835.html
Hausmann, R., Tyson, L.D. and Zahidi, S. (2011) *The Global Gender Gap Report 2011*. Online document: http://www.uis.unesco.org/Library/Documents/global-gender-gap-report-education-2011-en.pdf
Hawthorne, L. (2001) The globalisation of the nursing workforce: Barriers confronting overseas qualified nurses in Australia. *Nursing Inquiry* 8 (4), 213–229.

Horwitz, E. and Young, D. (1991) *Language Learning Anxiety: From Theory and Research to Classroom Implications*. Englewood Cliffs, NJ: Prentice Hall.
Ichimoto, T. (2000) *Globalisation, Higher Education, and the Re-creation of Japanese Femininity*. Paper presented at the the Australian Association for Research in Education (AARE), December, Sydney.
Ieda, S. (1991) *Ieroo kyabu: Narita o tabidatta onnatachi [Yellow Cabs: The Women who Took Off from Narita Airport]*. Tokyo: Kooyuu Shuppan.
Igata, K. (2001) *Itsuka igirisu ni kurasu watashi*. Tokyo: Chikumabunko.
Inglehart, R. (1982) Changing values in Japan and the West. *Comparative Political Studies* 14, 445–479.
Itsuka watashimo kaigai rongu stei [One day I will try a long overseas stay]. (2004) *Nikkei Woman,* 223 (January), 16–53.
Japan Association for Working Holiday Makers (2006) *Working Holiday,* accessed 16 January 2006. http://www.jawhm.or.jp/jp/index.html
J-Net 21 (2005) *Eikaiwa Kyooshitsu [English Conversation Schools]*, accessed 15 January 2006. http://j-net21.smrj.go.jp/venture/startup/jirei_h009.html
Johnson, S.K. (1988) *The Japanese through American Eyes*. Stanford, CA: Stanford University Press.
Kachru, B.B. (1992) *The Other Tongue: English Across Cultures*. Urbana: University of Illinois Press.
Kang, Y. (2003) The desire to be desired: Magic spells, agency, and the politics of desire among the Petalangan people in Indonesia. *Language and Communication* 23, 153–167.
Kanno, Y. (2000) Kikokushijo as bicultural. *International Journal of Intercultural Relations* 24, 361–382.
Kanno, Y. (2003) *Negotiating Bilingual and Bicultural Identities: Japanese Returnees Betwixt Two Worlds*. Mahwah, NJ: Lawrence Erlbaum.
Kanno, Y. and Applebaum, S.D. (1995) ESL students speak up: Their stories of how we are doing. *TESL Canada Journal* 12 (2), 33–49.
Kelsky, K. (1996) Flirting with the foreign: Interracial sex in Japan's 'international' age. In R. Wilson and W. Dissanayake (eds) *Global/Local: Cultural Production and the Transnational Imaginary* (pp. 173–192). Durham, NC: Duke University Press.
Kelsky, K. (2001) *Women on the Verge: Japanese Women, Western Dreams*. Durham, NC: Duke University Press.
Kelsky, K. (2008) Gender, modernity, and eroticized internationalism in Japan. In D. Blake Willies and S. Murphy-Shigematsu (eds) *Transcultural Japan: At the Borderlands of Race, Gender, and Identity* (pp. 86–119). London, New York: Routledge.
Kidder, L.H. (1992) Requirements for being 'Japanese'. *International Journal of Intercultural Relations* 16, 383–393.
Kiesling, S.F. (2002) Playing the straight man: Displaying and maintaining male heterosexuality in discourse. In K. Campbell-Kibler, R.J. Podesva, S.J. Robers and A. Wong (eds) *Language and Sexuality: Contesting Meaning in Theory and Practice* (pp. 249–266). Stanford, CA: CSLI Publications.
Kim, Y. (2011) Diasporic nationalism and the media: Asian women on the move. *International Journal of Cultural Studies* 14 (2), 133–151.
Kinginger, C. (2004) Alice doesn't live here any more: Foreign language learning and identity reconstruction. In A. Pavlenko and A. Blackledge (eds) *Negotiation of Identities in Multilingual Contexts* (pp. 219–242). Hawthorne, NY: Mouton de Gruyter.
Kinginger, C. (2006) The Sabrina Syndrome: Intertexuality and performance of identity in American students' narratives of learning French. Paper presented at the American

Association of Applied Linguistics and the Canadian Association for Applied Linguistics, Montreal, Canada.
Kinginger, C. (2008) *Language Learning in Study Abroad: Case Histories of Americans in France*. Oxford: Blackwell.
Kitamura, A. (2011) 英語は女を救うのか *[Does the English Language Save Women?]*. Tokyo: Chikuma Shoten.
Kitzinger, C. and Firth, H. (1999) Just say no? The use of conversation analysis in developing a feminist perspective on sexual refusal. *Discourse & Society* 10, 293–316.
Kobayashi, Y. (2002) The role of gender in foreign language learning attitudes: Japanese female students' attitudes towards English learning. *Gender and Education* 14, 181–197.
Koor Intercultural Programs and Education (2004) *Kaigai de hataraku [Working Overseas]*, accessed 4 November 2010. http://www.london.ne.jp/koor/kindy.html
Kress, G. and van Leeuwen, T. (1996) *Reading Images*. Victoria: Deakin University.
Kubota, R. (1998) Ideologies of English in Japan. *World Englishes* 17, 295–306.
Kubota, R. (2002) The impact of globalization on language teaching in Japan. In D. Block and D. Cameron (eds) *Globalization and Language Teaching* (pp. 13–28). London: Routledge.
Kubota, R. (2008) A critical glance at romance, gender, and language teaching. *Essential Teacher* 5 (3), 28–30.
Kubota, R. (2011) Learning a foreign language as leisure and consumption: Enjoyment, desire, and the business of *eikaiwa*. *International Journal of Bilingual Education and Bilingualism* 14 (4), 473–488.
Kulick, D. (2003) Language and desire. In J. Holmes and M. Meyerhoff (eds) *The Handbook of Language and Gender* (pp. 119–141). Oxford: Blackwell.
Lantolf, J.P. and Pavlenko, A. (2001) (S)econd (L)anguage (A)ctivity theory: Understanding second language learners as people. In M.P. Breen (ed.) *Learner Contributions to Language Learning*. Harlow: Longman.
Leech, G.N. (1983) *Principles of Pragmatics*. London: Longman.
Let's Go Overseas (2000) Atarashii jibun o mitsuke ni kaigai e iku tte koto [to go overseas to find a new self]. *One two Magazine*, 38.
Leupp, G.P. (2003) *Interracial Intimacy in Japan: Western Men and Japanese Women, 1543–1900*. London: Continuum.
Linde, C. (1992) *Life Stories: The Creation of Coherence*. New York: Oxford University Press.
Lucas, J. (1984) Communication apprehension in the ESL classroom: Getting our students to talk. *Foreign Language Annals* 17, 593–598.
Lukes, S. (1974) *Power: A Radical View*. London: Macmillan.
Ma, K. (1996) *The Modern Madame Butterfly*. Rutland, VT: Tuttle Publishing.
MacIntyre, P.D. (1999) Language anxiety: A review of the research for language teachers. In D.J. Young (ed.) *Affect in Foreign Language and Second Language Learning: A Practical Guide to Creating a Low-anxiety Classroom Atmosphere* (pp. 24–45). Boston: McGraw-Hill.
Macintyre, P.D., Baker, S.C., Clement, R. and Donovan, L.A. (2002) Sex and age effects on willingness to communicate, anxiety, perceived competence, and L2 motivation among junior high school French immersion students. *Language Learning* 52, 537–564.
Madison, D.S. (2005) *Critical Ethnography: Method, Ethics, and Performance*. Thousand Oaks, CA: Sage.
Magazine House (2002a, 12 June) Sukuuru ichioshi! Suteki na sensei daishuugoo [Recommended schools! Good-looking teachers are here]. *an an* 1319, 37.
Magazine House (2002b, 12 June) Tada eigo ga hanaseru dake dewa dame! [It is no good just to be able to speak English!]. *an an* 1319, 54–55.

Magazine House (2003, 06 August) Eigo master jyutsu [Method of mastering English]. *an an* 1375.
Marchetti, G. (1993) *Romance and the 'Yellow Peril': Race, Sex, and Discursive Strategies in Hollywood Fiction*. Berkeley: University of California Press.
Markus, H. and Nurius, P. (1986) Possible selves. *American Psychologist* 41 (9), 954–969.
Mathews, G. (2000) *Global Culture/Individual Identity: Searching for Home in the Cultural Supermarket*. London: Routledge.
Matsubara, J. (1989) *Eigo dekimasu [I Can Speak English]*. Tokyo: Bungei Shunju.
Matsuda, A. (2003) Incorporating World Englishes in teaching English as an international language. *TESOL Quarterly* 37, 719–719.
Matsui, M. (1995) Gender role perceptions of Japanese and Chinese female students in American university. *Comparative Education Review* 39, 356–378.
McKay, S.L. and Wong, S.L.C. (1996) Multiple discourses, multiple identities: Investment in agency in second language learning among Chinese adolescent immigrant students. *Harvard Educational Review* 66, 577–608.
Miles, B.M. and Huberman, M.A. (1994) *An Expanded Source Book of Qualitative Data Analysis* (2nd edn). Thousand Oaks, CA: Sage.
Misago, C. (2004) *Onibaba ka suru onnatachi: Josei no shintai wo torimodosu [Women Turning into Onibaba: Reclaiming Female Bodies]*. Tokyo: Koobunsha.
Miya, Y. (1997) OL o yamete kaigai e iku to iu koto [To quit working as an OL and go overseas]. In S. Ohira and T. Kato (eds) *Marugoto onna no tenki* (pp. 26–41). Tokyo: Asupecto.
Nakane, I. (2007) *Silence in Intercultural Communication*. Amsterdam: John Benjamins.
New Zealand Herald (2004) Japanese visitor pays $2400 to work for no pay in Christchurch, accessed 4 November 2010. http://www.nzherald.co.nz/section/story.cfm?c_id=1&objectid = 3557904
Nikkei Woman (2004) *Itsuka watashimo kaigai rongu sutei [One day I will try a long overseas stay]* (Vol. 223). Tokyo: Nikkei Business Publications, Inc.
Niño-Murcia, M. (2003) 'English is like a dollar': Hard currency ideology and the status of English in Peru. *World Englishes* 22 (2), 123–143.
Nishimoto, K. (2005) Tabi, Yumeno gotoshi [Deamy travel], accessed 07 August 2012. http://tabi.yumenogotoshi.com/enjo/gaijin.htm
Norton, B. (2000) *Identity and Language Learning: Gender, Ethnicity and Educational Change*. Harlow: Longman.
Norton, B. and Toohey, K. (2001) Changing perspectives on Good Language Learners. *TESOL Quarterly* 35, 307–322.
Odagiri, Y. (2004) Eigo bijin [English beauty]. *Asahi Evening* (23 February), 5.
Oguri, S. (2002) *Darling wa gaikokujin: Darling is a Foreigner*. Tokyo: Media Factory.
Oguri, S. (2004) *Darling wa gaikokujin 2: Darling is a Foreigner 2*. Tokyo: Media Factory.
Ohara, Y. (2001) Finding one's voice in Japanese: A study of the pitch levels of L2 users. In A. Pavlenko, A. Blackledge, I. Piller and M. Teutsch-Dwyer (eds) *Multilingualism, Second Language Learning, and Gender* (pp. 231–254). Berlin: Mouton de Gruyter.
Ong, A. (1999) *Flexible Citizenship: The Cultural Logics of Transnationality*. Durham, London: Duke University Press.
Ono, H. and Piper, N. (2004) Japanese women studying abroad: The case study of the United States. *Women's Studies International Forum* 27, 101–118.
Ootomo, S. (2004) *Renai English: Kantan fureizu de hanaseru renai ingurisshu [Relationship English: You Can Speak with Simple Phrases]*. Tokyo: Diamondsha.
Oxford, R. (1990) *Language Learning Strategies: What Every Teacher Should Know*. New York: Cambridge University Press.

Oxford, R. and Anderson, N. (1995) A cross-cultural variability in conversation interactions. *Language Teaching* 28, 201-215.
Ozawa, Y. and Shirakawa, M. (2004) *Shiawase wo tsukamu kokusai kekkon no susume: Unmei no hito wa umino mukou ni ita [I Found my Man of Destiny Overseas: Recommendation for International Marriage for Happiness]*. Tokyo: Nikkei BP.
Ozeki, N. (2002) *Dr. Ozeki no girl talk: Naisho no eikaiwa [Dr. Ozeki's Girl Talk: Secret English Conversation]*. Tokyo: McMillan Language House.
Ozeki, N. (2003a) *Dr. Ozeki no more girl talk: Danshi kinsei no eikaiwa [Dr. Ozeki's More Girl Talk: English Conversation, Boys Banned]*. Tokyo: McMillan Language House.
Ozeki, N. (2003b) *Koisuru otome no eikaiwa [English Conversation for Girls in Love]*. Tokyo: Kobunsha.
Papastergiadis, N. (2000) *The Turbulence of Migration*. Massachusetts: Polity Press.
Park, J.S-Y. (2009) *The Local Construction of a Global Language: Ideologies of English in South Korea*. Berlin: Mouton de Gruyter.
Park, J.S-Y. (2011) The promise of English: Linguistic capital and the neoliberal worker in the South Korean job market. *International Journal of Bilingual Education and Bilingualism* 14 (4), 443-455.
Pavlenko, A. (2005) *Emotions and Multilingualism*. Cambridge: Cambridge University Press.
Pavlenko, A. (2006) Bilingual selves. In A. Pavlenko (ed.) *Bilingual Minds: Emotional Experience, Expression and Representation* (pp. 1-33). Clevedon: Multilingual Matters.
Pavlenko, A. (2008) Emotion and emotion-laden words in the bilingual lexicon. *Bilingualism: Language and Cognition* 11 (2), 147-164. doi:10.1017/S1366728908003283
Pavlenko, A. and Piller, I. (2001) New directions in the study of multilingualism, second language learning, and gender. In A. Pavlenko, A. Blackledge, I. Piller and M. Teutsch-Dwyer (eds) *Multilingualism, Second Language Learning, and Gender* (pp. 17-52). Berlin: Mouton de Gruyter.
Pavlenko, A., Blackledge, A., Piller, I. and Teutsch-Dwyer, M. (2001) *Multilingualism, Second Language Learning, and Gender*. Berlin: Mouton de Gruyter.
Pennycook, A. (2001) *Critical Applied Linguistics: A Critical Introduction*. Manhwah: Lawrence Erlbaum.
Pennycook, A. (2007) The myth of English as an international language. In A. Pennycook and S. Makoni (eds) *Disinventing and Reconstituting Languages*. Clevedon: Multilingual Matters.
Pichette, M.J. (2000) The influence of gender on the acquisition of the Japanese language by white western men and women living and working in Japan. Unpublished manuscript, Temple University, Tokyo.
Piller, I. (2002) *Bilingual Couples Talk: The Discursive Construction of Hybridity*. Amsterdam: Benjamins.
Piller, I. (2003) Advertising as a site of language contact. *Annual Review of Applied Linguistics* 23, 170-183.
Piller, I. (2006) Cross-cultural communication in intimate relationships. In H. Kotthoff and H. Spencer-Oatey (eds) *Intercultural Communication: Handbook of Applied Linguistics 7*. Berlin: Mouton de Gruyter.
Piller, I. (2010) Sex in the city: On making space and identity in travel spaces. In A. Jaworski and C. Thurlow (eds) *Semiotic Landscapes of Globalization: Language, Image, Space*. London: Continuum.
Piller, I. (2011a) *Intercultural Communication: A Critical Introduction*. London: Edinburgh University Press.

Piller, I. (2011b) Multilingualism and social exclusion. In M. Martin-Jones, A. Blackledge and A. Creese (eds) *Handbook of Multilingualism*. London: Routledge.
Piller, I. and Takahashi, K. (2006) A passion for English: Desire and the language market. In A. Pavlenko (ed.) *Bilingual Minds: Emotional Experience, Expression and Representation* (pp. 59–83). Clevedon: Multilingual Matters.
Piller, I. and Takahashi, K. (2010a) At the intersection of gender, language and transnationalism. In N. Coupland (ed.) *The Handbook of Language and Globalization* (pp. 540–554). Oxford: Blackwell.
Piller, I. and Takahashi, K. (2010b) Language, migration and human rights. In R. Wodak, B. Johnstone and P. Kerswill (eds) *Sage Handbook of Sociolinguistics*. Thousand Oaks, CA: Sage.
Piller, I. and Takahashi, K. (eds) (2012) Japanese on the move: Life stories of transmigration, blog. http://www.languageonthemove.com/japanese-on-the-move
Piller, I., Takahashi, K. and Watanabe, Y. (2010) The dark side of TESOL: The hidden costs of the consumption of English. *Cross-Cultural Studies* 20, 183–201.
Prendergast, C. (2008) *Buying into English: Language and Investment in the New Capitalist World*. Pittsburgh: University of Pittsburgh Press.
Rumsey, A. (2003) Language, desire, and the ontogenesis of intersubjectivity. *Language and Communication* 23, 169–187.
Russell, J. (1998) Consuming passions: Spectacle, self-transformation, and the commodification of blackness in Japan. *Positions* 6 (1), 113–117.
Ryugaku Journal (2002) *ICS kokusai bunka kyooiku sentaa [ICS International Cultural Educational Center]*, 19 (4).
Said, E.W. (1978 [1994]) *Orientalism*. New York: Vintage Books.
Saito, T. (2003) *Hikikomori bunka ron [Cultural theory of hikikomori]*. Tokyo: Kinokuniya shoten.
Schumann, J. (1978) The acculturation model for second-language acquisition. In R.C. Gingras (ed.) *Second Language Acquisition and Foreign Language Teaching* (pp. 27–50). Washington, DC: Center for Applied Linguistics.
Seo, A. (1992) OLs abroad. *Look Japan* 37, 34–35.
Shuukan Diamond (2005) 10 nen go no daikigyoo [Large corporations in ten years], accessed 20 January 2006. http://www.gaba.co.jp/companyinfo/media/diamond050122.html
Tabuchi, H. (2012) Young and global need not apply in Japan. *The New York Times* (29 May). http://www.nytimes.com/2012/05/30/business/global/as-global-rivals-gain-ground-corporate-japan-clings-to-cautious-ways.html?_r=2&hp
Takahashi, K. (2009) Migration, gender and second language learning [Gender to dainigengo gakushuu: Iminjyosei no shigoto]. In C. Kawamura, A. Kondoh and H. Nakamoto (eds) *Living Together in a Multicultural Society: Approaches to Immigration Policy [Iminsaiaku eno approach: Raifusaikuru to tabunkakyousei]* (pp. 256–258). Tokyo: Akashi Shoten Publishing.
Takahashi, K. (2010a) Multilingual couplehood: Romance, identity and the political economy of language. In D. Nunan and J. Choi (eds) *Language and Culture: Reflective Narratives and the Emergence of Identity* (pp. 199–207). New York: Routledge.
Takahashi, K. (2010b) Who's inward-looking? *Language on the Move*, blog. http://www.languageonthemove.com/language-learning-gender-identity/whos-inward-looking
Takahashi, K. (2012) Multilingualism and gender. In M. Martin-Jones, A. Blackledge and A. Creese (eds) *Handbook of Multilingualism*. London: Routledge.
Talbot, M.M. (1997) 'An explosion deep inside her': Women's desire and popular romance fiction. In K. Harvey and C. Shalom (eds) *Language and Desire: Encoding Sex, Romance and Intimacy* (pp. 106–122). London: Routledge.

Toda, N. (1999) *Otokoto onna no suriringu: Eiga de oboeru renai eikaiwa [Men and Women, Thrilling for Men and Women: Learning Romantic English Through Movies]*. Tokyo: Shuueisha.

Toyota, M. (1994) *Kokuhatsu! Yellow Cab*. Tokyo: Sairyuu sha.

Tsuda, Y. (1995) *Eigo shihai no koozoo: Nihonjin to ibunka communication [Structure of English Imperialism: Japanese and Foreign Cultural Communication]*. Tokyo: Daisan Shokan.

Tsuda, Y. (2000) *Eigo heta no susume [A Recommendation for Poor English]*. Tokyo: KK Bestsellers.

Valentine, D. (2003) 'I went to bed with my own kind once': The erasure of desire in the name of identity. *Language and Communication* 23, 123–138.

Virgin English (2004) Ikemen gaijin kooryaku hoo damenzu gaijin gyakutai hoo [Strategy for getting a good-looking gaijin, strategy for getting rid of a bad gaijin]. *Author*, 1 (February), 48–51.

Wallace, R. (2011) Push to attract Japanese students here. *The Australian*. http://www.theaustralian.com.au/higher-education/push-to-attract-japanese-students-here/story-e6frgcjx-1226079461717

Weedon, C. (1997) *Feminist Practice and Poststructuralist Theory*. Oxford: Blackwell.

Wish International (2002) Oosutoraria & nyuujiirando atarashii ikikata hajimeyoo [Let's start a new way of life in Australia & New Zealand]. *Wish* 8, 13–41.

Yokota, K. (2004) Kare wa shiifu [He is a thief]. *S girl* (pp. 135–166). Tokyo: Bunka sha.

Yoshida Isogai, T., Hayashi, Y. and Mayumi, U. (1999) Identity issues and reentry training. *International Journal of Intercultural Relations* 23 (3), 493–525.

Yoshida, T., Matsumoto, D., Akiyama, T., Moriyoshi, N., Furuie, A. and Ishii, C. (2003) Peers' perceptions of Japanese returnees. *International Journal of Intercultural Relations* 27, 641–658.

Young, D.J. (1992) Language anxiety from the foreign language specialists' perspective: Interviews with Krashen, Ommaggio Hadley, Terrell, and Rardin. *Foreign Language Annals* 25, 157–172.

Zimmerman, D.H. (1998) Discourse identities and social identities. In C. Antaki and S. Widdicombe (eds) *1998* (pp. 87–106). London: Sage.

Zwei (2006) Kokusai renai, kokusai kekkonn doo omou? [What do you think about international relationship and marriage?], accessed 4 November 2010. http://woman.zwei.com/woman/counselor_010/coun_01.shtml

Index

age, 56–60, 84, 87, 96, 97, 118, 121, 140, 148, 156
Ahearn, Laura M., 7, 43, 90
akogare
  and language learning, 6–7
  antipathy towards, 146
  construction of, 14
  data on, 12–3
  ethnography of, 3, 14
  exploitation of, 99
  for English, 1–2, 8, 12–13, 122
  for terms of endearment, 69–70
  for the West 1–2, 4–5, 70, 122, 123–4
  for Western celebrities, 36–39
  for white men, 72–3, 75, 81, 83, 132, 147–8, 151–2, 154
  history of, 4–5
  in adolescence, 15–18, 51; *see also* desire and language desire
Alcorso, Caroline, 107
an-an magazine, 22–3, 24, 30, 161
Anderson, Neil J., 154
Andressen, Curtis, 11, 157
Applebaum, Sheila Dermer, 154
Appleby, Ros, xii, xv
Ashima, Shinobu, 145
Asian men, 73–74
Asians, 60–1, 65–7, 74, 97–8, 154
Atsumi, Reiko, 10
Australian/Aussie English, 54, 68, 94–5
Australians, 60–1, 63–8, 74–75, 79, 88, 93, 97, 99–101, 104, 108, 110, 126, 130, 133–4, 140, 142, 146

Bailey, Keiron Douglas, xv, 4, 9, 13, 21–2, 25–6, 151, 152
Balaz, Vladmir, 163
Bilingual Couples Talk, 6
Blackledge, Adrian, 154
Block, David, 112
Blommaert, Jan, xiv
Bora Bora Island, 105, 123–5
Bucholtz, Mary, 7
Burr, Vivien, 95
Butorac, Donna, 74, 107, 154

Cameron, Deborah, 7, 144
Canagarajah, Suresh, 90
Castles, Stephen, 157
Chang, Chu-Lin, 64, 74
Chang, Jackie, 13, 25
China, 4, 14, 17, 75, 134, 135–7
code switching, 134
Colic-Peisker, Val, 107
Constable, Nicole, 113
Coupland, Justine, 23
couple language, 131, 135
Cruise, Tom, 36–38
cultural supermarket, 111–3, 119

desire, 7–9, 13, 64, 69, 80, 89, 93, 96, 97, 108–10, 112, 154, 158, 162;
  see also akogare and language desire
discrimination, 66–7, 75, 88–9, 104–5, 107–8, 109, 161–2
Dörnyei, Zoltan, 89
Dower, John, 4, 5, 10

Eckert, Penelope, 7
eikaiwa school (English conversation school), 9–10, 20–1, 25–8, 139, 150
Ellis, Rod, 23
endearment, 69–70, 141
English conversation schools (see eikaiwa school)
English fever in Japan, 9
English language learning (ELL)
  and internationalisation, 160–1
  in Japan, 90
  Renai English (English for romantic purposes), 28–35
  strategies, 3, 8
  success in, 64, 67, 71, 88
ethnography, 1, 3, 8–9, 11–15, 19
Evans, Gillian, 53

Firth, Hannah, 34
Foley, Douglas, 14
Foucault, Michel, 7, 95
Freed, Barbara F., 64
friendship, 7, 12, 64–7, 74–75, 76, 79, 120, 132, 134

Gaba, 21, 22–3, 25–8, 31, 40
Gal, Susan, 152
Gardner, Robert C., 89,
gender equality, 51, 61, 98, 162–3
Gerteis, Christopher, 4
Goodman, Roger, 114

Habu, Toshie, 11, 157, 158, 160
Hall, Kira, 7
Hall, Stuart, 122
Harden, Blaine, 162
Hausmann, Ricardo, 162
Hawthorne, Lesleyanne, 107
Hernandez-Zamora, Gregorio, xii–xiii
heterosexuality, xv, 31, 34–5, 40–1, 139, 144–5, 146
Higgins, Christina, xiii
hikikomori (social withdrawal), 16, 50, 97–8, 109, 133, 142
Hollywood, xiv, 2, 16–7, 28–31, 35–7, 39–40, 47, 77, 88, 103–4, 124, 138–9, 145, 147, 159, 165

Home
  and international romance, 132–3
  as an ELL opportunity, 91–8, 141–2, 143
  choices of, 137
  multiple homes, 122, 137
  return to Japan, 111, 114–5, 122, 125
  Sydney as, 127, 129
homestay (host family), 53, 66, 91–2, 95–7, 108
Horwitz, Elaine, 154
hybridity, 112, 122, 134, 137

Ichimoto, Takae, 10, 11
Ieda, Shoko, 5, 145
Igata, Keiko, 145
Inglehart, Ronald, 157
intercultural communication, 147
internationalisation, 9, 145, 160–3

Japanese government, 4, 161
Japanese on the Move: Life Stories of Transmigration, 161
Japanese students in Australia, 1, 10–1, 64, 99, 141, 142, 156
Johnson, Sheila K., 4

Kachru, Braj B., 44, 139
Kamada, Laurel, xii
Kang, Yoonhee, 7
Kanno, Yasuko, 114, 154
Kelsky, Karen, xiv, 3–4, 5, 10, 13, 19, 21, 23, 24, 25, 46, 51, 77, 111, 122, 150, 151, 152, 157, 158
Kidder, Louise H., 114
kikokushijo (returnees), 114, 120–1, 161
Kim, Youna, 11, 157, 162
Kinginger, Celeste, 153, 154
Kitamura, Aya, 150, 151, 159, 162
Kitzinger, Celia, 34
Kobayashi, Yoko, 9, 46, 158
kokusaika (see internationalisation)
Kress, Gunther, 13, 22, 27
Kubota, Ryuko, xiii, xv, 9, 29, 158–159
Kulick, Don, 7, 144
Kumagai, Keichi, 11, 157

language choice, 77, 79–80, 130, 131–2, 146, 148–9, 161
language desire
   and ELL, 141, 153–6, 158–60
   and media, 20, 41, 145–6
   and migration, 149–50, 156–8
   and women's life choices, 150–3
   construction of, 138–9, 144–6
   effects of, 146–9
   for Chinese, 135
   notion of, 6–8
   racial implication, 36
language ideology, xiii, 25, 91, 157
language maintenance, 130–1, 117–8, 130, 131, 137, 143–4, 146, 148, 149–50,
Lantolf, James P., 90, 110
Leech, Geoffrey N., 104
Leupp, Gary P., 4, 10
life cycles, 60
Linde, Charlotte, 47
Lucas, Jenifer, 154
Lukes, Steven, 8

Ma, Karen, 5, 25, 72
MacIntyre, Peter D., 89, 154
Madison, Soyini D., 14
Marchetti, Gina, 41
Markus, Hazel, 89
Mathews, Gordon, 112–3, 119
Matsubara, Junko, 41, 51–2, 120
Matsuda, Aya, 52, 159
Matsui, Machiko, 11, 157, 158, 163
McKay, Sandra Lee, xiii, 90, 154
Media
   education, 159–160
   language desire, 145–146
   ryugaku, 43–46, 91–3, 139, 142
   work during *ryugaku*, 98–9, 106
Menard-Warwick, Julia, xii,
migration
   and gender, 157
   and SLL, 158
   cost of, 150
   desire for, 149–50
   international migration theory of, 9, 157
Miya, Yoko, 10
mobility, xiv, 111, 113, 130, 133, 136–7, 143, 153, 156–8, 162

motivation, xiii, xiv, 1, 6, 11, 27, 43, 51, 55, 59, 89, 153–6
multiculturalism, 53, 60–1, 108, 128, 134,

Nakane, Ikuko, 156
Nikkei Woman, 114–5
Niño-Murcia, Mercedes, 9
Norton, Bonny, xiii, 3, 6, 90, 98, 153, 154
Nurius, Paula, 89

Occupation period, 4
Oguri, Saori, 145
Ohara, Yumiko, 108
Ong, Aihwa, 113
Ono, Hiroshi, 9, 157–8
Ootomo, Sanae, 31–5, 145
Oxford, Rebecca L., 154
Ozawa, Yuko, 145
Ozeki, Naoko, 145

Panglish, 5
pan-pan, 4, 161
Papastergiadis, Nikos, 112
Park, Joseph Sung-Yul, 7, 9
Pavlenko, Aneta, 6, 76–7, 90–1, 96, 108, 110
Pennycook, Alastair, xiv, 7, 90–1
permanent residency, 97, 116, 123, 127, 143, 168
Piller, Ingrid, ix, xiv, 3, 6–8, 9, 13, 19, 20, 25, 29, 31, 90, 91, 96, 104, 107–8, 110, 118, 130, 145, 153, 159, 160, 161
pillow talk, 3
Piper, Nicola, 9, 157–8
Pitt, Brad, 36, 40, 87, 103–4, 124
poststructuralism, 3, 6, 90, 138
power, xi, xii, xiv, 3–4, 6, 7–8, 14, 25, 26–7, 29, 32, 40, 69, 72, 90–2, 94, 108–10, 146, 148–9, 153–6
Prendergast, Catherine, 9, 13

race, xi–ii, 25, 40, 66, 72–4, 107–108, 130–2, 135
racism, 89, 109–10
renai English (*see* English language learning)
returnees (*see kikokushijo*)
romance, xiv, 4, 5, 6–7, 12, 20–6, 29–32, 34–5, 40–1, 64, 68–71, 75, 76–80, 86,

95, 97, 114, 126–7, 130, 134–6, 139, 143, 145, 151–3, 154, 160, 162
Rumsey, Alan, 7
Russell, John, 25, 159–60
ryugaku (study overseas)
  age, 56–60, 140
  agents, 98
  and the media, 43–46, 91–93, 98–9, 114–5, 145
  Australia as a destination, 10, 46–56
  consequences of, 142–143
  gendered, 10, 130
  meaning of, 139–40
  success in, 64, 88
  the US as a destination, 10

Said, Edward W., 41
Saito, Tamaki, 50
Schumann, John H., 89
Seargeant, Philip, xiii
second language acquisition, xiv, 5–6, 8, 9, 25, 89, 90, 138, 153–4, 156–7
Seo, A., 10
Sex and the City, 31
Shirakawa, Momoko, 145
silence, 78, 156
study overseas (*see Ryugaku*)

Tabuchi, Hiroko, 162
Talbot, Mary M., 34–35, 41
Tilbury, Farida, 107
Toda, Natsuko, 145
Toohey, Kelleen, 90
Top Gun, 36
Toyota, Masayoshi, 5

Tsuda, Yukio, 20, 21, 25, 64, 72, 98, 151, 159
Tyson, Laura D, 162

Ushioda, Emma, 89

Valentine, David, 7
Valenzuela, Angela, 14
van Leeuwen, Theo, 13, 22, 27

Wallace, Rick, 162
Weedon, Chris, 6
WEF's Global Gender Gap Report 2011, 162
Western men (White men), 2, 3, 24, 21–30, 39, 69–71, 72, 126–7, 132, 139, 140, 147–8, 151–2
White woman, xiii, 39, 41
Williams, Allan M, 163
women's comics, 23–4
women's magazines, 13, 21–3, 28–30, 35, 44, 98–9, 139
Wong, Sau-Ling Cynthia, 90, 154
work as an ELL opportunity, 98–108, 120–1, 142, 151
working holiday, 12, 15, 47, 50, 52, 54–6, 57–9, 91–3, 99, 106, 142, 149

Yellow Cab, 3, 5, 160–1
Yokota, Kumi, 23–4
Yoshida, Tomoko, 114
Young, Dolly, 154

Zahidi, Saadia, 162

For Product Safety Concerns and Information please contact our EU Authorised Representative:

Easy Access System Europe

Mustamäe tee 50

10621 Tallinn

Estonia

gpsr.requests@easproject.com

www.ingramcontent.com/pod-product-compliance
Ingram Content Group UK Ltd.
Pitfield, Milton Keynes, MK11 3LW, UK
UKHW022217250326
4937IPUK00005B/31